M000287345

"Lila Balisky's investigation into the s‍ to become a classic in the power of theologizing ‍ midst of suffering. Her intimate understanding of the Ethiopian context, having lived through the Ethiopian Marxist revolution (1974–1991) with local believers, brings authenticity to the depth of Tesfaye's testimony in songs that sustained Ethiopian Christians during severe persecution. It will force you to think more deeply about God and His ways."

—Roberta R. King
Professor of Communication and Ethnomusicology,
Fuller Theological Seminary, Pasadena, CA

"Writing and researching from a posture of humility, and with nearly 40 years of cross-cultural ministry in Ethiopia, Lila Balisky has written a superb study of the life narrative and songs of Ethiopian singer, composer, and church leader Tesfaye Gabbiso . . . Vividly aware of the challenge of translating meaning from one language and medium to another, Balisky takes the necessary precautions and gets it right. She has given us a wonderful study that celebrates both musical creativity and deep indigenous worship."

—Darrell Whiteman
Missiological Anthropologist, Global Development

"Tesfaye, Ethiopia's most distinguished and renowned gospel singer has inspired, encouraged, and uplifted millions of Ethiopians through his theologically sound, but musically superb songs, which he has composed and sung. This is particularly true of the songs he produced when the church came under fire during the times of the Ethiopian Revolution.
This book represents a significant addition to the study of music in Ethiopia and marks a major step in introducing the Ethiopian dimension of ethnomusicology to the larger scholarly conversation."

—Tibebe Eshete
Department of Religious Studies, Michigan State University

"*Songs of Ethiopia's Tesfaye Gabbiso*, by Lila Balisky, is a solid work in research methodology and analysis of a modern musical saint and his contribution to Ethiopia and world hymnody. Thanks to Balisky for shedding theological and cultural light on the person, life and ministry of Tesfaye Gabbiso."

—J. Nathan Corbitt
Professor Emeritus of Cross-Cultural Studies, Eastern University

Songs of Ethiopia's Tesfaye Gabbiso

American Society of Missiology
Monograph Series

Series Editor, James R. Krabill

The ASM Monograph Series provides a forum for publishing quality dissertations and studies in the field of missiology. Collaborating with Pickwick Publications—a division of Wipf and Stock Publishers of Eugene, Oregon—the American Society of Missiology selects high quality dissertations and other monographic studies that offer research materials in mission studies for scholars, mission and church leaders, and the academic community at large. The ASM seeks scholarly work for publication in the series that throws light on issues confronting Christian world mission in its cultural, social, historical, biblical, and theological dimensions.

Missiology is an academic field that brings together scholars whose professional training ranges from doctoral-level preparation in areas such as Scripture, history and sociology of religions, anthropology, theology, international relations, interreligious interchange, mission history, inculturation, and church law. The American Society of Missiology, which sponsors this series, is an ecumenical body drawing members from Independent and Ecumenical Protestant, Catholic, Orthodox, and other traditions. Members of the ASM are united by their commitment to reflect on and do scholarly work relating to both mission history and the present-day mission of the church. The ASM Monograph Series aims to publish works of exceptional merit on specialized topics, with particular attention given to work by younger scholars, the dissemination and publication of which is difficult under the economic pressures of standard publishing models.

Persons seeking information about the ASM or the guidelines for having their dissertations considered for publication in the ASM Monograph Series should consult the Society's website—www.asmweb.org.

Members of the ASM Monograph Committee who approved this book are:

Paul V. Kollman, University of Notre Dame
Roger Schroeder, Catholic Theological Union
Bonnie Sue Lewis, University of Dubuque Theological Seminary

Recently Published in the ASM Monograph Series

Friedman , Matthew. *Union with God in Christ: Early Christian and Wesleyan Spirituality as an Approach to Islamic Mysticism*

Chin, Clive S. *The Perception of Christianity as a Rational Religion in Singapore: A Missiological Analysis of Christian Conversion.*

Hubers, John. *I Am a Pilgrim, a Traveler, a Stranger: Exploring the Life and Mind of the First American Missionary to the Middle East, the Rev. Pliny Fisk (1792–1825)*

Songs of Ethiopia's Tesfaye Gabbiso

Singing with Understanding in Babylon, the Meantime, and Zion

BY LILA W. BALISKY

Foreword by Vernon Charter

American Society of Missiology Monograph
Series Vol. 37

☙PICKWICK *Publications* · Eugene, Oregon

SONGS OF ETHIOPIA'S TESFAYE GABBISO
Singing with Understanding in Babylon, the Meantime, and Zion

American Society of Missiology Monograph Series 37

Pickwick Publications
An Imprint of Wipf and Stock Publishers
199 W. 8th Ave., Suite 3
Eugene, OR 97401

www.wipfandstock.com

PAPERBACK ISBN: 978-1-5326-3494-9
HARDCOVER ISBN: 978-1-5326-3496-3
EBOOK ISBN: 978-1-5326-3495-6

Cataloguing-in-Publication data:

Names: Balisky, Lila W., author | Charter, Vernon, foreword

Title: Songs of Ethiopia's Tesfaye Gabbiso : singing with understanding in Babylon, the meantime, and Zion / Lila W. Balisky; foreword by Vernon Charter.

Description: Eugene, OR : Pickwick Publications, 2018 | American Society of Missiology Monograph Series | Includes bibliographical references and index.

Identifiers: ISBN 978-1-5326-3494-9 (paperback) | ISBN 978-1-5326-3496-3 (hardcover) | ISBN 978-1-5326-3495-6 (ebook)

Subjects: LCSH: Spirituals (songs)—Ethiopia—History and criticism. | Christianity—Ethiopia. | Music—Ethiopia.

Classification: LCC ML420.T53 B2 2018 (print) | LCC ML420.T53 (ebook)

Manufactured in the U.S.A.   11/07/18

To
Paul, my beloved husband, scholar, friend
and

creators of song

in Ethiopia

Contents

Figures

Tables

Foreword

IN 2001, I TRAVELED to Ethiopia to research the history of music in the churches of that country during the years of the Ethiopian Marxist revolution (1974–1991). While there, I was privileged to meet and converse with Tesfaye Gabbiso, whose songs are the focus of this book. Tesfaye Gabbiso in 1979 spent seven years in prison during a period when many Christians were the objects of persecution by the revolutionary government. Tesfaye's songs, forged in the furnace of affliction, are precious to Ethiopian Christians of all denominations and stand as a volume of rich lyrical theology, a call to radical discipleship, and an impetus to passionate, authentic worship.

During the 1960s and 1970s, a powerful spiritual awakening swept the country of Ethiopia. The impact of this movement of the Spirit of God continues to be felt to the present day. One of the remarkable features of that revival was the emergence of gifted young musicians like Tesfaye, whose songs greatly enriched the worship, discipleship, and outreach of Ethiopian churches, and provided a source of great hope and comfort for Ethiopian Christians during the dark years of revolution, civil war, and persecution that gripped the country between 1974 and 1991. During that period, hundreds of churches were closed by the *Dergue* (revolutionary council), their buildings were confiscated, and many church leaders and musicians were imprisoned because of their commitment to Christ and their perceived disloyalty to the Marxist agenda of the revolutionary regime. Through the sovereign power of God and the faithfulness of those who endured the fires of persecution, the churches were greatly enriched in their worship, outreach, and numerical growth through those painful years.

I felt greatly honored to have an extended conversation in 2001 with Tesfaye at the home of Paul and Lila Balisky in Addis Ababa. Among the many details of his story, Tesfaye stressed the fact that young people in every denomination were primary objects of persecution during the 1970s and 1980s. Beginning in the 1960s, Christian youth from every denomination were at the forefront of the revival movement, and, as Tesfaye said, their generation was being uniquely prepared to meet the coming challenge to suffer for Christ: "God was raising a generation of young people, igniting our hearts in righteous zeal, to stand for Christ in the face of severe persecution."

Tesfaye Gabisso is one among a handful of musicians who have been called "fathers of Ethiopian church music." As a historian and ethnomusicologist, I find it significant that the songs that were appearing during the three decades covered by Lila Balisky's study (1960s through 1980s) comprised the first truly indigenous music that was eventually embraced by virtually all evangelical churches in Ethiopia. Neither the translated western hymns nor the "antiphonal hymns," which prevailed before 1960, took root in all of the Ethiopian churches in the way that the music from Tesfaye's generation did. Recordings of their songs spread throughout the country and the "new music" took root in churches everywhere. Their theological content, poetic imagery, and cultural authenticity established this music as a standard for generations of songwriters to follow.

In this book, Lila Balisky has given the church a valuable resource for discipling worship leaders and congregations in the stewardship of their singing. Her comprehensive analysis of the texts of Tesfaye's songs offer a template by which to evaluate the themes and the content of the sung repertory of any worshiping community. Using Roberta King's "Global Church Worship Matrix," she demonstrates that the texts of a church's songs reflect how fully its members are living out (or not living out) God's calling to participate in the *missio Dei*, in their personal lives, in their conformity to the Word of God, in the life of the faith community, and in the missional context of communicating the Gospel worldwide.

I warmly recommend this volume to Christian musicians and poets everywhere, with the hope that Tesfaye's life and artistry will help to shape fully their vision as servants of Christ and his church. Missionaries and missiologists will find here a compelling case study of contextualized worship in a specific cultural setting. At the same time, Balisky's book would serve admirably as a cross-cultural textbook for students of missiology and ethnodoxology whose life vision will be to facilitate authentic biblical worship among the nations of the world. It is also worth emphasizing the value of the excellent English translations for the 104 songs selected for this study. I challenge worshipers everywhere to study and internalize the substance of Tesfaye Gabbisso's songs and allow them to define and reshape the core and essence of their worship.

Vernon Charter, D.W.S.
Professor Emeritus/Music/Worship Arts/ Ethnomusicology
Prairie College, Three Hills, AB, ToM 2Ao, Canada

Abstract

THIS PROJECT EXPLORES THE song career and lyrics of a prominent contemporary Ethiopian soloist, Tesfaye Gabbiso. From the middle of the twentieth century until the present, thousands of indigenous "spiritual songs" have emanated from an emerging generation of musicians in the evangelical churches of Ethiopia. Approximately 20 percent of Tesfaye's total output of songs was produced during a seven-year period of acute suffering while he was incarcerated for his stand in the faith during the Ethiopian revolution from 1974 to 1991. The 104 songs studied comprise Tesfaye's cassettes 1–7, which are included in English translation at the end of this book. This case study presents a sociohistorical and religious context of the singer's life narrative as well as various forms of content analysis. Tesfaye's own commentary through writing and speaking contributes grounding to the study. Inquiry is made into the meaning and significance of his songs as they represent a position of suffering and endurance as well as a challenge to discipleship in the musical arts.

Acknowledgments

THIS MONOGRAPH IS THE unexpected culmination of a long journey in which I took action, step by step, almost subconsciously. God through His Spirit has led me all the way, and my gratitude finds expression in these words of Tesfaye Gabbiso:

> Oh, Lord, bless us with a blessing. Enlarge our spiritual territory.
> May Your hand be upon us. You are our hope. (Song VI–6)

A host of friends, through a period of many years, are to be acknowledged for their contributions to my life and this study of Ethiopian songs.

The first acknowledgement is to Tesfaye Gabbiso himself, the creator and singer of the songs in this study. He agreed that such a reflection on his songs could possibly be a positive and spiritually challenging exercise at this stage of both his own song history and in the life of the Ethiopian church. I thank him for allowing this work to proceed in such a way that we both acknowledged the goodness and leading of God's Spirit and the *kairos* of the moment.

I further acknowledge the influence of professors, writers, and musicians who have encouraged me to "do something" with my Ethiopian music experience. John Parratt, in 1991 at New College, University of Edinburgh, inspired me regarding the concept of oral theology and encouraged the use of my translated collection of songs as the basis for a paper in his class on African theology. Other encouragers at strategic points along the way have included Andrew Walls, Darrell Whiteman, Jonathan Bonk, Nathan Corbitt, James Krabill, Marianne Nilsson, Kay Shelemay, and Hugo Ferran. I kindly thank two friends and scholars, Tibebe Eshete and Vernon Charter, for their willingness to assist in reading this paper and give helpful suggestions.

Ethiopian friends who have stimulated my thinking include Ezra Abate, Meheretab Beraki, Gezahegn Mussie, Eyob Denio and Zelalem Mengistu.

My sincere thanks go to Haile Jenai who, over a period of twenty years, worked tirelessly whenever I called upon him for his language and translation skills. He listened and transcribed seven Amharic cassettes, then translated all of the Amharic material into English. Yohannes Desta's assistance in translation is also much appreciated. Zenebe Gebrehana and all at the SIM Press in Addis Ababa are to be thanked for their skills in producing the diglot hymnal in Amharic and English entitled *Yetesfayé Gabbiso Mezmuroch: The Songs of Tesfaye Gabbiso.*

A great debt of gratitude goes to SIM Canada for approving this study as a project even though we were already retired from active service in Ethiopia. As a result, many friends were enabled to contribute to this project's tuition and travel costs, and I am truly grateful for God's provision. I trust my work will be of value to the developing world-wide emphasis on the arts in mission.

To my own family, I owe a great debt. My husband, Paul, shared my inspiration to undertake this task and has been a gentle, understanding mentor throughout the process, listening ceaselessly to my ideas, always encouraging me throughout the process. Our three sons, Allen, Loren, and Kevin, with their families, have cheered me on in various ways.

Two musical friends who traveled with me to teach "Worship and Music in the Church" in Ethiopia were Aurelia Keefer, a soul friend and scholarly source of inspiration, and Moges Berassa, singer and guitarist, who added much richness to our joint teaching.

In Grande Prairie, Alberta, Canada, I thank three friends: Willa Myers, Janice Orr, and Maxine Shantz, whom I conscripted as a support group while I studied at Fuller.

I give special thanks to my three ethnomusicology colleagues within a larger Fuller cohort: Amelia Koh-Butler, Megan Meyers, and Sue Whittaker. This was a one-off remarkable Fuller SIS (School of Intercultural Studies) cohort with the combined wisdom and teaching talents of my mentor, Roberta King, as well as Sherwood and Judith Lingenfelter. I shall be forever grateful for the golden opportunity to study at Fuller Theological Seminary. Many times our cohort was encouraged and blessed by Roberta King leading us in singing the responsive: "The Lord bless you." The Lord's face shone upon us and gave us peace through four wonderful years of study together.

Abbreviations

EGST	Ethiopian Graduate School of Theology
EKHC	Ethiopian Kale Heywet Church
EOTC	Ethiopian Orthodox *Tewahedo* Church
RVOG	Radio Voice of the Gospel
SIM, Int'l	Serving in Mission (formerly Sudan Interior Mission)
WES	Wolaitta Evangelical Seminary
EC	Refers to the Ethiopian Calendar which follows the western calendar dates by 7 to 8 years. The "EC" is maintained when helpful for future researchers in relation to Amharic printed materials.

THE FOLLOWING FURTHER ABBREVIATIONS were created to aid in the challenge of dealing with both English and Amharic languages in this book.

(Song VII–14). Any song from the source songbook will be indicated by cassette number using Roman numerals followed by a hyphen and the song number (Arabic) within the cassette. The entire body of songs with Table of Contents is found in Appendix C.

(Tesfaye, BG, 57). References with this configuration refer to the Amharic book *Beziyan Gizé* written by Tesfaye Gabbiso about his prison experiences. The page numbers refer to the Amharic book. An English translation, entitled *Those Days*, is to be published in Ethiopia in the near future.

(Tesfaye, #7). This code refers to Amharic articles in Ethiopian publications. Abbreviation has been used to enable the flow of the reading because the Amharic titles are complex and often there is no specific author. Page numbers are not referenced within the text because all the articles are relatively short. But all necessary details are listed at the end of bibliography in a special collection entitled, "Amharic Articles: Tesfaye Gabbiso Special Collection."

Transliteration and Formatting

TRANSLITERATION OF AMHARIC TO English: The transliteration system employed is a basic and consistent method of dealing with the Amharic *fidel* (Amharic alphabet). It does not indicate doublings or *fidel* with varied orthographic history. But it is suitable for both Amharic and English readers.

Vowels:
e as in "bed"
u as in "too"
i as in "bead"
a as in "sad"
é as in "state"
ï as in "his"
o as in "cone"
Consonants:
(These indicate what is commonly known as "explosives" in Amharic)
ch = ç; k = ķ; p = p (no regular "p" in original Amharic); t = ţ; ts = ş

Formatting notes in Amharic:

1. There is no "capital" form of Amharic *fidel*. Therefore, in titles, the use of a "small" case *fidel* is accurate.

2. All foreign language forms are required to be in italics, so this renders proper formatting of bibliography entries difficult. I have endeavored to be consistent in making the format clear enough that a given bibliography entry may be sufficient for research in either English or Amharic.

3. "EC" written after a date refers to "Ethiopian Calendar" which is 7 to 8 years behind (depending on the month) the western calendar.

Formatting Ethiopian names in the bibliography differs from the English style in that I have followed the Ethiopian preference, which cites first name then last name. Also, both names are cited in footnotes for Ethiopian authors.

Prologue

Experiential Journey into Ethiopian Song

> *When we are looking for African theology we should go first to the fields. . . . We must look at the way in which Christianity is being planted in Africa through music, drama, songs, dances, art, paintings.*[1]

IN 1967, AS A young missionary under the auspices of SIM, Int'l, I had the privilege of going "first to the fields." I began to hear the songs of Ethiopia. At that time, out of a general interest in music, I started listening to the "spiritual songs" of the Ethiopian evangelical churches, especially those within the Kale Heywet Church (EKHC) with roots in the SIM. Little did I know where this interest in the music of our adopted country would eventually lead me. In the years following, I eagerly acquired any available Ethiopian songbook I came across in any of the evangelical churches. I also explored songs in the two other Trinitarian churches present in Ethiopia: (1) The Catholic churches (1 percent of the population) and (2) the Ethiopian Orthodox *Tewahedo* Church (EOTC), which comprises 40 percent of the population. I collected songbooks from both traditions and supervised translation of many Orthodox choir songs.

My actual experience of writing and teaching on Ethiopian music began with authoring an article in *Missiology* (1997): "Theology in Song: Ethiopia's Tesfaye Gabbiso." This article was originally inspired by a course in African theologies, which I took under John Parratt at New College, University of Edinburgh, from 1990 to 1991. In 1996, I was invited by Andrew Walls to present a well-received seminar lecture on Ethiopian music at New College. Back in Ethiopia, during the 1980s and

---

1. Okullu, *Church and Politics*, 54.

1990s, I was privileged to create and teach "Worship and Music" courses in the Ethiopian Kale Heywet Church diploma schools and the Evangelical Theological College in Addis Ababa. In 2008, I taught an ethnomusicology course at EGST (Ethiopian Graduate School of Theology).

In 2010, I facilitated the publication of an English-Amharic diglot of the songs of Tesfaye Gabbiso. These songs were translated from Amharic to English with the expert collaboration and giftedness of Haile Jenai. In 2013, through a series of fascinating connections and the interest of Hugo Ferran, French-Canadian ethnomusicologist, my entire collection of Ethiopian music was digitalized.[2] In the 2013 online edition of *Canterbury Dictionary of Hymnody*, the writing of an article on Ethiopian hymnology is shared by Ralph Lee (Orthodox section) and myself (New Churches' section).

Now to the subject of this book: I have chosen to study the lyrics of one songwriter, Tesfaye Gabbiso, with whom we have been associated for over forty-five years. He represents a long and fruitful era of solo-singers in Ethiopia, and my desire is to capture the essence of his lyrics as an academic record and legacy for future scholars of Ethiopian church music. I do this as a "sacrifice of praise" for the many years of service that God granted my husband, Paul, and me in Ethiopia.

As young missionaries, having just arrived in Ethiopia in 1967 under the auspices of SIM Int'l, we spent a year studying Amharic and then were assigned to our first post in Aletta Wondo, Sidama. With three small sons, I was busy in the home, but God brought Ethiopian music into our new home, and thus began a journey that has brought me half a century later to this book. The story follows.

In 1970, my husband, Paul, was instructing in a local Kale Heywet Church Amharic Bible School for church leaders in Aletta Wondo, Sidama, southern Ethiopia. One student who enrolled was Gabbiso Doyamo, a venerable elder both in community and church. He came from the countryside bringing with him his young son, Tesfaye, who joined in the SIM mission school on the compound for his middle years before high school. Tesfaye was a sturdy, short, smiling, alert young lad. As we were parents of three sons ourselves, all a bit younger than Tesfaye, the neighborhood gang soon joined forces and became great friends. Tesfaye and his friends were often at our house, and I soon realized how he liked

2. See https://hugoferran.wordpress.com/publications 2013. "Lila W. Balisky Private Ethiopian Music Collection." The original collection is held in Grande Prairie, Alberta, Canada.

to climb up on a stool and turn on the radio on our high kitchen shelf to listen to "new music." It was at that stage I began my journey into Ethiopian songs. The new music was coming from Radio Voice of the Gospel (RVOG)[3] and was beginning to replace the older translated Swedish/ American gospel songs which had earlier been translated into Amharic. These new spiritual songs were being created by young people and sung to indigenous tunes, and here was a new genre for my investigation.

Within a short time, Tesfaye and his friend Estifanos found themselves being asked to sing in the local Ethiopian church assembly on Sunday mornings. They would sing songs heard on the radio station RVOG as well as new songs Tesfaye himself was creating.[4]

After leaving Aletta Wondo in 1971, we were not in contact with Tesfaye again until he came unexpectedly to visit us in Jimma, Ethiopia, on November 12, 1977. By now, Tesfaye's solo ministry was well-established, and several cassette tapes had already appeared in Ethiopia's music stores. I remember some of his comments that day. He noted that some folks were saying his tunes were hard to sing, but the general public was greatly appreciating his songs. He reminded me that I had challenged him as a young boy that he might become a blessing to the entire Ethiopian church in the future if he accepted and used his obvious gift of music for God's glory. Little did either of us know that within a few months following, he would be detained with others and spend seven years in prison because of his Christian commitment.

The next time we met was fifteen years later in Addis Ababa in 1991. At that time, I did a lengthy recorded interview with Tesfaye in order to capture his life journey to that point. I became more fully aware of his expanding reputation as a prominent Ethiopian singer. An excellent Amharic-English translator had earlier begun informally working with me on translating Tesfaye's cassettes, and so by the late 1990s, I had a complete hand-written version of Tesfaye's Amharic cassettes in the English language.

In 2005, we retired to Canada from full-time service in Ethiopia, but when we returned to Ethiopia in 2008 for a six-months' teaching stint at the Ethiopian Graduate School of Theology (EGST), the idea of a diglot (English and Amharic printed side by side) of Tesfaye's songs came to

3. RVOG (Radio Voice of the Gospel) was a prominent Lutheran World Federation international radio station, founded in 1963 and based in the Ethiopian capital, Addis Ababa.

4. See photo in Appendix A.

mind. This project could be the consummation of the long years in which Haile Jenai and I had labored together in translating and checking the first seven cassettes of Tesfaye's solos. After summoning up the courage and rationale for such an idea, I discussed this, first with Tesfaye, then with the appropriate people in the SIM Media department. Such a publishing project was an entirely new thought for all of us, but we all agreed we should give it a try. The first printing was small, as the SIM Media Department had never produced anything like this and were not sure what the response would be to such a book. A modest number of copies appeared as a first printing with the title: "The Songs of Tesfaye Gabbiso: *yetesfayé gabbiso mezmuroch.*"

As of 2015, the third printing was completed, and Ethiopians all over the world appreciate the book. To God be all the glory.

This doctoral program has been thrust upon me as a holy calling. I could not ignore the opportunity. I enrolled at Fuller Seminary with the idea of comparing the solo and choir songs of the evangelical and Orthodox churches, but was soon convinced by my professors and cohort members that I was attempting an impossible amount of material. They queried: "What smaller, contained body of songs might you consider?" In an epiphany during that class period, I suddenly realized that I must write about the songs of Tesfaye Gabbiso as found in the very diglot that we had published a year or two earlier. In tears of humility and amazement, I bowed to the task, and a doctoral dissertation was the result.

I will now take you, the reader, to the field.

1

Introduction

COME WITH ME TO the campus of Addis Ababa University on September 14, 1997. Excitement was in the air as a rally of Christian students was in progress. There was freedom again to meet in public and express faith after the weary restrictions during years of the Marxist revolution (1974 to 1991). We gathered outside under tall eucalyptus trees and listened to three well-loved soloists, Addisu Werku, Tamrat Haile and Tesfaye Gabbiso. They were "fathers" of the spiritual song revival that was in progress. All three men sang their most famous songs while we, the gathered throng, exploded with ïllïlta the ululation or trill of joy commonly used in Ethiopia. The root of this Amharic word is the same as the Hebrew, the «hallel» which appears in the English word Hallelujah. That day, Tesfaye chose to sing "When God Assists" (Song V–11), one of his much-appreciated prison songs. The tune of the chorus matches the words as it marches in bold pentatonic movement down the scale: "God . . . when he comes down . . . from the heavens." The event was an exclamation mark of excitement and thanksgiving in the life of the Ethiopian churches. Who is this Tesfaye Gabbiso with such impact through his songs?

This case study explores the songs of Ethiopian soloist Tesfaye Gabbiso within the context of his life narrative as a singer. The research is situated within the socio-historical and religious history of Ethiopia from 1960 to 2010 and considers how the critical moments of his musical career have been shaped by his life context. Particular emphasis is given to the Marxist revolution (1974 to 1991) that greatly impacted the life of the singer. A published book of 104 Amharic song texts, as found in the Amharic/English diglot, published in 2011, is the basis of the study. It is

1

presented as a case study employing narrative biography, realist ethnography, and content analysis.

STATEMENT OF THE RESEARCH QUESTIONS

1. How have the critical moments in the lived experience and musical career of Tesfaye Gabbiso been shaped by the socio-historical and religious Ethiopian context of the latter 20th century, with particular emphasis on the Marxist revolution of 1974 to 1991?

2. What are main themes in the 104 song texts, focused by Tesfaye's life narrative, as found in *The Songs of Tesfaye Gabbiso?*

3. What has been the impact of the singer and his songs on the life and worship of the Ethiopian evangelical church?

4. What interpretations and synthesis will be discovered that will sustain a tradition of rich hymnody in the churches' worship and mission?

DELIMITATIONS

This study is limited to the 104 songs contained in *The Songs of Tesfaye Gabbiso* an English/Amharic diglot based on Tesfaye's first seven cassettes. In 2012, Tesfaye Gabbiso published a larger compendium of his songs entitled, "His Mercy Never Ends" (*mïhïretu ayalḵïmïna*) which is not part of this study. An eighth CD, released since the genesis of this dissertation, is also not included in this study.

This work focuses primarily on the song texts; discussion of the musicological dimensions is minimal. There has been no effort to maintain rhythm or meter in the translation process.

This dissertation is not a biographical treatise on the life and career of Tesfaye Gabbiso. It does not include his pastoral and teaching ministries except as related to his singing.

Though I address this dissertation to the Trinitarian churches of Ethiopia, I acknowledge that my examples and the main emphasis of my writing as well as the context of my experience is mostly with the evangelical churches. However, I believe the study of Tesfaye's life and lyrics will be applicable to all the churches.

DEFINITIONS

Spiritual songs: During the past half-century, thousands of indigenous spiritual songs (*menfesawi mezmuroch*) have been composed by a younger generation of Ethiopians in Orthodox, Catholic and Evangelical churches. These songs were a new genre created in the minds and hearts of earnest Christians as a new way of expressing their deepest spiritual experience.

Younger generation: The roots of the spiritual song movement are to be located within groups of university students and other church young people beginning in the 1960s. These were youth and young adults in contrast to traditional church elders and hierarchy. In the Orthodox churches, songs were created for use outside the ecclesiastical liturgical setting and in the more informal afternoon preaching and singing times for children and laity within Orthodox Church compounds.

Trinitarian churches: This term has been used by Seleshi Kebede to include all the Christian churches in Ethiopia.[1] Ethiopia is a unique nation with a mix of long Orthodox Church history, long Catholic Church mission activity, and today a grand array of other church groups which may be described as evangelical. Most of them are charismatic in worship and may even describe themselves as Pentecostal at the present time. See the following definition:

Evangelical: A large number of church groups in Ethiopia today who do not position themselves in the Orthodox or Catholic Churches but have a loose organization called the Evangelical Churches Fellowship of Ethiopia (ECFE). Hence, I have chosen the word Evangelical, capitalized when deemed appropriate, to denote those churches as the third group within the Trinitarian churches cluster.

ASSUMPTIONS

The songs of Tesfaye Gabbiso have been very popular in Ethiopia over the past forty years. He is still composing and singing and is considered a "father" of Ethiopian evangelical music. Therefore, his songs are worthy of study.

The English translation of the Amharic songs is deemed accurate for academic study, although both languages are carefully considered in the word studies and analysis.

1. Seleshi Kebede, "Cooperation of Trinitarian Churches," 25.

The spiritual song tradition of this one soloist is presumed to be an adequate and true representation of the greater Ethiopian evangelical song environment.

The selected songs as defined by the first seven cassettes are assumed to be an adequate sample of Tesfaye's entire corpus of songs.

Research into the song lyrics will yield significant insights into the personal spirituality of Tesfaye Gabbiso as well as into the theology of the evangelical churches, especially during the years of the Ethiopian revolution, 1974 to 1991, a period of deep suffering for the church.

SIGNIFICANCE

Firstly, this study supplies a scholarly addition to Ethiopian academia in an area that has previously been largely unaddressed. Very little has been written representing evangelical Ethiopian Christians (20 percent of the Ethiopian population) and their involvement in the arts. This study will provide insights and analysis into lyric theology as found in one singer's spiritual songs.

Secondly, the results of this study should encourage conscious consideration of the social, theological and missiological impact of song lyrics. This study will be influential in the process of deepening theological understanding in the Ethiopian church. It will stimulate discipleship among Christian musicians as they purposefully contribute depth and beauty to personal and corporate worship. It will challenge Ethiopians in the diaspora and in mission service as they carry their song in witness beyond Ethiopia.

Thirdly, this work will stimulate academic study by Ethiopian scholars. The rich heritage of song must be preserved and serve as a foundation for the church's future song. It is the intent of this study to open up further avenues of thinking, research and practical action.

Fourthly, this study holds the potential to be a catalyst in strengthening bonds between the Trinitarian church bodies in Ethiopia as they consider their common history, especially through a period of persecution. Too easily, we forget. Ethiopia holds a unique heritage on the African continent with its mix of Orthodox, Catholic and evangelical traditions. All of the Trinitarian churches appreciate and sing the songs of Tesfaye Gabbiso. People listen to his devotional songs in their homes and churches. One hears them blaring out from song shops or even bus radios. His songs are sung at many public events ranging from funerals to large Christian conferences.

Lastly, may this study also be an embodied vision and challenge to Christian commitment globally as to the value of spiritual songs which influence the totality of life, witness and worship in our world of trials and suffering. Song, rooted in the flow of *missio Dei* and motivated aesthetically by the eternal beauty of God, is perhaps the greatest testimony that may be lived out in our complex world.

2

Literature and Theoretical Moorings

SONG IS A MODE of communication finding foundation and interpretation through various disciplines such as missiology, theology, anthropology, and history. In this chapter I discuss literature that pertains to applied research in various fields and theoretical aspects which impact song, especially as it pertains in the Ethiopian setting.

Song, as phenomenon, is vital to the very heart and expression of the *missio Dei* which is the surging mission of God throughout his creation. The Christian scriptures narrate a history of song that begins with the stars singing together and culminates at the throne of God. Missiological principles have shown the relationships and inter-relatedness of various disciplines with music in world community, church context, personal life and place of the Word. I will apply, for example, the image of a theodrama to explain the Christ-event enculturated in the life and practice of singer Tesfaye Gabbiso.

MISSIOLOGICAL CONCEPTS

Under missiological concepts, I consider two areas which are applicable in this discussion. The first is the Global Church Music Matrix which is a way of organizing our thinking. I will also consider the place of song in the larger scope of what is called the *missio Dei*.

MATRIX FOR STUDIES IN GLOBAL CHURCH MUSIC

The relationship of music to other disciplines may be studied by using a "Matrix for Studies in Global Church Music" approach, as put forward by

King in ethnomusicological studies.[1] Through the four lenses that affect each other and intertwine, I will have a tool to study the life and songs of Tesfaye Gabbiso.

Four-Arena Approach

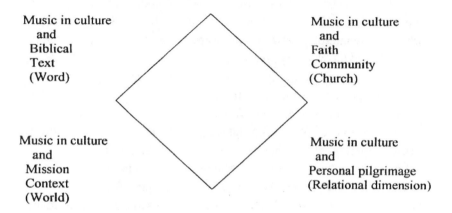

Music in culture
and
Biblical
Text
(Word)

Music in culture
and
Faith
Community
(Church)

Music in culture
and
Mission
Context
(World)

Music in culture
and
Personal pilgrimage
(Relational dimension)

Figure 1: Matrix for Studies in Global Church Music
(Adapted from King, "Beginnings," 13)

This model is employed again in Chapter 9 in Figure 5 where the framework is used to consider the various arenas in which Tesfaye lives and sings. I also gradually expand this approach into a thicker model in Figure 6 with the undergirding of the *missio Dei* as the foundation and aesthetics or the beauty of God over-arching the whole model.

SONG IN THE *MISSIO DEI*

By using the concept of *missio Dei*, I accept the definition of David Bosch as he speaks of the sending of God, his self-revelation, and a deeper universal mission that lies beneath and beyond what the church does in "mission." We as the church are "privileged to participate" in this eternal impetus.[2] I see the spiritual song of a person as a minute but powerful part of this triune thrust or surge undergirding the church and the world. The spiritual song of one person into the world should reflect this sending; it not only reflects but is a part of the sending of God.

---

1. Henceforth called "Global Church Music Matrix" in this dissertation.
2. Bosch, *Transforming Mission*, 10.

African writers contribute to discussing song in the inculturation of Christianity. Lamin Sanneh speaks of the *missio Dei* and transmission of scripture which opens a new world of the Supreme Being, bringing the Christian message "within range of popular piety."[3] Song may be included as both "prayer" and "popular piety." Africa's expression in song may be the most accurate expression that is to be found, of the inculturated message. Kwame Bediako agrees with Sanneh that Christians live and work "in the interplay between prayer and action; it has never achieved its mission to the world by precept alone."[4]

Furthermore, Calvin Stapert points out that "the song the church sings, as described in the New Testament, is a joyful response to the works of God, stimulated by the Word and the Spirit. It is sung by humans to God and to each other, with the saints and angels and all creation."[5] Again, Stapert points out that God is the "primary audience" of our song; but meanwhile "another audience, the prisoners, the nations, is also listening" like the Philippian jailor in Acts.[6] I appreciate Stapert's concept of song that is sung everywhere in creation, and his thoughts have stimulated my thinking as to what a song means in whatever situation it may be sung.

The overarching beauty or aesthetics of God in my model is proposed based on N. T. Wright's concept of the eternal beauty. A song is one of the highest forms of beauty we know in this world. It is a part of the wholeness expressed in Romans chapter eight, which holds an "integrated worldview, and with a theology of both creation and new creation."[7] There is a delight in beauty which leads us to God and the new creation.

At the end of the dissertation, I propose a synthesis of the undergirding and over-arching mission and aesthetics of God in creation that will envelop the total message of singer and song.

THEOLOGICAL CONSTRUCTS

In this section, I explore both African and Western theologians' contributions to our topic. In particular, what do African writers say about theology in song? Theologies of resistance and survival, of suffering and

3. Sanneh, "Horizontal and the Vertical," 170.
4. Bediako, "Christ in Africa," 456–57.
5. Stapert, *New Song*, 28.
6. Stapert, *New Song*, 23.
7. Wright, *Surprised by Hope*, 222–24.

lament, pertain to Tesfaye's songs. What should the focus of one's song be? We are invited to see the singer as part of theodrama, the Christ-event being lived out in real life.

Theodrama

Kevin Vanhoozer's concept of theodrama insists on the Christ-event as the core of all truth as it is lived out as mission in local contexts. "Christians demonstrate understanding of the biblical script, and hence of what God was doing in Jesus Christ, not through academic treatises and commentaries but through their individual and corporate lives; Christian speech and action are forms of performative knowledge."[8] Vanhoozer's "canonic principle" would insist that Scripture is what our stories (songs) must follow and, further, that "every fitting performance of the gospel must also take account of our present speech and action."[9] A singer's performance fits the definition of "improvisation" in Vanhoozer's terms as a form of "disciplined spontaneity" which leads me to suggest that a soloist singing his song in an appropriate manner is an example of continuing "the evangelical action by responding to the offerings of Word and Spirit in culturally (and intellectually) appropriate manners."[10] That is, the gospel is "infinitely translatable" and "infinitely performable."[11] I see Tesfaye, the soloist, standing in the middle of the Global Church Music Matrix, as shown in Figure l, demonstrating this truth of the theodrama.

African Theology

Discussions by Stinton, Bediako, Molyneux, and Howell stimulate thought in the area of African theology and how it should be done. Stinton is concerned about "'home-grown' or authentic, indigenous faith reflections in the midst of particular life circumstances." [12] She faithfully enables African voices such as Magesa's who give such thoughtful reflection on African spirituality.[13] Howell collects not only songs, but proverbs, sermons, local poetry, and has recorded many a conversation at

8. Vanhoozer, "One Rule," 112.

9. Vanhoozer, "One Rule," 113.

10. Vanhoozer, "One Rule," 114–115.

11. Vanhoozer, "One Rule," 116.

12. Stinton, "Africa," 106.

13. Magesa, "African Christian Spirituality," 68–78.

evening firesides. She confirms the power of Kasena songs of Ghana and concludes that they are "natural expressions" of the people's theology.[14]

One may study the topical subjects appearing in a singer's repertoire. A focus on God appears to be predominant in the songs: God's work, his salvation and his power. Dealing with the forces of evil is also a dominant theme. King's "*Lex Canendi, Les Credendi*," ("How one sings is how one believes") also explains that our theology is expressed in the song.[15] One of my goals is to understand the concerns of Tesfaye Gabbiso in his lyrics, especially regarding suffering. His theology, enfolded in Scripture, was hammered out on the anvil of physical and emotional suffering. But rather than dwell only on suffering, Tesfaye has stated that he prefers his songs to concentrate on themes of Gospel and discipleship.[16]

The Psalms as Song

The work of Christopher Wright, especially on the Psalms, forms a biblical backdrop for this study in revealing the broad scope of the *missio Dei* and the place of song.[17] The old songs of Israel become the new songs spreading through the world. This biblical use of song leads to the question of what is song in the life of an individual? The wide usage of Psalms both in worship and daily life is detailed to sound very similar to the usage of the spiritual songs in Ethiopia. Stapert elaborates on the use of Psalms as "house music" and the importance of song in the everyday life of the Jews.[18] This carries into the New Testament. Stapert discusses the issue, alive today in Ethiopia, as to what is involved in singing a "new song" in an "old" world.[19] This pertains to the church song development in the 1960s. As we shall see, Tesfaye's style was "new" for that era in a church and political setting that was growing weary.

Walter Brueggemann's insights on metaphor and the language of the Psalms contribute to this discussion in his reflections on our experience of "touching the Psalter" and how metaphorical language liberates us to interpret it for our own experiences, the more perilous, the more poetic. He writes lucidly about psalmic poetry in the midst of life's extremities,

---

14. Howell, *Religious Itinerary*, 216, 275.

15. King, "Bible," 117.

16. Interview with Tesfaye Gabbiso, Hawassa, January 9, 2015.

17. Wright, *Mission of God*, 474–84.

18. Stapert, *New Song*, 155–56.

19. Stapert, *New Song*, 131–48.

disorientations, chaos, raw hurts, and living at the edge.[20] We will discover how Tesfaye breathes the Psalms and resonates with the life of David.

Resistance and Survival

An Ethiopian scholar, Tibebe Eshetu, has discussed the songs of the evangelical church during the Ethiopian revolution as a form of resistance.[21] Tesfaye makes some references to the Revolution that are quite direct to the Marxist philosophers. For example, in Song II-12, he says, "Man, thinking he knew, did a lot of searching. Loving sin, and living for judgment, man folded his hands and said, "The Lord doesn't exist." Music was "among the many targets of intimidation and arrest by the authorities because of the perceived 'subversive' character of their music, as well as their resistance to government attempts to co-opt their music for political purposes."[22]

Vernon Charter, relying on Durkheim's theory of ritual politics, says that people make political commitments on the basis of emotions, not just rational argument.[23] It does not seem that Tesfaye's songs reflect any Ethiopian nationalism in particular. There are no symbols of the power of Haile Selassie or traditional Lion of Tribe of Judah, but the fact that there was a new kind of popular religious music being sung was enough to disturb the new Marxist government.[24] Song has a powerful place in resistance as Don Saliers suggests in his speaking of the "power of biblical canticles" and how they can have political "soundings."[25] This phenomenon will be seen in Tesfaye's prison interactions with government officials.

Girma Bekele, an Ethiopian Christian scholar now living in Canada, is currently writing to the Christians of Ethiopia challenging them to be the "in-between" people, the salt and light in society, the healers of the ethnic breaches, the carriers of life to the poor. He challenges the Christians of Ethiopia to "resist the norms, forsake prejudice and be active in the nation."[26] But one might question his plea to be "in-between" people

---

20. Brueggemann, *Praying the Psalms*, 1–15.
21. Tibebe Eshete, *Evangelical Movement*, 278–83.
22. Charter, "Contested Symbols," 1.
23. Charter, "Contested Symbols," 3.
24. Tibebe Eshete, *Evangelical Movement*, 245–51.
25. Saliers, *Music and Theology*, 43–50.
26. Girma Bekele, *In-Between People.* 266–75.

when they were actually enduring an oppressive regime that incarcerated Tesfaye and his friends for seven years. Tesfaye's songs challenged and resisted the existing Marxist regime with an alternative allegiance to the Kingdom of God.

Suffering and Lament

Suffering and lament are common themes in the Psalms. Tesfaye identifies with David in a very deep way. Eleonora Hof makes the suggestion that "lament cannot be voiced from a neutral location."[27] It is significant to hear the voices of those removed from the dominant culture or structure, which certainly was Tesfaye's case for seven years. She argues that "those suppressed by the dominant symbolic order enjoy a certain 'surplus.'[28] This means that they are able to have knowledge that is hidden from those who are maintaining the symbolic order."[29] Then when a prisoner sings, no less, there is even an extra surplus that befuddles the captor. As she quotes Wolterstorff,

> Lament, at heart, is giving voice to the suffering that accompanies deep loss, whatever that loss may be. Lament is not about suffering. Lament is not concerning suffering. Lament is the language of suffering, the voicing of suffering. Behind lament are tears over loss. Lament goes beyond the tears to voice the suffering."[30]

Tesfaye laments. Begbie adds to this discussion with his lengthy concept of time which is involved in lament, and thus the title of this dissertation hints at being in Babylon, the Meantime and on into Zion, all of which is possible to experience at once.[31] The passing of time and endurance are important aspects in thinking about songs in a period of persecution.

CULTURAL CONSIDERATIONS

What is the relationship between Gospel and culture? Ethiopia is a nation rich in culture that dates back hundreds of years. There are several aspects that should be considered as relevant to the discussion of song.

27. Hof, "Missiology of Lament," 323.
28. Hof, "Missiology of Lament," 323.
29. Hof, "Missiology of Lament," 325.
30. Hof, "Missiology of Lament," 330.
31. Begbie, *Theology, Music and Time*, 71–126.

As a starting point, I look at Zimbabwe's Chitando and his excellent work on Gospel music.

Gospel and Culture

Chitando's work on Gospel music in Zimbabwe helps me to understand the relationship between gospel and culture. He speaks of gospel music as "a valuable entry point" into the study of culture and Christianity being converted to culture, but "also converting Christianity to African cultural realities."[32] As "cultural workers," singers are vitally involved in the whole *missio Dei* through their creation and expression of song.[33] They are blessed and revitalized personally as they sing the word both in community and to the world. They are contributing to community and being ministered to at the same time as the community responds. They are being evangelized as well as doing evangelism as they sing. And they are making music created from within themselves and then sung by themselves. Just as Chitando described Zimbabwe singer Manyeruke taking Zimbabwean gospel music to international audiences, so also Tesfaye sings to Ethiopian diasporas in many different countries. As with Manyeruke, it is also said of Tesfaye that "people of various religious persuasions have found solace and entertainment in his music."[34]

Ethiopia's Dichotomy, Spiritual Songs and Worldly Songs

Where do Ethiopian songs originate? This dichotomy resonates historically back to St. Yared and the songs he received from God which were considered spiritual in origin. Throughout world church history, the battle has not lessened between sacred and secular, especially in the church.[35] And as decades and centuries pass, the old "secular" inevitably moves to acceptability in the church, and music forms continue to evolve and travel. The Amharic for "spiritual songs" is *menfesawi mezmur.* In the current evangelical parlance, it would seem that songs not emanating from the church are considered "worldly." In classes I have taught where I asked about cultural songs such as work, lullaby, sports and national anthems, there was a questioning in students' minds whether they are

---

32. Chitando, *Singing Culture*, 91.
33. Chitando, *Singing Culture*, 8, 51.
34. Chitando, *Singing Culture*, 52.
35. Best, *Music Through the Eyes of Faith*, 40–41.

really legitimate for Christians to compose and sing. There seems to be a lack of appreciation for songs in the middle, songs that are cultural but not necessarily spiritual. These songs I am speaking of are somewhere "between" what is considered spiritual song and the traditional *zefen* music which is for secular dance and entertainment in a manner that does not meet with the approval of church folks.

This dichotomy between *zefen* and *mezmur* is discussed by Jan Magne Steinhovden in a recent master's thesis. Do spiritual songs come directly from God through the Spirit? What is the function of the person through whom the song is given?[36] This concept is explored by K. Gordon Molyneux, as well in the context of the Kimbanguist hymns in the Democratic Republic of the Congo.[37] Tesfaye, who is definitely a composer and singer of "spiritual songs" is a strong supporter of the idea that songs come from God through the singer. There is an eternal conflict between what is of God and what is of the evil one. Tesfaye firmly believes in the gifts of the Spirit which energize the genuine spiritual song.

There is a sense in which Christians are always singing against evil in culture, but their song may, at the same time, also be a strong witness into the culture. Rich Hansen, a recent comer to Ethiopia, lecturing at the Ethiopian Graduate School of Theology (EGST), traces the history of dualism in Ethiopian thinking. He contends that dualistic thinking may be used "by Satan to distort and frustrate the growth of God's kingdom."[38] Tesfaye has put into verse the reality of darkness and light, the kingdom of God and the kingdom of Satan. Many would testify that Tesfaye's songs have promoted the growth of God's kingdom, not distorted it. The church in Ethiopia is therefore challenged to worship and speak into culture in new and vital ways for this generation and its unique challenges, just as Tesfaye has done in a past generation.

Ethiopian Literary Devices

Vivid images from the natural world, with which Africa is so familiar, are an important dimension of Ethiopian literature. Claude Sumner, former Jesuit professor at Addis Ababa University, has described the phenomenon:

---

36. Steinhovden, "*Mäzmur* and *Zäfän*," 25–38.

37. Molyneux, *African Christian Theology*, 151ff.

38. Hansen, "Transforming the Dualistic Worldview," 140.

> The basic images that [Ethiopians] use bathe in a pool that is common to the Semitic world . . . to the Hebrew Bible in general, and the Psalms in particular. We are here dealing, as it were, with the two levels in the human psyche: the conscious and the unconscious . . . The image lies deeper than the idea.[39]

This use of metaphor is one of the very strong points in Tesfaye's songs. I find it difficult to synthesize what he is saying on any given topic because his use of metaphor is so rich, and I do not want to deprive the reader of actually seeing and hearing his varied descriptions.

Wax and Gold

There is much ambiguity and double meaning in Ethiopian poetry known traditionally as "wax and gold" (*sem ïna werk̲*), the wax holding the real meaning and gold the hidden meaning. Donald Levine speaks of the roots of this form being from the Ge'ez but points out that "constructions also appear in some types of secular verse in the vernacular Amharic, and indeed, at times inform Amharic conversation."[40] It is a basic means of communication and the entire country is historically influenced through the Amharic by this concept. Poems, created by common people, are popular at weddings and other public functions and always bring great delight to the audience.

Although there is metaphor infused in this style, there is also a certain playful duplicity indicated which is not characteristic of the new spiritual songs, albeit they are full of metaphor. I therefore have mentioned the concept of wax and gold only because it is universally connected with Ethiopia and the Amhara culture. As for religious poetry or k̲ïné, one Ethiopian has said that it "is as distinctive of Ethiopian spiritual culture as t̲éff, a species of grass grown as a cereal grain only in Ethiopia, is distinctive of her material culture."[41] Tesfaye's songs are really outside these traditional Amhara writing styles, but certainly Ethiopian writing in whatever genre is influenced unconsciously by these literary aspects of the prevailing culture.

Though not pertaining directly to Ethiopia's wax and gold concept, I found the entire discussion in Lakoff and Johnson's *Metaphors We Live By* a creative commentary on how we as humans live and speak

---

39. Sumner, *Ethiopian Philosophy*, 61.
40. Levine, *Wax and Gold*, 5.
41. Levine, *Wax and Gold*, 8.

metaphorically in all our speech.[42] There is room for ambiguity as one interprets another's writing or song. A certain mystery always remains when we delve into the thoughts and writing of another person.

Minstrel and Holy Man Concepts

Minstrel (*azmari*) and holy man concepts are common in Ethiopian culture. Ruth Finnegan discusses the "independent professional poets" of Ethiopia and the existence of court poets where freelance tradition was common. "It is not surprising then to find frequent instances of the coexistence in one society of both official poets at courts, and roving poets in other spheres."[43] Anne Bolay describes the *azmari* as keeping the oral tradition alive and that they may be involved in singing blessing songs in religious processions.[44] The minstrel and holy man concepts are also discussed in Steven Kaplan[45] and Brian Fargher.[46] One may ask if an evangelical singer's career would in any manner reflect the Ethiopian historical minstrel (*azmari*). These singers, who wandered from court to court, exposed the short comings of those in power by poetic song that contained double meanings.

It would seem, rather, that the ground swell of spiritual songs in the 1960s, of which Tesfaye was a part, came from a new impetus in the hearts and minds of a young generation infused with religious fervor. Tibebe Eshete has accurately described this phenomenon of the "torrent" of new songs with local tunes, use of instruments such as accordions and guitars, and borrowing of cultural forms such as clapping, ululation and swaying, as representing a new freedom and creativity of expression.[47] Aside from the above comments by Tibebe Eshete, there seems to be little academic scholarship, as yet, on the evangelical spiritual songs written from within an Ethiopian indigenous perspective. There are, of course, many more informal articles on Ethiopian singers and their songs.

In this connection, as well, A. Scott Moreau has used the Tesfaye story in describing Tesfaye under the classification of "Initiator as

---

42. Lakoff and Johnson, *Metaphors We Live By*, 3–6.

43. Finnegan, *Oral Literature in Africa*, 94.

44. Bolay, "*Azmari*," 75–76.

45. Kaplan, *Monastic Holy Man*, 45–87.

46. Fargher, "Charismatic Movement in Ethiopia," 356.

47. Tibebe Eshete, *Evangelical Movement*, 279.

Pathfinder-Organic."[48] In Moreau's schematic presentation, the reasons for Tesfaye's inclusion as "pathfinder-organic" is that his songs originated "within local settings" and, as an insider within his local culture, he "charts a new path rather than mimicking outside paths."[49] By "organic" Moreau is indicating a flow which is free, or liquid, and whose ministry "flows in multiple directions . . . they may focus on orientations of con-textualization rather than methods, such as the metaphoric pictures of contextualization as a living tree . . . a river we navigate . . . or a drama in which we improvise."[50] Tesfaye's life is an example with an emphasis on spiritual outreach, basing his approach on "dynamic critical realism" and "emic initiators" at the root of his ministry.[51] Tesfaye makes "the gospel come to life in creative ways in new cultural settings." [52] There is the danger of a pathfinder/initiator, as Tesfaye is defined, of facing accusations of heresy or syncretism from fellow believers. This was not the case with Tesfaye because his songs are deeply immersed in scripture.

Ethiopian Evangelical Churches Literature on Spiritual Song

Within the Ethiopian evangelical churches are several who have criti-cally appraised the spiritual song as defined in this paper. Tibebe Eshete describes the beginnings of the spiritual song outburst in the 1960s. He contends that at this time, "religious songs were socialized and became part of popular culture. Music took evangelical Christianity into the public arena through channels that were not easy to track, like cassettes, which were becoming increasingly available."[53] He writes of the effect of the Ethiopian revolution (1974 to 1991) on the church and refers often to Tesfaye Gabbiso's experience of persecution but also of the power of his songs in that situation.

Scholarly occasional papers by Zelalem Mengistu, written for the Ethiopian churches and musicians, have been presented in various ven-ues. He deals with the necessity for correct theology in song composition. Gezahegne Mussie directs Living Worship International Ministries from Addis Ababa. He speaks and writes extensively on the current spiritual

---

48 Moreau, *Contextualization*, 266.

49. Moreau, *Contextualization*, 272–73.

50. Moreau, *Contextualization*, 193.

51. Moreau, *Contextualization*, 264.

52. Moreau, *Contextualization*, 273.

53. Tibebe Eshete, *Evangelical Movement*, 279.

song scene in Ethiopia. Eyob Denio, director of Wolaitta Evangelical Seminary (WES), has written short books in Amharic on the creation of songs and expectations regarding the spiritual vitality of both solo and choir singers.[54] There is a similarity and convergence of ideas in their work in that all three men are active in their concern for a greater depth of spiritual understanding among young song writers and more care in selection of metaphors used in song. In Chapter 10, I discuss at length the specific contributions of these three men whose ideas about spiritual songs in the evangelical church converge in leading for change.

As regards this subject of song and the literature, there are available sample lyrics as raw data of Ethiopia's early evangelical church history.[55] Depending on the location, antiphonal songs were sometimes sung in tandem with translated hymns from the Swedish hymnbook *Sibhat L'Amlak* ("Praise to God"). For example, I remember the weekly women's classes at the Bonga Kale Heywet church where we would sing choruses in the local language of Kefinya along with Amharic translated songs from the printed hymnbook. Both were popular. According to an email from Tesfaye Gabbiso, dated August 29, 2014, his songs were definitely influenced by the stanza and chorus format of the translated hymns.

COMMUNICATION IN SONG

I turn now to consider what it means to communicate in song. What does a song mean in culture? What does music mean in God's kingdom? What does a song mean as it is sung and also heard by others? Roberta King argues: "Song texts function as valid theological indicators due to their 'home-grown' nature, originating from the people themselves as they interact with Christian teaching."[56] This is a very accurate description of the young Ethiopian soloist. Tesfaye, as he bases his lyrics on the teaching of Scripture as he understands it, utters a song in his particular setting. Thus, his songs become "valid theological indicators" of his understanding and place in the world.

---

54. Eyob Denio, *Song and the Singer's Life.*

55. Balisky, "African Indigenous Songs," 23–38; Balisky, *Wolaitta Evangelists,* 157–59.

56. King, *Pathways in Christian Music,* 138.

Pathway of a Song

In the article "Toward a Discipline of Christian Ethnomusicology: A Missiological Paradigm," King describes and defends the use of the Global Church Music Matrix, a four-arena missiological diagram that I use and build upon in this dissertation. She stresses the importance of theologizing through encouraging "culturally appropriate songs for use in ways that function at deep cultural levels."[57] King writes, "Recognizing the importance of the song's content, the method seeks to shape a song's message in ways that penetrate the thought process of a people."[58] Tesfaye's songs, written from his heart and mind without intentional directed stimulus from outside, would be more an opposite of what King is describing. In my use of King's Global Church Music Matrix, I am not directing the act of creating appropriate lyrics but rather coming at an analysis of what has already been written.

James Krabill was the first ethnomusicologist with whose writing I became familiar. It was his book that influenced me to think about various facets of a church's hymnody such as tracing the "itinerary" of a particular song.[59] As I delved deeply into the horrific prison experience suffered by Tesfaye and others, the Biblical drama of suffering and alienation reflected in Tesfaye's songs became very apparent to me. Irene Ai-Ling Sun, writing on the "Songs of Canaan" in China, offers excellent categories for looking at songs and their impact.[60] Sun's work and mine correspond in the fact that she was dealing with revolution in China with similarities to the experience in Ethiopia. Especially helpful in my thinking was her discussion on imagery and theology in the Canaan Hymns. The power of metaphors from nature is also true of Tesfaye's songs, and as she writes, "Allegories from nature serve as effective means to invite non-believing listeners to consider the existence of God."[61] Tesfaye used this effectively in several of the songs he sang to his prison keepers (see Chapter 10). A specific example concerns Song IV–10 where God delivers his people from the "vultures" and takes them home on His powerful wings. Who were the vultures? This was my question where I presumed from the beginning that "vultures" was a metaphor. But in later email discussion

---

57. King, "Toward a Discipline," 300–301.
58. King, "Toward a Discipline," 300–301.
59. Krabill, *Hymnody of the Harrist Church*, 308–31.
60. Sun, "Songs of Canaan," 1–9.
61. Sun, "Songs of Canaan," 2–3.

with Tesfaye, he wrote to clarify for me that the word "vultures" could be taken literally "because if our bodies were left dead somewhere in the forest unburied, the fate would have been to become the vultures' meal. Sometimes bodies were not allowed to be buried properly in those days if the victims were considered anti-revolutionaries."[62]

Oral Theological Expression

Oral theological expression is emblematic across African Christianity. Molyneux suggests that rudiments of the Christian life are taught in Africa through powerful and effective means outside the usual rubric of western missiology.[63] Oral theology is produced in songs that may never be documented, at least beyond a composer's notebook. This is indeed true of the great majority of the spiritual songs in the Ethiopian evangelical churches. However, modern technology is rapidly changing that picture. The Orthodox Church choirs have done an excellent project in the past few years getting a goodly number of their choir songs into print. In my possession are four choir books with lyrics for well over 1300 spiritual songs of these Orthodox choirs.

The writing of Mary McGann is helpful in describing the total experience of song. The song is part of the total liturgy, although I later explain how the church of Tesfaye Gabbiso's experience is not "liturgical" in the historical sense. But as McGann states, singing is vital to the larger ritual of worship and is inseparable from the context and persons who make the music.[64]

Song in Culture

Clifford Geertz's work on "thick description" and religion as a cultural system assists in placing song into a cultural framework. He questions whether a song is to be objectively interpreted, or if it exists as its own interpretation? "A good interpretation of anything, a poem, a person, a history, a ritual, an institution, a society, takes us into the heart of that of which it is the interpretation."[65] And, "The guiding principle is the same:

---

62. Email from Tesfaye Gabbiso, April 27, 2017.
63. Molyneux, *African Christian Theology*, 151ff.
64. McGann, *Exploring Music*, 21.
65. Geertz, *Interpretation of Cultures*, 18.

societies, like lives, contain their own interpretations. One has only to learn how to gain access to them."[66]

Furthermore, most research consists of studying a people's culture, which is itself "an ensemble of texts," and the researcher is only peering in.[67] Bruno Nettl adds definition to a person being studied within society by noting: "One may look at culture, at music, at music-as-culture from the perspective of a member of the society being studied or from the viewpoint of the analyst. This is probably the most basic of all ethnomusicological issues."[68] Both Nettl and Geertz conclude that a researcher's getting inside a culture and endeavoring to see with an emic viewpoint is the more advantageous method and, of course, the most difficult, if really possible at all. Geertz, employs a concept of "thick description" which attempts to describe the process of some action within its total setting. He also writes,

> Religion is: (1) a system of symbols which acts to (2) establish powerful, pervasive, and long-lasting moods and motivations in men by (3) formulating conceptions of a general order of existence and (4) clothing these conceptions with such an aura of factuality that (5) the moods and motivations seem uniquely realistic.[69]

Song, of course, may be included within this description of religion.

Saliers persuades us that theology requires music. He writes that ". . . we are asked to say some things that we do not truly think we believe until we sing them, or hear them in appropriately complex activities." [70] Significantly, he argues that when "great theologians wish to speak of the deepest realities, they move toward poetry and music, heightened speech, as an attempt to 'sound' spiritual matters." [71]

Music in the Kingdom

Music functions within societies in various ways. Nathan Corbitt suggests a way of examining various functions of music in a full-orbed church ministry: priest, prophet, proclaimer, healer, preacher and teacher.[72]

66. Geertz, *Interpretation of Cultures*, 453.

67. Geertz, *Interpretation of Cultures*, 452.

68. Nettl, *Study of Ethnomusicology*, 228–29.

69. Geertz, *Interpretation of Cultures*, 90ff.

70. Saliers, *Music and Theology*, 6.

71. Saliers, *Music and Theology*, 72.

72. Corbitt, *Sound of the Harvest*, 18–20.

Tesfaye Gabbiso's life and songs illustrate almost all the functions of music identified by Corbitt. Indeed, Corbitt cites Tesfaye Gabbiso as particularly illustrative of the prophet role. "Drawn from a meditative life in Scripture and prayer, his songs preached hope to the faithful people of Ethiopia during the communist rule in the 1970s and 1980s."[73] Also, Corbitt names him a preacher, emphasizing Tesfaye's disciplined life as much as his song, in his ministry to the nation of Ethiopia.[74] As I have argued previously in another context,

> Tesfaye's voice leads Ethiopia in prayer for God's kingdom to come on earth, as it is in heaven. His songs are oral theology for the women, men, and children of Ethiopia. He sings the work of God; the people believe and are challenged by the influence of his personal life to be built up in the most holy faith and to live authentically as Christians ... a significant body of truth bearing great influence as largely oral theology on the minds and hearts of Ethiopia's people. Listen to the song.[75]

In this way, the songs of Tesfaye are representative of an oral theology.

Inculturation of Faith

Catholic scholars in Ethiopia are much appreciated as standing at a vantage point outside both the Orthodox and Evangelical churches. Beyene Tewelde, speaking on evangelization and inculturation in the history of Ethiopian Christianity, suggests that blame must not be put on former missionaries, but that there must be a present inner renewal.[76] Abba Emmanuel Fritsch is also concerned with "a deep and responsible participation of the lay people so that 'the Word of Christ may dwell among them with all its richness' (Colossians 3:16)."[77] This illustrates the concern of both these Catholic Church leaders for their church that sometimes may be more apt to know the liturgy without experiencing it deeply. I believe Tesfaye is an illustration of a lay person in whom Christ dwells richly. Samuel Wolde-Yohannes presents a politico-philosophical perspective on the view of man versus Marxist philosophy. In traditional Ethiopian thinking, everything is connected to God in contrast to Marxist

73. Corbitt, *Sound of the Harvest*, 102.

74. Corbitt, *Sound of the Harvest*, 185.

75. Balisky, "Theology in Song," 455.

76. Tewelde Beyene, "Inculturation and Evangelization," 7.

77. Fritsch, "Liturgy and Culture," 70.

thought.[78] This speaks to the idea that all song naturally comes from God, which is what Tesfaye believes about all his songs. The tension arose in a historically pious and God-fearing country when Marxist philosophy set in. For example, Tesfaye's singing in prison with his understanding of God in his personal life and in his song, went completely against the Marxist thinking which Ethiopia was supposed to be espousing.

SUMMARY

In this foundational review of scholarly thinking I have looked at various basic categories of literature that pertain to this investigation. The primary missiological concept utilized in this study is King's "Global Church Music Matrix." In theological considerations, I have looked at the Psalms as song plus pertinent subjects regarding resistance and suffering. Ethiopia, rich in culture and arts, offers interesting literary constructs as well as the on-going debate between spiritual and worldly music. Influences of the Orthodox Church through history are also part of the story. In the last section, I have explored ethnomusicological concepts pertaining to oral expression as well as song in culture and in the kingdom.

As I argue throughout this work, "Tesfaye Gabbiso, song composer, theologian, and soloist, greatly contributed to the expansion of gospel songs, both before and after his imprisonment."[79] The new churches formed a strong legacy as they sang, representing a whole new genre of spiritual songs. What then lies behind Tesfaye's songs and the creation of an emerging genre of spiritual songs that nourished the nation? What were the methods and process for this study? These questions are considered in the next chapter.

78. Samuel Wolde-Yohannes, "Vision of Man and Humanity," 93–99.
79. Tibebe Eshete, *Evangelical Movement*, 282.

3

Methodology

THIS CASE STUDY DEVELOPS an understanding of the songs of one singer-composer within his life setting and narrative. It is not a complete biography of Tesfaye Gabbiso but deals only with his song career. The chapter opens with an explanation of the foundational structuring of the research followed by a discussion of the two main methods of inquiry: ethnographic research and content analysis. An element of autoethnography is included because of the writer's close association with the subject of the study. Finally, a schedule of research activities outlines the progress and shape that the study has taken. The validity of the research is argued at the end of the chapter.

STRUCTURING THE RESEARCH

The overarching model for this dissertation finds its foundation in the area of Christian music communication as diagrammed by Roberta King in the "Model for Doing Christian Music Communication Research."[1] The scope is confined to the following diagram, as presented by Roberta King as a cycle to follow in development of this study.

---

1. King, *Pathways in Christian Music Communication*, 25.

Christian Communication Theory Research Cycle

1. Historical Religious and Social Context
2. Life Narrative of Tesfaye Gabbiso
3. Content Analysis of Song
4. Themes and Interpretations
5. Impact Diachronic Study
6. Metaphor Analysis
7. Lyric Theology in Contemporary Milieu

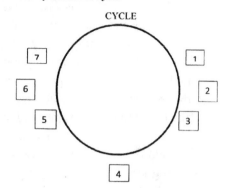

Figure 2: Case Study Cycle

King's cycle allows for exploration of the main facets of a case study as it seeks to answer a set of research questions. One can enter the cycle at any point with the material overlapping in various ways. It demonstrates the basic content of the research and is also broadly reflected in the chapter headings. The chapters of the thesis, beginning with Chapter 4, follow generally through this cycle.

John Creswell's suggested approach and order of components was also a guideline. This approach is advantageous because it enables injection of personal narrative into the larger study. Creswell suggests the following approach and order of components in which the issue is identified, with purpose, method of study, and how it came to be within the surrounding circumstances. He suggests opening with a vignette or story to develop a sense of time and place. Then the following steps are taken:

- Issue is identified, with purpose and method of study and how it came to be, plus the surrounding circumstances

- Extensive description of case and context, data

- Issues to explain complexity of the case, building through references to others' and the writer's understanding

- Further probing of issues

- Assertions presented and conclusions arrived at
  Ending with a closing vignette or experience[2]

---

2. Creswell, *Qualitative Inquiry*, 195–96.

The framework in which this study is placed demanded an episte-
mological assumption because I have been an insider to the subject and
have collaborated and "positioned" myself within the local setting for
many years.[3] Qualitative inquiry is used to present a case study that is
"a good approach when the inquirer has clearly identifiable cases with
boundaries and seeks to provide an in-depth understanding."[4] Over a
period of forty years, I unwittingly gathered a great deal of data and in-
formation on the subject of this dissertation. Also, a diglot songbook in
Amharic and English provided a bounded text for content analysis.

Following Creswell, this study is a "single instrumental case study"
revolving around one individual[5] and serves as a "clearly identifiable
case with boundaries."[6] Analysis of the bounded songbook lyrics,
through the process of purposeful sampling and coding of apparent
themes, especially of suffering and endurance, leads to an "intrinsic
case study" because "the focus of the study holds intrinsic or unusual
interest"[7] in the fact that the composer personally experienced persecu-
tion and incarceration during the Ethiopian revolution of 1975–1991.
Another point of "unusual interest" is that Tesfaye has kept his domicile
in Ethiopia throughout his life, whereas most of the "fathers" of this
song movement migrated to western countries.

"Taking cultural inventory" applied to my work in terms of sys-
temizing cultural aspects and establishing categories for organizing my
writing and interpretation.[8] While much of the information was garnered
from written material such as Amharic articles and Tesfaye's own auto-
biography of the prison years, I have also been a participant observer of
Tesfaye's life for forty-five years.

ETHNOGRAPHIC RESEARCH

What was the historical, political, social and religious context in Ethiopia
that was a setting for the life narrative of Tesfaye Gabbiso? How do his
songs reflect the tumultuous times in which he sings? What has been the
influence of his songs on the church and wider society of Ethiopia?

3. Creswell, *Qualitative Inquiry*, 17.

4. Creswell, *Qualitative Inquiry*, 74.

5. Creswell, *Qualitative Inquiry*, 131.

6. Creswell, *Qualitative Inquiry*, 74–75.

7. Creswell, *Qualitative Inquiry*, 244–45.

8. Spradley, *Participant Observation*, 156–57.

Ethnographic research into the context of Tesfaye Gabbiso's life narrative or lived experience called for extensive use of various types of data collection. Creswell suggests Yin's six types of information to be collected."[9] The details below illustrate my use of all six kinds of information: documents, archival records, interviews, direct observations, participant observations, and physical artifacts. Archival information included personal letters and emails, narrative interviews with the soloist, magazine articles in English and Amharic, formal and informal interviews, Balisky diaries, the soloist's autobiographical writing and online sites. The information below gives a sampling of my ethnographic research:

Approximately one dozen personal letters dating back to the 1990s after his release from prison, including a printed invitation to the wedding of Tesfaye Gabbiso to Hanna Goshu on September 2, 1995, at Full Gospel Believers' Church of Hawassa, are a part of the literature. More recently, approximately ten emails with various parties and over twenty exchanges of email with Tesfaye have answered questions or clarified information.[10]

In 1990, the first time of meeting upon release from prison, Tesfaye visited us in Addis Ababa and I did a two-hour taped narrative interview with him about his life up to that point. This comprehensive interview included his views on singing and his status as an accomplished soloist. I somehow felt compelled to do this interview as it was a crucial time when he was coming out of isolation back into society. This was the first time we had seen him since his release from prison. In his characteristic humility, Tesfaye specifically requested that I keep all that information personal. I typed up the interview and deposited it in my private files, thus honoring his request for privacy. However, when it came time to write this dissertation about fifteen years later, he granted me specific permission to use the content of that interview.

One of the challenges for me was to discover what has been written in Amharic magazines that would pertain to Tesfaye and his music. I knew, only generally, that a good number of articles and interviews had been published through the years, but where would I find them? The only article I had in my files had appeared as a profile in a British publication from Keston College.[11] This was while he was in prison and in response

9. Creswell, *Qualitative Inquiry*, 75.

10. Refer to listing of emails at end of bibliography.

11. This newsletter, with offices in England, reported on religious freedom, especially in relation to communist countries and profiled Tesfaye's experience of

to an account sent to Amnesty International. In a June 8, 2013 interview with Tesfaye in Addis Ababa, I asked if he had any list or file of articles about his life. He immediately responded, "Just a minute" then phoned a friend of his. After the phone conversation, he told me that I would soon receive some papers. The following day a thick manila envelope containing ten Amharic articles was delivered by Tesfaye's colleague to the guest house where we were staying. This was a gold mine, because no indices or library repositories are kept of Amharic Christian magazine articles. This most significant collection of articles was made by a friend of Tesfaye's, Binyam Negussie Gebre/Heywot, who had kept all the articles pertaining to Tesfaye's life and song in a special collection through the years since the first pre-prison article in 1978 to 1979.[12]

Interviews, mostly informal, were held with fourteen individuals, ten of them in Ethiopia and four in Alberta, Canada. These included a range of informed friends: faculty members of Yared Music School and Mekane Yesus Jazz Music School, Ethiopian church leaders, Ethiopian writers in Canada, personal Ethiopian friends in Grande Prairie, and a French-Canadian ethnomusicologist studying Ethiopian spiritual songs in Montreal. I recorded Tesfaye's story and views on song in 1990, not knowing that fifteen years later it would become a major source of information.

Multiple sources contribute to the data. First, my personal diaries from 1967 to the present afford accurate dates and detailed information from our first contact with Tesfaye as a young lad at Aletta Wondo, Ethiopia in 1971, through his significant visit in Jimma on November 12, 1977, shortly before his imprisonment, to the most recent interview in Addis Ababa on January 9, 2015.[13] Second, the soloist's autobiography of his prison years, *Beziyan Gizé* (Those Days), became an unexpected important resource, as it was just published in Amharic in 2010. The book will be printed in English in the near future.[14] Third, online audio-visual sites have included YouTube presentations of Tesfaye singing in various

persecution in *Keston News Service (Profile)* #217, 22.

12. A complete listing of the ten articles is located in a special collection at end of bibliography.

13. Fortunately, I have kept a daily diary as well as guest-book through the years 1967 to the present.

14. I have given this book, though not yet available in English, a code (Tesfaye, BG, page #) in all future notes referring to it. BG stands for *Beziyan Gizé*, the Amharic title for what will be known as "Those Days" in the upcoming English translation.

events, including the 2013 Luis Palau crusade "Love Ethiopia" with Tesfaye singing at the final event in Addis Ababa.[15]

The collection of ten Amharic articles on Tesfaye Gabbiso, appearing in Ethiopian magazines over the years, is a vital source of information because these interviews and commentaries supply a resource which reveals the response of the Christian public towards Tesfaye. In order to define and highlight the quantity of information in all this written material, when not quoting directly but indicating other "voices" which are speaking, I have chosen to employ a different font as suggested by Gregory Barz.[16]

Additionally, direct observation was used in my research. Most of this observation took place before this study began, so I might name it archival direct observation. I briefly describe several occasions when I have personally observed Tesfaye in concert:

1. Aletta Wondo, Sidama. In the early 1970s Tesfaye often sang in the local Kale Heywet Church on Sunday mornings with a friend Estifanos Negash. They were about fourteen years old at the time and were singing some of the new songs they had learned from the radio. It was rather unusual that two young boys would be an accepted part of the church worship program. [17]

2. Addis Ababa University campus, September 14, 1997. This was an historic occasion when three "father" singers of Ethiopia sang their most loved songs at an ECFE (Evangelical Churches Fellowship of Ethiopia) outdoor rally. Tesfaye Gabbiso, Tamrat Haile and Addisu Werku were the singers. All three sang their own songs, Tesfaye singing "When God Assists" (V–11), his famous prison song. Fortunately, my diaries have assisted in recalling such occasions and the actual songs which were sung. It was a thrilling experience for me to be present at that university concert.

15. Several sites offer information regarding Tesfaye Gabbiso and others singing together at Ethiopian Love Concert in Addis Ababa. 1) "Love Ethiopia Press Release" of May 22, 2014, at http://www.palau.org in 2013. 2) Tesfaye Gabbiso singing at Love Ethiopia Concert, www.youtube.com/watch?v=eu02-3Uic-w. Last accessed on May 1, 2015.

16. Barz, "Confronting the Field(note)," 206–10. In order to clarify the flow of script when not quoting directly (with quotation marks), I use a different font, suggested by Barz, to indicate Tesfaye's "voice." These Amharic sources are identified under "List of Abbreviations" in the front matter.

17. See Appendix A for a photograph of the singing lads.

3. Tesfaye's home church in Sidama on a Sunday morning (c. 2000). We were in Sidama to visit Tesfaye and his parents on that weekend.

4. Song-Fest at SIM Addis Ababa chapel while I teaching an EGST (Ethiopian Graduate School of Theology). Tesfaye came at my request as a surprise guest to the Song-Fest on April 3, 2008.

5. Tesfaye singing at a conference of the Ethiopian fellowship in Los Angeles on February 11, 2011. One of the songs he sang was V–7, "But I Know One Thing."[18] This was on a preliminary trip to Fuller when I made my final decision in the Fuller Prayer Garden to move ahead with a doctorate. We did not realize Tesfaye was in Los Angeles until we arrived here and learned from Ethiopian friends that he would be singing at a conference in downtown Los Angeles that week.

AUTOETHNOGRAPHY

Autoethnography was employed at certain junctures, drawing from my own experiential part in the story.[19] Although the validity of the autoethnograhic method is debated by some, I have employed a partial use of the method as a unifying factor and method of triangulation in my presentation. I have followed Ellis in the following ways in order to understand and interpret the subject. Ellis writes about understanding "cultural experience", the use of personal vignettes or "epiphanies" then building "layered accounts. . .focus[ing] on the author's experience alongside data, abstract analysis and relevant literature."[20] As per Ellis, I have the agreement of Tesfaye that he is represented fairly and ethically. Personal diaries, taped and live interviews and letters of Lila Balisky and Tesfaye Gabisso have verified the reliability of past common experiences.[21] I am aware of some of the possible drawbacks of an autoethnographic approach[22] and have sought to avoid issues of bias as discussed by Sue Butler.[23]

18. This is the same song that Tesfaye sang at the Love Ethiopia Crusade.

19. Creswell, *Qualitative Inquiry*, 123.

20. Ellis, "Autoethnography," 1–5.

21. Ellis, "Autoethnography," 6–7.

22. Higashi, "Musical Communitas," 166.

23. Butler, "Considering 'Objective' Possibilities," 295–99.

CONTENT ANALYSIS

Following the ethnographic study, the main task of this dissertation employs content analysis to study the texts of 104 songs of Tesfaye Gabbiso as contained in the songbook: Tesfaye Gabbiso, "*Yetesfayé Gabbiso Mezmuroch* : The Songs of Tesfaye Gabbiso" (an Amharic/English diglot compiled by Lila Balisky and translated by Haile Jenai). Text analysis was used employing a grounded theory approach that begins with the data to "develop a theory."[24] Data analysis, both quantitative and qualitative, was involved in the process of studying the 104 songs. Using open and axial coding, I used various methods of studying the songs from word coding to theme sampling and selective coding. Assertions and findings from the song texts are presented and conclusions drawn.

This content analysis has also involved a study of a substantive amount of (1) written and (2) spoken word (interviews) by Tesfaye from Ethiopian magazines. This investigation, then, is an examination on "forms of human communication" in order to add to the findings in the songs.[25]

The question of language translation arises. As is well-known, it is difficult to translate poetry. I have made every effort to be as accurate as possible in assessing the meaning. I have not attempted to make the songs singable in English. Haile Jenai, a very talented translator from Amharic to English, was very consistent in his translation so that coding was simplified. All translation was checked by Tesfaye himself for accuracy of meaning. I did some word adjustment to make the English text flow as poetically as possible. Both men have been highly appreciated as professional colleagues in this project.

A form of analysis that was probably the most important aspect to me was an idea that occurred well into my dissertation studies. Using the Global Church Music Matrix, I wanted to discover how the life and songs of Tesfaye would emanate from the center of the diagram to the four quadrants. This was undertaken using three sources: (1) Events and evidence from his lived experience, (2) Statements, both written and spoken and (3) Song content. As you will read, this proved to be a very successful exercise.

---

24. Leedy and Ormrod, *Practical Research Planning*, 146.
25. Leedy and Ormrod, *Practical Research Planning*, 148.

SCHEDULE OF RESEARCH ACTIVITIES

It was an advantage to my work that I was able to return to Ethiopia three times during the years of specific research for this document. From October 2011 to January 2012, I coordinated translation of both Orthodox and Evangelical songs, working with various local translators in Addis Ababa. At that point, the definite focus of the future dissertation was unclear. Having moved permanently to Canada in early 2005, I found this trip valuable as I was a participant observer of different musical events in Addis Ababa where Tesfaye's songs continue to be widely used.

In Addis Ababa during June and July 2013, I carried on the following pilot research using the following methods: (1) translation of relevant materials for the historico-religious and cultural context. This included supervision of the translation of printed materials in the form of magazine articles about and by the soloist through a period of thirty-three years. (2) self- administered questionnaires, (3) informal interviews and conversations, (4) personal interactions with the song writer, Tesfaye Gabbiso, on two significant occasions, and (5) a preliminary English translation of Tesfaye's latest autobiographical account of the prison years. Sample coding with a second coder, Haile Jenai, was used to begin the work of song text analysis.

These pilot projects were a significant foundation for further research. However, the topic of the dissertation was later narrowed from a comparison of evangelical and Orthodox songs to just the one book of Tesfaye Gabbiso's songs, so the early research was not directly useable in this investigation. In terms of participant observation, I observed the use of Tesfaye's songs in Addis Ababa at a wedding on June 23, 2013 and also at a memorial service for an SIM theologian and mission leader, Steve Strauss, on June 25, 2013. On June 26, 2013, I employed the use of a questionnaire while teaching a one-time class on church music at the Ethiopian Graduate School of Theology.

On June 28, 2013, I conducted an Amharic song chapel at the Addis Ababa SIM main offices with the Ethiopian colleagues, guiding them through their own church history of song and observing their appreciation and knowledge of Tesfaye's songs from memory. In July 2013, at the International Conference on SIM History in Africa, held in Addis Ababa, at which occasion academics from East and West Africa were assembled, I was privileged to organize a concert evening with Tesfaye Gabbiso singing and speaking of his own pilgrimage in song. Though the West African delegates did not know Amharic, it was part of my personal observation on that occasion to appreciate the power of song even in a foreign language. The visitors to Ethiopia were "moved by the Spirit" (their description) in listening to Tesfaye sing and expressed a great urgency to take CDs back to their countries with them. With some degree of flurry on the part of the conference organizers, enough CDs were acquired overnight before the return flights to various countries of West Africa.

On January 6, 2015, I interviewed Gezahegn Mussie, musician and singer, who works in collaboration with Tesfaye Gabbiso to hold seminars and conferences on worship and music in Ethiopian churches.

On January 9, 2015, during a third short-term trip to Ethiopia, we were blessed to spend an evening in the home of Tesfaye and Hanna in Hawassa, 270 kilometers south of Addis Ababa. This is only the second visit we have paid to their home over the forty-five years we have known Tesfaye. He showed us recent videos of his ninety-three-year-old mother singing in Sidaminya. He also read to us from his own memoirs that he is presently compiling on computer. This was valuable field experience.

From January 20 to 22, 2015, a planned songwriters' workshop was facilitated in Wolaitta, Soddo, by Eyob Denio and myself to inspire twenty young songwriters presently involved in church music ministries.[26]

SUMMARY

This case study combines ethnographic studies and content analysis of song texts. The initial questioning and coding of the songs was determined by the life experiences of the singer, especially in relation to suffering and endurance. However, other themes that arose during the study were also analyzed. Other approaches to inquiry were used in exploring aspects outside the experience of suffering. Examples include looking at the Trinity, views on growth and discipleship, poetic aspects of metaphor in the art of his songs, plus Tesfaye's obvious emphasis on David and the Psalms. These are only samplings of additional studies that could be undertaken.

I believe that validation has been achieved through a "confluence of evidence that breeds credibility, that allows us to feel confident about our observations, interpretations and conclusions."[27] In particular, triangula-

---

26. See a brief description of this workshop in Appendix B.

27. Creswell, *Qualitative Inquiry*, 204—a statement by E. W. Eisner.

tion has been used through "multiple data sources" to verify the work. These multiple data sources include the song texts themselves, what Tesfaye writes/speaks, what others say, and the contextual facts surrounding the case. Through this study, I also seek to "raise new possibilities, open up new questions, and stimulate new dialogue."[28]

Based on the findings, I now commence a study on the historical and cultural background and the context of the singer's spiritual formation. This will include a brief history of church and state, with special focus on the impact of the Marxist revolution.

28. Creswell, *Qualitative Inquiry*, 205.

4

Background of Tesfaye Gabbiso's Life

I am known in the Book of Life. To the end, my life will
stand firm, strengthened in You. (VI–1)

To GAIN A VIEW of Tesfaye's life, I briefly consider the historical and re-
ligious context into which he was born. Of special import is the impact
of the Marxist revolution (1974 to 1991) that profoundly affected the life
of Tesfaye. I consider his family narrative and the context of his spiritual
formation.

Ethiopia as a nation in Africa holds a unique position geographi-
cally, culturally, and historically. Andrew Walls, in describing the larger
"Ethiopian" movement in Africa, is, after all, describing the actual nation
of Ethiopia:

> Ethiopian stands for Africa indigenously Christian, Africa *pri-*
> *mordially* Christian; for a Christianity that was established in
> Africa not only before the white people came, but before Islam
> came; for a Christianity that has been continuously in Africa
> for far longer than it has in Scotland, and infinitely longer than
> it has in the United States. African Christians today can assert
> their right to the *whole* history of Christianity in Africa, stretch-
> ing back almost to the apostolic age.[1]

The early Christian witness in Ethiopia defines its church heritage
as a unique one in the continent of Africa. It stems back to the fourth

---

1. Walls, *Cross-Cultural Process*, 91.

century when Syrian missionaries entered Ethiopia. We have the amazing story in written form which has endured to the present.

If Andrew Walls has described the uniqueness of Ethiopia, there is further enigma in trying to categorize or fit Ethiopia into the larger continent. Kay Shelemay, from an ethnomusicology stance, writes that Ethiopia is "not properly African, not sufficiently Middle Eastern, not mainstream Christian, and not postcolonial. Ethiopia fits no scholarly category (or stereotype) beyond that of a vaguely defined 'other.'"[2]

The years of which I write (1960s to early 1990s) were times of trouble, anxiety and persecution for the Trinitarian churches of Ethiopia. Patriach Tewoflos of the Ethiopian Orthodox Tewahedo Church (EOTC) and Guddinaa Tumsaa, General Secretary of the Ethiopian Evangelical Church Mekane Yesus (EECMY) were both executed in July 1979.[3] These two examples were the extreme, but many Christians were persecuted, and churches were closed. Tesfaye represents that era. This chapter describes the life and times that were a setting for Tesfaye as a younger man.

The Ethiopian Revolution, Marxist in philosophy, was an influential period and bears heavily on the subject of this paper because songs proliferated during those years of the revolution. The significance of the revolution is examined through the lenses of several writers as regards the religious milieu in Ethiopia between 1974 to 1991. It includes a consideration of the general ferment of the 1960s, the development of youth movements and beginnings of the choir and soloist phenomena. In countries where there is an oppressive government, music is often viewed as a powerful agent in destabilization of the people.[4] Therefore, the government questioned all the musical creativity going on in the churches.

OVERVIEW OF ETHIOPIAN CHURCH HISTORY

The histories of the Orthodox and Evangelical churches differ significantly. Ethiopia holds two streams of Christianity: (1) the early Orthodox church stream beginning in the fourth century and (2) the broader mission history, via the West, in the evangelical stream. As Walls suggests,

---

2. Shelemay, "Crossing Boundaries," 17.

3. Eide, *Revolution & Religion*, 3, 11.

4. Begbie, "Powers of Music in Worship," 109; and Tibebe Eshete, *Evangelical Movement*, 280.

the conversion of the Ethiopian eunuch[5] indicates that "with the Gospel all roads do not lead to Rome [but] that the gospel travels on other highways too."[6]

In order to understand the context in which Tesfaye began singing, a brief consideration of the genesis of the Orthodox Church in the fourth century must be mentioned. Orthodox Church roots carry the story of music in the church with the accompanying received story of Yared, the work of the *debtera* (church musicians), church structure, renewal movement and Sunday School songs, orality and memorization.[7] Christine Chaillot writes of the development of Orthodox lay religious organizations starting in the 1950s as well as renewal movements of the 1960s among the growing evangelical churches, which were reflective of changes taking place in society.[8] Traditionally, "Literature, art, music and most facets of organized expression were virtually wholly ecclesiastic, and the religion of the state determined the scope of all artistic expression."[9]

Song History of the Evangelical Churches

The entrance of European missions to Ethiopia may be traced back several centuries to a few Europeans travelers and missionaries and translators, but actual mission entrance began with the Lutherans from Scandinavia in the latter part of the nineteenth century. The Swedish Lutheran historian, Gustav Aren, though not writing specifically about music, makes many fascinating comments about early mission music-making. He describes what it was like to train a choir to sing translated songs to western tunes:

> Despite their linguistic and metrical imperfections these hymns were much loved. They expressed concepts and sentiments dear to the Bethel people and their successors. It may be regretted

5. Whether or not the Ethiopian eunuch was from the exact territory of present Ethiopia is debated.

6. Walls, "Globalization and the Study," 71.

7. Kimberlin, "Music of Ethiopia," 232–52.

8. For details, see Chaillot, *Ethiopian Orthodox*, 110–14, regarding the renewal movement beginning in the 1960s, especially on the work of the Orthodox Church *debteras* (official singers) and the "Sunday Schools" in the church, which appeared in the same period that the evangelical churches were beginning to create their own spiritual songs.

9. Ullendorff, *Ethiopians*, 159.

that these hymns were not adapted to indigenous rhythms and tunes; but such a thing could hardly be expected at that time.[10]

Early editions of these songs eventually evolved into various editions of the Amharic hymnal of translated western hymns *Sïbhat L'Amlak* ("Praise to God") that Tesfaye and friends sang from while in high school and before the new songs took precedence. This history of translated western hymns is traced in "Evangelical Hymns in Amarinya" by Marianne Nilsson and also a *Canterbury Dictionary of Hymnology* article on Ethiopia by Lila Balisky and Ralph Lee.[11] These translated songs have been significant in Tesfaye's spiritual pilgrimage.

The later work to the south, especially of SIM, the largest mission organization, finds expression through Brian Fargher who emphasizes the foundations of the Bible-based mission work.[12] Paul Balisky has followed on in describing the history of the evangelists who were responsible for extensive church growth in the south of the country.[13] The evangelists carried songs with them from their own ethnic areas and these early believers, with "no contact with other Protestants hundreds of miles away, developed a sort of antiphonal song that made use of a leader."[14] The evangelists taught the new believers throughout the southern areas of the country.[15] The leader began with a song topic and a simple tune using three to five tones of a pentatonic scale, then the people replied in an antiphonal manner with a pre-determined and repetitious response.

> Much theology is thus imparted and reviewed for children, illiterates, and unbelievers. The singing is conducted in a very orderly fashion, no bodily motion other than the tapping of a finger or toe. Frequently a switch to a related topic . . . is signaled by the leader by an ingenious device, raising the pitch a tone.[16]

---

10. Aren, *Evangelical Pioneers*, 301.

11. Nilsson, "Evangelical Hymns," 80–172; and Balisky and Lee, "Ethiopian Hymnody."

12. Fargher, *Origins of the New Churches*, 26–59.

13. Balisky, *Wolaitta Evangelists*, 307–16.

14. Wallace, "Hymns in Ethiopia," 271.

15. A contemporary example of this was described to me in August 2012 by ethnomusicologist Hugo Ferran, who encountered Ethiopian evangelists teaching songs to the Ma'ale people in southwest Ethiopia.

16. Wallace, "Hymns in Ethiopia," 271.

The musical style is a major third. Usually two syllables would be sung on the lower note, then one on the upper third. The leader would sing one line, followed by the people with a refrain that he had taught them at the beginning of the song. There was also some indicator (which I have not discovered) as to when the song would end. Everyone knew the cue. Tesfaye heard and participated in this type of singing as a young child in his home church.

Impact of the Marxist Revolution

With the beginning of the revolutionary years under Marxism, one turns to the political dynamics at work in the 1960s before the revolution. Fargher includes the Orthodox and Evangelical into one religious entity, "the church in Ethiopia," and describes the music scene thus:

> Three types of singing had been common in the churches: translated hymns set to western tunes, traditional antiphonal singing, and chanting by priests and deacons. All three lacked the one thing which the renewal movement stressed: the expression of relevant spirituality. Within the brief space of about five years (approximately 1973 to 1978) almost every congregation in the country had at least one gowned young people's choir.[17]

Other dynamics of the times included the dissatisfaction of the young people that leadership was being held in the hands of an older generation with no opportunity for the young ones to rise to responsibility. There was a geographic movement of young people to urban centers where they were questioning tradition and experiencing in the "older" churches "ethical laxity, sterile worship and legalism" which were stifling.[18] The growing renewal brought new spiritual life and enthusiasm engendering a new song form that Tesfaye illustrates. This music form is further described later on. Fargher asks, "What would have happened to the church of Ethiopia during the first seven tough years of the Revolution (1974 to 1980) if the renewal movement had not already effected many beneficial changes by that time?"[19] The new song being created in the hearts and minds of the younger generation gave a new spiritual vitality to the churches. It was a time in the history of the church for a revival of mind

---

17. Fargher, "Charismatic Movement," 355.
18. Fargher, "Charismatic Movement," 345–47.
19. Fargher, "Charismatic Movement," 345.

and spirit. The new songs in the hearts of the younger generation gave them the power to endure in a time of persecution.

FAMILY NARRATIVE OF TESFAYE GABBISO

In this general setting in southern Ethiopia, I now consider the specific family narrative of Tesfaye Gabbiso. Tesfaye was born in 1954 in the Sidama Region of Southern Ethiopia, in the rural district of Aletta Wondo and local area Degorra Elmete (TG, #7). His mother tongue was Sidaminya. He lived his childhood among the Sidama people group found in the Omotic cluster. The geographic setting of fertile hills and valleys lies between Hawassa to the north and Dilla in the middle south. Most families were subsistence farmers where cattle are a measure of wealth. In the lush and fertile rural area, Tesfaye's father Gabbiso Doyamo, could produce almost all the family needed for daily life: fermented cows' milk and butter, false banana tree (*insette*) which is a staple food for the southern peoples as well as *werķé*, prepared with butter and cheese, oranges, coffee, chickens, mules, growing grain, self-sufficient on their own place. Hawassa, the region's main center, where Tesfaye Gabbiso and his family currently live, is now a modern metropolis where Tesfaye has served as lead pastor of a Mulu Wongel (Full Gospel) mega-church.

Religiously, Tesfaye's grandparents and parents had practiced the animistic traditional religion of the area. However, missions influenced the Sidama area beginning just prior to World War II and the Italian invasion of Ethiopia. Religious groups that influenced the Sidama people included the Orthodox and Catholic Churches, present in the area for centuries, Mekane Yesus Lutheran, interdenominational Sudan Interior Mission, Heywet Birhan (Light of Life) and other smaller organizations. His family was most influenced by the Christian community of the Kale Heywet Church, historically related to SIM Int'l (formerly known as the Sudan Interior Mission), which first entered that area with the gospel in 1928.

In 1948, Tesfaye's grandfather was possessed of a spirit and after the offering of sacrifices and fulfilling various requirements to appease the spirits of the traditional religious system, the grandfather died. The oldest son, Gabbiso Doyamo, inherited the spirit of his father, believed to be sent by *Megano* (the tribal high god), and therefore became the *ķalicha* (religious practitioner) for that local area. In 1949, soon after this experience of his father's death, he heard the gospel of Jesus preached by an evangelist and became a believer, giving up the spirit possession practices and eventually joining preaching tours and studying in Aletta Wando Bible School from 1968 to 1971.[20]

Tesfaye, as he remembers personal conversations with his father, has a slightly different version. He says he never heard from his grandfather regarding spirit worship. Rather, according to Ato Gabbiso, he stopped serving his mother's spirit and became a believer before his mother passed away. Gabbiso told Tesfaye and the family that he inherited the spirit of his mother, believed to be sent by Megano (the tribal high god), and therefore became only a "candidate" to be a *ķalicha* (religious practitioner) for that local area. He never actually served in that position.[21]

The coming of Gabbiso Doyamo to Aletta Wondo to join the Bible School was the cause of Tesfaye's coming into the larger center as well. Tesfaye was then about twelve or thirteen years of age and came from their country farm with his father to Aletta Wando to join a higher-level school.[22] Tesfaye had begun his elementary schooling in a local church-run school in his home area then attended grades four to six in the SIM elementary school at Aletta Wondo. It was at this time that he became part of the life of the Balisky family who were living at SIM Aletta Wondo. He remembers playing with the three Balisky sons, enjoying a special small student dwelling in the Balisky yard where he and his friend Estifanos lived and were involved in various humorous childhood tricks. He remembers Mr. Paul's whistling, his dedication to teaching the church leaders, plus his trekking out to visit rural church areas on the weekend. Tesfaye remembers Lila as a gardener and musician who was intrigued with young Tesfaye's interest in singing. Tesfaye also remembers when he received an academic award for his school performance from the hand of SIM principal of the school, Mr. Harry Atkins.[23]

Tesfaye does not remember a distinct influence of the Orthodox Church in his home area, but there was an unconscious influence of the Orthodox Church in his religious life. The southern ethnic groups kept the traditional names for their high god in the Bible translations rather than using the Amharic word for God. In other words, the concept of the high god was kept strong in their own culture.

20. This Bible School was a theological institution for training church leadership under the direction of the Kale Heywet Church and SIM.

21. Email from Tesfaye Gabbiso to Lila Balisky, April 27, 2017.

22. Balisky, *Wolaitta Evangelists*, 233–35.

23. Interview with Tesfaye Gabbiso, Hawassa, January 9, 2015.

> Most obviously the tradition of a people may include a Being who, when that people came into contact with a God-centered religious tradition (Orthodox), will be invested with all the characteristics of the Supreme Being; or the tradition may in some other way recognize the ultimate unity of the transcendent world, a single principle underlying life.[24]

In my most recent interview with Tesfaye in Hawassa on January 9, 2015, Tesfaye elaborated on the powerful effect of his mother on his life. "She was a worship leader and a holy woman who loved to sing and pray— even better than my Dad." How had she come to faith? Gabbiso a believer, had led her to Christ as a young girl when he was teaching the Amharic alphabet (*fidel*) in the church. But she was not yet learning to read. One of the relatives, observing this young girl's inclination towards learning, proposed to her brothers that she should abandon her traditional leather clothing for a dress made of cotton. She had also been pouring coffee at the center-pole of the house, as was customary religious practice, but she stopped immediately at the suggestion of Gabbiso who advised her that if she was learning, she should not follow this practice any more. She became an eager student under the tutelage of Ato Gabbiso and then later became his wife.

Tesfaye's mother had an unusually strong influence on her son's verbal and musical skills. She was the main Bible reader in their home, reading aloud from the Amharic. She was able to read without glasses until well into her eighties. During the January 9, 2015 interview with Tesfaye, I was privileged to have him show me a video of his mother, at age ninety-three, reading aloud from John chapter 14. She was reading the Amharic Bible in a strong voice, with accuracy and beautiful expression. On the same video, she also sang a song she had composed which Tesfaye translated as follows:

> Why don't the people listen quietly while I am singing?
> The time has come for people to make their decision.
> Christ was crucified for our sins.
> Let the gathering of Christ be blessed in heaven and on earth.
> Everyone will receive his wage.
> The place where people divide is at the gate before Christ.
> Forget about your wealth and be concerned about religion where faith
>   is strengthened.

24. Walls, *Missionary Movement*, 122.

Life is in Christ.

The Devil is released to deceive people.

Be strong in your faith. [25]

CONTEXT OF SPIRITUAL FORMATION

In Tesfaye's personal published account of his years in prison, he says,

> Since my parents were members of the Kale Heywet Church, I
> had the chance of getting to know Christ through them right
> from my infancy. However, it was only after 1973 that I came to
> experience tangible spiritual formation in my life. This occurred
> in that very year in Yirga Alem . . . I don't exactly remember the
> time . . . in that year (1965 EC) I gave my whole heart to Christ
> and a big change took place. (Tesfaye, BG, 12; TG, #1)[26]

The media and any written materials during Tesfaye's childhood
were sparse. Many evangelicals read or listened only to Bible reading,
there was nothing else to read. Young people are used to memorizing
in Ethiopia, and no doubt Tesfaye memorized volumes of scripture and
song as a young lad. Tesfaye confirms that from the age of eighteen, he
began to read the Bible seriously. His Christian high school friends en-
couraged him to begin this habit.

Thus far, I have grasped a snapshot of Tesfaye's childhood setting as
well as some insight into the earliest years of his Christian experience.
One of the Christian brothers (fellow believers) who had a great influence
on Tesfaye was Tekeste Tekle, instructor at the Teacher Training Institute
in Yirgalem and later director of the hostel owned and administered
by the Evangelical Church Mekane Yesus (EMCY). Tesfaye appreciated
Tekle as a broad-minded Christian brother (Tesfaye, BG, 14).

---

25. Other Ethiopian mothers have been marvelous singers. Ashenafi Kebede,
prominent musician and orchestra conductor in Ethiopia, deceased in 1998, also tells
a moving story of his devout and musical mother, Fantaye Nekere. "She wrote beauti-
ful semi-sacred verse and poetry, and recited from memory several of Saint Yared's
melodies. She chanted praises to Virgin Mary every day, and sang for Ashenafi the
Psalms of David, playing on the *begena*, every night. She had a great influence upon
his artistic soul. Unfortunately, she died when he was only nine years old. He still
remembers her with a profound sadness" (Fikre Tolossa, *Ethiopian Herald*, 21).

26. This style of reference is used from here to the end of the book to refer to the
Amharic articles pertaining to Tesfaye Gabbiso. Refer to "Transliteration and Format-
ting" in the front matter.

DESCRIPTION OF TESFAYE'S MINISTRY

Tesfaye has said he belongs to the whole church in Ethiopia, because the three largest church groups have been his home at different stages of his life. He was born into a family that attended and served the Kale Heywet Church. During his teenage years and early adulthood, he was mentored and active in the Mekane Yesus Church in Yirgalem. But as he matured, he became a vital part of the Mulu Wongel Full-Gospel church and has remained with them in several capacities, serving in their theological school and also as pastor of a large church in Hawassa for a number of years.

Tesfaye's young manhood was, of course, severely influenced by his seven years in prison. He had a late start in post-high school education but was eventually able to attend and complete a degree at Daystar University in Nairobi, Kenya. In more recent years he has also completed a master's degree at the Ethiopian Graduate School of Theology in Addis Ababa.

Back during the prison years, one of the many visitors who would come to encourage him was a young Christian woman, Hanna. It was allowed, occasionally, that friends and relatives could bring food to the prisoners, and sometimes they could talk over a fence. Hanna became his wife after the prison years, and they now live in Hawassa, Ethiopia, where Hanna has recently completed a biblical degree at Shiloh Bible College. They are parents of two sons, Tsegaw and Tsenatu.

The Christian public at large and various magazines seem to have been interested in Tesfaye's comments about life and ministry through the years. Two of the favorite subjects for their consideration have had to do with how he understands himself and his career.

Shepherd and/or Singer

A question was asked to Tesfaye as both a shepherd (pastor) but also a singer.

> You are not only a shepherd but also a singer. Another question considers the types of songs. Many songs are considered OK. But though some are good in every aspect, some distort the Gospel message in that they focus on worldly things rather than on the Gospel message. Then, we also hear that the life purity of our singers is questionable. How do you see this? (TG, #7)

Tesfaye's answer is interesting, and here I begin using a second font to indicate discussions using Tesfaye's "voice" as it comes through in various interviews and his own writing.

It is difficult as a singer to judge and compare songs and singers. It is better if the larger community evaluates the singer. God is always raising up servants (TG, #7). From this comment, the reader will note that Tesfaye often displays a sense of humor that puts the onus back on the questioners and eliminates his talking very much about himself.

> A yoke or burden was put on me and my friends. I myself am a beneficiary of others' songs, both present and past singers. One singer I have benefitted from, among a long list of others, is Addisu Werqu. Even now, I know my life is being built by the ministry of new singers. (TG, #7)

After these beginning comments, Tesfaye advises that song lyrics should contain advice and edification.[27] The words of songs should give advice and edify. Just because a song has a pleasing tune does not mean that it necessarily contains a spiritual core. All spiritual songs should agree with the Word of God, glorify the Lord, and at the same time be acceptable to the present generation. They should proclaim the Gospel and bring people to Christ. While singing in public places, the singer's ministry should be supported by his personal life style. A singer's walk with God, knowledge of the Bible and connection to God's people should all be exemplary. All connections with church and the people around us need to be sound and healthy—to walk well, keep a straight path and cling to the Lord (TG, #7).

Prophet and/or Priest

Tesfaye's life and ministry exhibit the characteristics of both prophet and priest as well as musician. Evangelicals in Ethiopia would resonate with the Old Testament "priest." But, of course, the priest in the Orthodox Church is a common part of the Ethiopian scene. In the evangelical churches, the common word for the church leader and preacher role is "pastor." The chart below (by Hiebert, Shaw, and Tienou) skillfully presents qualities and descriptions of both Prophet and Priest. I have added to the chart by putting an asterisk before qualities I see as characteristic

---

27. As per Barz, footnoted earlier in chapter 3, I make use of a second font to indicate Tesfaye's "voice" in discussing what he writes or says. This style will continue to appear when appropriate.

of Tesfaye. The reader will note, in many cases, that both "prophet" and "priest" are checked with an asterisk.

Tesfaye would show qualities of both roles. During his earlier years in prison and during the revolution, he definitely was in a prophetic role speaking through his own song and self-possession to many revolutionaries. But since the early 1990s, he has served more in a priestly role during a relatively stable era in which he still serves the church and educational institutions, most recently as the pastor of a large Mulu Wongel (Full Gospel) church in Hawassa. He has been sure of his divine call both singing and pastoring roles. His songs reveal a long-term focus on the past and into eternity as he dwells on God's work through time, but he also lives very much in the present, singing into today's realities. His leadership in the song world has a distinct charisma as he is highly regarded by people of all ages and all church traditions. In lifestyle, he and his family live in a modest dwelling and do not flaunt wealth or means. However, he is treated royally when he travels amongst the Ethiopian diaspora. I have seen him being ushered around with some degree of dignity when he was ministering in Los Angeles.

Table 1: Prophet and Priest

(Adapted from Hiebert, Shaw, and Tienou: *Understanding Folk Religion*, 328, Figure 12.2. Used by permission from Baker Academic, a division of Baker Publishing Group)

	PROPHETS	PRIESTS
FOUND	*when old structures are inadequate for new situations; times of social turbulence, political turmoil and spiritual crisis	*during times of relative social stability and prosperity
APPOINTMENT	*through inner certitude of a divine call to a particular task and human obedience	*through the religious system; election, training, installation, appointment, promotion
FOCUS	*on broad issues, idealistic, and a concern with past and future	*procedures, rituals; realistic, concerned with the present
LEADERSHIP	*charismatic	bureaucratic
LIFESTYLE	*frugal, simple, emphasizes communal living	*adapted to the community, preserves individual privacy

	PROPHETS	PRIESTS
BEHAVIOR	emotionally expressive, eccentric	*calm, temperate, programmed
ATTITUDE TO SIN	*intolerant, iconoclastic	*allows for human failures and imperfections
COMMUNICATION WITH GOD	*seeks direct access to God through personal revelation	*seeks knowledge of God through public revelation
SPIRITUALITY DEFINED	*inner piety and social involvement	living in harmony with sacred tradition
NORMS	*God speaks to the specific time and situation	*timeless laws and universal principles
AUTHORITY	*personal charisma and spiritual	office and work
ROLE AND FUNCTION	*moral and ethical preacher, foreteller, exhorter of people to turn back to God	*teacher of orthodox doctrine, guardian of tradition, minister at the altar in worship
TRAINING	*apprenticeship on the job	*formal training prior to ministry
RELATION TO SOCIETY	*outside to judge and call to repentance	*inside to maintain the religious culture
RELATION TO CHURCH	*reformer, critic, detached, no territorial ties, no place in hierarchy	*guardian of tradition and creeds, tied to specific congregations, empowered, appointed and legitimatized by hierarchy
SELF-IDENTITY	outsider	*member of the religious organization
CHANGE AGENT	*social and spiritual reform, gives up forms, acts on existential truth, calls for dynamic changes	*liturgical renewal, legislative reforms without schism, restrains change, makes moderate reforms

Tesfaye's personality and behavior are certainly "calm, temperate and programmed" as he exhibits life disciplines like honoring schedules, daily disciplines, reporting to authorities, caring for family, and humbly living what he sings. The "attitude to sin" category was one of the strong attractions of this chart for me because Tesfaye's songs reveal such a deep sorrow and disgust for sin and evil, but he also writes often of longing for the sinner and wanderer to be restored. His "norms" are a balance between knowing distinct holy times with God but also appreciating the healthy principles of daily life and work. In his training, a great deal of his apprenticeship was on the job in prison. Yet since prison years, even though his education was delayed, he has completed theological studies through graduate school.

SUMMARY

In this chapter I have inquired into the background of Tesfaye's life in the context of both Ethiopian church history and also the impact of the Marxist revolution on the Christians of that time. I have learned about his forebears who became believers through the witness of Ethiopian evangelists. I heard how Tesfaye was nurtured in singing through his childhood, especially by his mother. I see how his life led to leadership positions both in the church and in music ministries as he matured. His life exhibits characteristics of both prophet and priest. It seems that the evangelical community finds it unusual that he can live inside both of those roles plus, at the same time, be a soloist. In the Ethiopian mind, the soloist holds a high position of honor which many young people want to attain. Through the Spirit's enabling, Tesfaye appears to hold, both gracefully and humbly, all five of these titles of acclaim: pastor, prophet, priest, shepherd and soloist. He is a complicated and gifted individual in the areas of church leadership as well as in song. In the next chapter I concentrate on his song career.

5

Song Career of Tesfaye Gabbiso

Oh, my Soul, He is the Lord; worship Him;
To my merciful Lord, let praises abound.
Let me obey Him with all my life.
Let me tell of His kindness and sing of His mercy. (V–9)

DURING THE PAST HALF-CENTURY thousands of indigenous "spiritual songs" (*menfesawi mezmuroch*) have been composed by a younger generation of Ethiopian Christians. Though songs have been created in many of Ethiopia's approximately eighty-five languages, this study concentrates only on a bounded number of songs composed by one soloist, Tesfaye Gabbiso, in the official language of Ethiopia, Amharic. This phenomenon had its genesis in the 1950s and 1960s prior to the Marxist revolution that lasted from 1974 to 1991. In this chapter, I examine the song career of Tesfaye Gabbiso through various lenses, including his development as a singer. Much of the information is drawn from his own spoken and written reflections about song.

CHILDHOOD EXPERIENCE OF SONG

As a small child, Tesfaye would have heard his mother singing. The lullabies his mother sang would have been created either by her or perhaps spiritual or cultural songs in her mother tongue of a Cushitic language called Sidaminya. Both mother and father were very devout Christians, so he would have heard truth in the songs from his earliest days. Soon, as a growing lad, Tesfaye sang antiphonal songs in his parents' church in which biblical narratives and doctrinal truths were expressed. Any one song might mention up to twenty biblical stories or characters.[1] Some songs used in his congregation were from *Sïbhat L'Amlak* (Praise to God) that included missionary-translated hymns.[2] Tesfaye recalls that the only book or magazine in their house was an Amharic Bible that he used to pick up and read from time to time. Tesfaye also notes that in the early Sidamo churches, many times the women would lead the antiphonal singing in church services. Tesfaye recalls his mother singing to him as a young boy. "Our mother was the incessant singer. . .I would often sing along with her." She taught her children to sing and sang with them. In the church, Tesfaye also heard and closely observed his mother's younger brother, Ato Galalcha as he sang. He also recounted, "When I listened to him sing, I would rejoice in my heart." [3]

In the following paragraph, I choose to introduce a different type style. In attempting to capture the essence of Tesfaye's own words (albeit translated), I will use a different font, beginning in this chapter, for situations where I am not using his exact words, or a song's exact translation. However, it is a paraphrase which offers the reader a closer resemblance to the exact language and style used in the songs themselves, as well as in the spoken words of Tesfaye and the translated articles.

At the same time, as a growing boy, after he left home for middle school, Tesfaye listened to *zefen* (worldly song, in opposition to *mezmur* which was spiritual song) on the radio. However, he did not have the boldness to sing worldly songs, even though in high school he was tempted and learned them little by little. He would go to coffee and tea shops with his school friends and listen to the radio. Being young, the youth wanted to look like city people and be savvy and contemporary. Temptations were there, but Tesfaye acknowledges that he never succumbed to harmful practices such as smoking, drinking or chewing chat. In addition to these influences, there was the new ideology of that period "for instance, the no-God ideology" (TG, #7).

---

1. Balisky, "African Indigenous Songs," 30.

2. The first printed edition of a songbook by this name appeared in 1925. It was printed in Asmara. However, there had been earlier translated songs in print back as far as the 1880s by Swedish missionaries.

3. Interview with Tesfaye Gabbiso, Hawassa, January 9, 2015.

DEVELOPMENT AS A SOLOIST

During Tesfaye's teenage years, a new style of Amharic songs began to be heard over Radio Voice of the Gospel (RVOG). These songs were making an impression on him as he weighed and evaluated the words. New songs were being created by a group of university students in Addis Ababa. The songs were different from the translated hymns. They had new tunes that were distinctly Ethiopian in style. Suddenly young people were realizing they could create for God's glory themselves, both lyrics and tunes.[4] Was this phenomenon something for Tesfaye to explore in his own way?

In my interview with Tesfaye in 1990, he recounted that he received "much blessing and grace from this radio ministry, the Mulu Wongel choir, the university student choir and the Araya family, also soloists such as Tsegaye Habtemer and Addisu Werku." He remembers Addisu Werku being personally interviewed on RVOG when Addisu sang *tïz yileñal ya medhané, beïnçet laï yemoteu sïlené* (I remember that Savior who died on a wooden cross for me). "These songs entered into my soul and heart," says Tesfaye. Addisu said in the radio interview that without a doubt there were young people listening to him at that moment who could write and sing songs as well as he was doing. Tesfaye remembers,

> When I heard this, it just did something to me in my heart. The service or ministry of the radio in my own life is something— what shall I say, a large gift to me. After I grew up and my life had been changed, after I knew what it was all about, and from the radio and other people, I began to write the songs they were singing in my own little notebook. I didn't realize at that time that I had a gift for singing.[5]

The first time he heard a solo with accompaniment was in 1966 in Aletta Wondo. The first time he saw a guitar was in 1969. In 1973, at a Hawassa conference, he saw a choir that had come from Heywet Birhan church in Jimma that was accompanied by guitar, accordion and saxophone. One evangelist had an accordion. The first instrument Tesfaye himself owned was a little harmonica which he learned to play on his own in 1971–72. The first time he handled a guitar was in 1974 in Yirgalem

4. Interview with Yigezu Desta by Vernon Charter and Lila Balisky, Addis Ababa, July 9, 2002.

5. This 1990 interview was very significant in that it was the first time we had held a conversation since his release from seven years in prison.

under Ato Tekeste Teklu, and in 1975 he received his first private guitar as a gift with a note attached anonymously.

The group of faithful believers in Yirgalem was a significant influence in Tesfaye's spiritual and musical growth. As a young man, he was ordained there by the body of believers (Tesfaye, BG, 21). The choir of the local church was arrayed with choir gowns and accompanied with musical instruments (guitar). He recalls that the songs or hymns that the Lord blessed them with were for the first time recorded on audio cassettes and distributed to the Christian public beginning in 1978 (Tesfaye, BG, 21).

CHARACTERISTICS OF EVANGELICAL CHURCH MUSIC

We now turn to consider the characteristics of evangelical church music as it developed in Ethiopia during the period of the 1960s and 1970s. It is important to remember that prior to this time, the songs of the evangelical churches in the urban areas were mainly western hymn texts sung to western tunes. The translation was in Amharic, the official language. In the more rural areas, the churches might sing short songs in the local language. The "new music" that sprang up was a new form altogether, with both words and tunes created in the hearts and minds of young people. It was not western; nor was it in the Orthodox chant style. Except in the Mekane Yesus churches, traditionally Lutheran-related churches, there was no "formal" liturgy. I might say that the informal liturgy of these evangelical churches was largely defined by the music. As Charter suggests, "In sum, it may be said that music has become the dominant liturgical symbol in most churches since the 1980s through the new prominence given the solo singer, the choirs, and the congregation."[6]

Usually there is a choir or a worship group on the platform that leads the singing. A soloist is an honored guest. Ethiopian singers, in general, report the creation of words and tune occur in both directions. John Blacking speaks of "how words generate melody which develops a force of its own and in turn generates new words."[7]

The great majority of soloists' tunes are pentatonic. The usual rhyme scheme is couplets, probably most influenced by traditional Ethiopian poetry rather than a Euro/American hymnbook legacy.[8] Rhyme is frequent in the Horn of Africa and is used in classical Ethiopic Ge'ez verse.

6. Charter, "Contested Symbols," 11.

7. Blacking, "Structure of Musical Discourse," 21.

8. Email from Marianne Nilsson, February 6, 2014.

The style of rhyming is called *yebét memcha* meaning "to come home" and is used in strophic poetry of the Oromo, in Amharic royal songs and other cultural songs.[9]

As indicated earlier, during the 1960s and 1970s, the previous use of translated mission hymns into Amharic began to wane, and the development of renewal movements resulted in new initiatives of lay creativity. Newer songbooks were printed, one of the most well-known series being a set of four books entitled *Weddase Amlak* (Praise to God). There were many songwriters included, but as an example of the popularity of Tesfaye's songs, 16 percent of the total number of songs in *Weddase Amlak* No. 2 are by Tesfaye Gabbiso.[10] These "spiritual songs" were an informal expression of spiritual knowledge and experience springing from the hearts and minds of the ordinary laity.

Periods of Ethiopia's evangelical song history may be divided into three, according to Tesfaye:

1. The Ethiopian Orthodox Yaredawi Style

2. The Missionary European Style

3. The Evangelical Integrative Style[11]

Time frames for the above styles would approximate the following dates: Style 1 from the 6th century to the present; Style 2 from late 19th century to the present (still used occasionally in both public and home gatherings and in the official songbooks of the Mekane Yesus Church); and Style 3 is the eclectic, global style of songs originating in the 1960s and continuously evolving in the present. Tesfaye's own songs fit into Style 3.

The "integrative style" borrows from Styles 1 and 2 plus ethnic styles. In private conversation, I heard a pastor confirm that Tesfaye is willing to adapt and sing to newer music styles in such ways as using studio instrumental backup, changing rhythms, humming, adding harmony.[12] Additionally, a current trend to string song choruses together, based on musical qualities and rhythm, and forgetting about the stanzas that hold the strong teaching details, is representative of this style. It

9. Finnegan, *Oral Literature in Africa*, 74.

10. This set of songbooks is described in detail in Balisky and Lee, "Ethiopian Hymnody."

11. Tesfaye Gabbiso, "Music and Worship," 21–22, 37.

12. Conversation with Pastor Yohannes Girma, Addis Ababa, January 7, 2015.

appeals to the congregation because all the songs are well-known. I heard a Christmas medley like this in Addis Ababa in 2014 and was amazed with the beauty of what the small group of singers could produce musically, but my impression was that the words were extremely repetitive and lacking in substance.

TESFAYE'S MINISTRY AND MUSICAL STYLE

How widely known and appreciated are Tesfaye's songs? First, we look at his songs in print. It is to be remembered that songs in print are a minute number compared to the aural distribution on cassettes, CDs, and online. It is of interest to note several instances in which his songs have made their way into print. I mention three particular Ethiopian songbooks.

Ïgziabhér Ale ('God Is Here: Fifteen Songs from Ethiopia') was a mimeographed booklet of fifteen songs, two of which were composed by Tesfaye Gabbiso. Produced by Ethiopian Evangelical Church Mekane Yesus for the All Africa Council of Churches conference in 1981, it appeared as two mimeographed booklets: one in English, one in Amharic. However, the booklets never arrived at their destination due to internal political pressures and events in Ethiopia. It was duplicated and ready to have been mailed to the upcoming conference on the very day that the Derg confiscated the Mekane Yesus Seminary campus. The songs had been translated by Hartmut Schoenherr with Jim and Aurelia Keefer, with music transcriptions by Marianne Nilsson. They represented an era of suffering in the Ethiopian church and the Preface to the songbook notes that the songs "give witness to God and His mighty deeds" in a time of trouble. Tesfaye's songs IV–9 and IV–10 were the ones included—both apropos to the Ethiopian sitiuation at that time.

Mïhïretu Ayalḳihïmïna ('His Mercy Never Ends') was published by Tesfaye Gabbiso and the Hawassa Mulu Wongel Church in 2012. The book contains the lyrics to over 200 songs composed by Tesfaye Gabbiso from 1973 to 2012. Tesfaye Gabbiso has in recent years been pastor of this mega-church in Hawassa, Southern Ethiopia, but he also travels as a soloist invited by the Ethiopian diaspora around the world. His songs are much appreciated and widely sung in many different settings beyond the church such as dedications, graduations, public conventions and conferences.

Wedasé Amlak ('Praise to God') is a series of four Amharic songbooks with words only which was published by Geja Ethiopian Kale Heywet Church, a local large Addis Ababa congregation and member church of EKHC. This set of hymnbooks became widely used by many church congregations and groups throughout Ethiopia. To illustrate Tesfaye's impact, in book #2, with a total of 155 songs, twenty-seven of the songs are composed by the soloist, Tesfaye Gabbiso.

What is it like to hear Tesfaye sing? I now describe the musical style of Tesfaye's singing, his voice quality, instruments and style of songs. His role as a singer is defined. Tesfaye will also speak about his own music.

Musical Style

Typical of Ethiopian singers, Tesfaye sings an embellished or decorated melody line and utilizes the popular strong nasal quality. As a young singer, when he realized he was receiving the gift of music, he learned to play the guitar by ear. In fact, there is no written musical notation, chording, or accompaniment except for a very few small booklets that have appeared through the years. As is normative in oral societies, everyone plays by ear. Tesfaye's songs are written in Amharic, the national language, rather than in his mother tongue of Sidaminya, though he has translated some songs back into his mother tongue through the years.[13] Tesfaye commented in 1990 that his songs usually come to him with words and tune at the same time. Often his inspirations would come in early morning walks when he was alone with God.

In accompaniment styles, Tesfaye sings to guitar and accordion accompaniment, but also plays and accompanies himself on the traditional Ethiopian *krar*, a six-stringed traditional lyre. It is an important traditional instrument, but in a period when evangelical churches were giving up cultural instruments in order to play accordions, guitars and keyboards, Tesfaye was both a modernizer and traditional figure in occasionally accompanying himself with a *krar*.[14]

Most authentically, Tesfaye accompanies himself on a guitar. That is the picture of him usually seen, for example, on YouTube videos. However, as time moves on, Tesfaye has adapted accordingly, using studio instrumental accompaniments. In several recent public events, such as the Luis Palau "Love Ethiopia" crusade in late 2013, Tesfaye asked Dawit Getachew, an innovative musician, to arrange and play the accompaniments for him.[15]

---

13. Email from Tesfaye Gabbiso, September 4, 2013.
14. Telephone interview with Tibebe Eshete, July 8, 2015.
15. Interview with Dawit Getachew, January 27, 2015.

With an accompaniment crew of one or more musicians, all playing by ear, the present musicians handle intricate electronic accompaniments and experiment in unique ways with even some use of harmonization and more of what might be called a "major chord mode," neither of which is traditional in Ethiopia. This adds contemporary appeal. Thousands of young people listened with spirit and enthusiasm to Tesfaye singing at the Luis Palau "Love Ethiopia" crusade in 2013. As Tesfaye understands it, his structure of stanzas and chorus is influenced by the mission-translated hymnbook *Sïbhat L'Amlak*.[16]

Tesfaye has never written down the tunes to any of his over 200 songs. They are all in his memory, although recorded CDs and cassettes offer another kind of "memory." This is not unusual, as I know that the majority of world music is not notated.

Perhaps the most telling feature of Tesfaye's songs is the overwhelming response. Why do people weep, cluck and respond so fervently while listening to these songs? Jeremy Begbie, British theologian in the arts, makes a point that there are many "extra-musical phenomena" to musical sounds. People respond emotionally to music, and as Begbie notes: "It will be our contention that this interplay can be of considerable interest to the theologian."[17] People and sound are in relationship, tied together and shared.

> Music always, to some extent, embodies social and cultural reality, no matter how individualistically produced, no matter how autonomous with respect to intended function, no matter how intertwined with the circumstances of a particular composer.... Music-making and hearing arise from an engagement with the distinctive configurations of the physical world we inhabit.... Musical practice is inescapably bodily, another matter of theological potential. Our own physical, physiological and neurological make-up mediates and shapes the production and experience of sound to a very high degree ... It has long been recognized that music has very strong connections with our emotional life.[18]

Therefore, music is socially and culturally "embedded," occurs in the physical world, is created and produced through a human body, and has strong connections to emotion. So, what is happening when Tesfaye is

16. Email from Tesfaye Gabbiso, August 29, 2014.

17. Begbie, *Theology, Music and Time*, 13–15.

18. Begbie, *Theology, Music and Time*, 13–15.

creating his own words and tunes, plus his own voice is the instrument?[19] I answer this question later.

Description of His Role

Two important roles for Ethiopians, as far as leadership in the church is concerned, are the positions of pastor (or shepherd) and solo singer. It seems that the evangelical community finds it unusual that Tesfaye can live inside both roles. Through several interviews with Tesfaye found in Ethiopian Christian magazines, I gain an understanding of Tesfaye's own self-perception and his beliefs about the roles in the church. When asked the question, "What should we call you, Pastor or Singer?" Tesfaye responds, "You can choose either if you want, or just call me Tesfaye" (TG, #4). His identity lies in both roles, and he embraces both.

"Service" or "ministry" (*agïlgïlot*) is an important and somewhat vague term in Ethiopian evangelical parlance. Again, a question: "What is ministry? And what is singing?" Tesfaye responds, "Ministry is doing the will of God, and singing is the same" (TG, #4). The question ensued, in this particular article, as to which he gives priority. Tesfaye's only response was that one should be faithful to commitments made. The tendency is for singers to respond to an invitation but then just neglect completing the assignment if something more appealing appears on the horizon.

Comments are made that Tesfaye preaches through his songs. For example, "Listening to Tesfaye's songs is like opening the Word and reading. Not just listening to a song but like entering a theological school and learning. It's like studying a full course on the Christian life" (TG, #9). This same writer has suggested that Tesfaye is serving his generation in four capacities: Apostolic father, apologist, polemicist and scientific theologian. Tesfaye, through his life experiences, preaching and singing is as one who has been with Jesus, willing to suffer, pass on the faith to another generation, combat earthly philosophies, strong in preaching, and a runner not just looking on the race from the sidelines (TG, #9).

Comments by Tesfaye on His Own Music

Through his writing, interviews, and the texts of his songs, an impressive amount of information can be assessed about Tesfaye's understanding of his own music. Tesfaye insists that his songs are given "from God" (TG,

---

19. Begbie, *Theology, Music and Time*, 28.

#2). When he began singing as a child, he first sang the songs of others, but people encouraged him to pray and believed that he would receive songs. He wondered about that advice and how it could come about? He relates how he thought of Mary's question to God, "Since I don't know a man, how can I bear a child? How can this be?" And Tesfaye, in similar fashion, wondered how could he sing songs of his own instead of others'? He thought of the words to Mary, "The Holy Spirit will come upon you." When the Spirit did come upon him, he knew the answer, as God's Word says in Zechariah 4:6, "By the Spirit of God, not by might or by power"). Only by the Spirit could he see new things that are revealed. This understanding helped him. He studied others and learned much and was honored and blessed. He says he did not count this lightly. "The words and tune were anointed by God, and I asked how this could be. This kind of life was full of the Spirit, and how was it possible to find such a thing?" After a time, he experienced the truth of these things. In about 1973, his understanding grew from singing along with others to singing as service to others (TG, #2).

Tesfaye confirms that in 98–99 percent of all the songs, God brought the songs to him. He hears from many people that his songs have a depth to them, and he declares that it is God who gives the word and God's spirit leads him in writing (TG, #2). Tesfaye therefore stands firmly in the *mezmur* tradition of song as contrasted to the *zefen* tradition or any undefined place between the two traditions. This has to be true. How can one person authentically create speech, utter truth, theology, compassion, tune, let alone be the only one who can issue this to the world? He is not mimicking anyone else. He is not singing the art of someone else. The whole "event" is totally from within the musician.

TESFAYE'S TEACHING ON SONG

Tesfaye himself has written extensively and been interviewed about his songs and style. Often, in writing and interviews, Tesfaye expresses his appreciation for what he has learned from the life of David in the Bible. Below is my summarization of an article Tesfaye wrote about David (TG, #5).

Tesfaye on the Life of David

David was a skilled musician and played the harp, even making music to minister to a king who was in mental anguish. David himself was weak in some aspects of his life, but he always turned to the Lord for forgiveness and strength. As for David's service in song, his singing ranged over his whole life from shepherding to ruling as a monarch. The Psalms include praise and sorrow. He was gifted as an individual with both poetry and tune and ability to sing and play the harp. The music, the singer and his words and life all came together in his life. David organized singers in the temple; and in so doing, he passed his songs on to other singers. The following is, therefore, a brief overview, translated, of some of the lessons Tesfaye learned from David and his singing:

1. Songs of a true singer are gifts from God. One must confirm and retain that gift carefully seeking to live a credible life with fruitful service.

2. What David sang for God he also sang to God. So, the singer, in order to honor God and also serve people, must humble himself and avoid ego trips.

3. The singer, being a messenger of creator God, must continually live close with God. The singer is not a teller of fables, but he must be a revealer of God's word, a true prophet and servant of God.

4. A singer's life must reveal God's thought so that the church will benefit. One must sing for his own time, so that the people are strengthened. He gave leadership at times and at various levels, and through it all, he created and utilized his singing.

5. The singer is like David. Thirsty, hungry, running, or ruling, he must control himself and live as a humble person. David's generation didn't find any problem in him; instead, he was a good example. For a cultural model, Tesfaye looks at the accepted story of the father of Ethiopian Orthodox church music, St. Yared, who lived in the 6th century. When Yared began to receive songs from heaven, he did not ask for silver or gold. He was willing to live alone and be poor, but he left a great legacy for the church. He lived with integrity and followed his conscience through hunger and thirst and suffering.

6. A singer must watch his moral life and holiness. If he slips, he must speedily get out of the tempting situation. David slipped in spending too much time alone and was tempted by lust. James 1:14 relates how many are tempted by their own lust and devoured. It wasn't the fault of Bathsheba; it was David's fault. Today, it is laziness (*sinfina*) from which we must protect

ourselves. We must be in a place where we see only God so that lustful thoughts cannot permeate our minds and bring disaster.

7. David was humble. The one who can ask "Who am I?" will not have a proud attitude and will give glory to God. Let us shut up and be quiet. The humble person will learn and will have a heart to receive the advice of others. See Proverbs 12:1, 2 Timothy 2:21 and Philippians 2:5–8 (TG, #5).

Tesfaye Singing about Song

Within the lyrics themselves, as composed by Tesfaye, I find a rather comprehensive view of music and song:

- Personal holiness as a foundation. He often combines preaching and singing together, and so he should, as his career has included both. However, the Ethiopian Christian public tend to draw a distinct line between the two gifts. The singer exudes more drama and emotional excitement. In Song I–3, Tesfaye writes: "If I sing you a song while I am not made right inside, or if I preach without knowing my defect, what fruit will there be? It is running in vain."

- Reason to sing. Tesfaye declares his reason for singing in Song II–8 that we must sing for our God and King. We must sing with understanding through all of life, in whatever season. He tells his own soul in Song V–9 that he wants to compose and sing a song of praise, a song that tells of his kindness and mercy. Song is an innate part of himself and the worship we all must bring.

- Quality of our praise. It is a privilege to present praises to the King of Hosts (Song V–15). And the magnitude of all that we praise him with is "precious": priests with trumpets, singers with musical instruments, voice going forth in unison with shouts of joy and hallelujahs (*illilta*). The earth says hallelujah and heaven applauds! (See Songs IV–7, IV–10, V–15, VII–4, VII–8).

Within the prison, he composed Song VI–1: "As I sing hymns of praise, I rejoice in you." Two prison songs speak specifically of singing. He rejoices in God as he sings hymns of praise and trusts in God who is his only hope, the One who completes the battle for him in the presence of his enemies. He rejoices that though the world cancels him out, he is known in the Book of Life (Song VI–1). Also, in Song

VI–11, "As a stranger in the land I sing today" speaks of his location as a prisoner and his commitment to trust God's leading in the way he should walk for the rest of his life.

Singing is effectual for these reasons: firstly, singing is effectual against the enemy. On a bloody street, victory is the Lord's (Song IV–5) and God stops the joy-cries of the enemies (Song III–4). In VI–4, he sings that we will destroy the fortress of the enemy "by the hymn of our praises." He has seen the successful fight of those who extol God and has learned from their song (Song I–9). Secondly, in Song III–5, he sings in the midst of unbelievers, giving his testimony. And thirdly, in the future, in our "songs of praise and hymns of joy" when the earth actually shakes with the joy-cries of the righteous, we will see greater things that God will do (Song VII–12).

In addition to the actual vocabulary of "sing" and "song" (the verb *zemere* and the noun *mezmur*) as used in Amharic, Tesfaye uses other distinct exclamations of praise to God in the songs as listed below:

> Hallelujah (*halé, haléluya*), Songs IV–9, VII–11
>
> Joyful hurrah (*ïséï*), Song VI–5
>
> Let us rejoice (*des yibelen*), Song III–9
>
> Exalting in praise (*kef kef ïnadergalen*), Song VII–4
>
> Shouts of joy (*beïlilta sïgedulet*), Song IV–10
>
> Praise (*mamesgïn*), Songs VII–3 and 5

In one of his Psalmic songs, VII–8, as a descriptive conclusion to this section, I quote stanza 4:

> Your priests and trumpets,
>
> Singers with musical instruments,
>
> Their voices went forth in unison.
>
> They highly exalted Him in their songs of praise.

All of the above about song is actually taught to us through his songs. He is not consciously teaching planned lessons on song. He is poetically expressing many different thoughts, but in the process of doing that, he is unconsciously giving listeners his views on song. In other words, his mind and heart ring with the vocabulary and spirit of song within his song lyrics.

TESFAYE'S STATEMENTS IN PRINT ON SONG AND SINGERS

Tesfaye is presently serving, alongside his solo ministry, in the elder leadership of the Believers' Full Gospel Church in Hawassa, Ethiopia. He therefore has many opportunities to write and speak on many topics. He is publicly identified in Ethiopia as a "singer and pastor." For example, in a magazine article in 2002 EC (Tesfaye, #10) [20], the author is listed as "Tesfaye Gabbiso, soloist and pastor". In this same article Tesfaye is asked what he thinks about songs in this generation. Tesfaye replies that song is a good movement for spiritual awakening. The Bible should be taught in a powerful way and the words of God should be in our songs (Tesfaye, #10). He has a high public profile through communications, both written and oral.

Through the years, Tesfaye has kept his domicile in Ethiopia, but he also travels quite extensively in other countries among the Ethiopian diaspora. Wherever he goes, he always preaches as well as sings. Tesfaye has sung for Ethiopian diaspora communities in the following countries: Kenya, South Africa, Dubai, Germany, Sweden, Norway, Belgium, Great Britain, the Netherlands, Italy, Australia, Canada, and the United States.[21]

Overcoming the Enemy

An interviewer from *Miliat* magazine (Tesfaye, #7) asked Tesfaye how we can overcome temptations and hardships that come from the Enemy. In response Tesfaye emphasizes three important disciplines: the Bible, prayer, and a determined heart. If these disciplines are actively followed in our lives, we will be fruitful for the glory of God. Tesfaye quotes the Apostle Paul, "Take the sword of the Spirit, which is the Word of God" (Ephesians 6:17). In the magazine interview, he relates how, as prisoners, they had a great thirst to find a Bible and read it. It was the Bible that prepared them for persecution. He says, "We tried as hard as we could to keep it printed inside us." He speaks of how the prisoners memorized the Word as David writes in Psalm 119:11: "I have laid up your word in my heart that I might not sin against you." And again, "Deal bountifully with your servant that i may live

---

20. Sources with the format (Tesfaye, #1, 10) are Amharic articles, often in third person, about Tesfaye or quoting him through interviews. See listing of magazine articles at the end of the bibliography.

21. Email from Tesfaye Gabbiso, May 7, 2015.

and observe your Word" (Psalm 119:17). Further in verse 38: "Confirm to your servant your promise which is for those who fear you." In prison the Christian group spent time studying the Word. When they got into difficulty the memorized word helped them stand firm. "It was just like a sword coming from inside us during the time of persecution and was an answer in time of trouble and suffering" (Tesfaye, #7).

Tesfaye says, "So I want to remind you that the Word which we place in our hearts will benefit any generation, at any time and into the future" (TG, #7.) He further advises to "Keep the Word of God printed inside you. Memorize it." He acknowledges that knowing the scriptures was like a sword "coming out from inside us during the time of persecution and was an answer in time of problems, difficulties and suffering. It benefits any generation." "We need to stick to the study of Word of God, as a baby clings hard to its mother's breast" (TG, #7).

On the television series, The Day of Salvation (*yemedan ken*),[22] Tesfaye speaks of the utmost primary need of prayer. Prayer and God's word, as necessary to ministry, are stressed verbally by Tesfaye in the program using a sort of double emphatic in amharic "*beṭam wana*" (meaning extremely important). Secondly, one must pray without ceasing and, thirdly, one must protect a determined heart to follow the Lord. A spiritual struggle is useful for one's life (Tesfaye, #7).

Gifts of the Spirit

A topic of great interest and concern in the Ethiopian church is the gifts of the Spirit. Tesfaye, in an interview with the magazine *Miiraf* (TG, #6), speaks of the importance of the Word in the lives of believers in order to fulfill God's purposes and use the gifts of grace wisely. He cautions the church not to over emphasize the gifts or distort their use; therefore, it is of utmost importance to follow the teaching of Scripture. There are those who do not seek the truth and it is difficult to bring them back to the truth of Scripture. "It is only by God's Word that these things can be corrected. Because they don't know their mistakes, they may grow old with them." His words to such people are stern. We must boldly consider correction that is needed, and only God's Word can give the necessary direction. The main thing to ask is "What does the Word teach us?" (TG, #6).

---

22. Tesfaye Gabbiso on Yemedan Ken (*yemedan ken*) www.yemedanken.net, part 1 with Kebede Mergia in 2011.

Error and Correction

Tesfaye also gives advice on the subject of not quenching the Spirit (TG, #6). His main points are that the gifts are given for the purpose of service and we must be very careful not to fall into error in their use.

> Many times we either don't know the Word of God or haven't studied it properly. That takes great effort. For those who have veered off course but still appear like disciples, it is hard to bring them back to the truth. They may grow old with their faults. Can we discern between seed and chaff? We must be willing to look boldly at correction, with careful fear and honor of God. It's too easy to let things slide and say, 'It's just a small thing', either to forgive their own error or dismiss someone else's error. If there is error in the church, we have to take responsibility to correct it. (Tesfaye, #6)

Tesfaye does not mince words when speaking his mind on what he feels is correct lifestyle and appropriate teaching in the church. But he always speaks very wisely and carefully, including himself in the plural "we", as evidenced in the above rebuke.

Church Focus

Tesfaye says we focus on short term encouragement or comfort in our churches. Never mind the songs, there is a lack in the teaching. Revival is necessary, but we must be rooted in teaching. He sees a kind of worship and living which is drawing people away from sound teaching and righteous living (Tesfaye, #8). He thinks that songs are important and should be encouraged. It's a good movement for spiritual awakening. In general, when the Bible is taught, it should be in a strong way so that the words of god should be in the songs (Tesfaye, #10).

Tesfaye notes that he tends to write "on discipleship and evangelism."[23] This remains his focus even now into his mature years in his late fifties. When he writes songs and people say the songs "exude deeper meaning," Tesfaye says that is not evident to him personally. "These are not things I do on purpose. I know that I express them as I am inspired by the Lord, or as the Spirit of God enables me to write them, and as He guides my thoughts and gives me discernment" (Tesfaye, #2).

Finally, in summing up his message to this generation of singers, he emphasizes that if the singers aim at content, getting their message

---

23. Interview with Tesfaye Gabbiso, Hawassa, January 9, 2015.

from the Word of God (not directly, necessarily, but the ideas) they will be a blessing. Firstly, it is mandatory to be biblical and to be in fellowship with God in prayer and sometimes in fasting. The second thing: one must take care of one's spiritual life. The messenger and message have to be reinforced by each other. He concludes with this advice: "Although we are not angels, we can aspire to live and serve in holiness."[24]

Temptations and Traps

Ministry is a privilege, but it has temptations, says Tesfaye. The Apostle Paul said, 'A door full of work is opened for me and oppositions are many.' The more we serve the more traps there are. Traps include money, defiling our personal life, temptation to be famous, non-submission to the church. We need to be diligent and keep close to a local church. But traps can also come from those who are believers and claim to be servants of God. Traps of pride, rebellion, despising the Word, disliking advice, lack of purity and wrongful love of advantages. We must resist all that. Sometimes the singers get all the criticism, but our churches are guilty too. Another area where fidelity of the singer is required is in the acceptance of invitations to sing, not to measure them according to prestige or profit but to honor one's prior commitment. Sometimes singers will cancel one commitment with the lure of a greater opportunity, perhaps internationally (Tesfaye, #4).

Traps are present, even for those who claim to be servants of the Lord. Pride, rebellion, despising the word of god, ignoring advice, lack of purity and getting tied up with love of advantages lead us astray. Even Christians, presenting themselves as servants of the Lord, may tend to lead us to destruction. We need to be careful. Be careful. Don't fall into the trap (Tesfaye, #7).

One of the problems mentioned is that singers who are invited to come and sing will dart into the church for their singing appointment. But they fail to stay for the sermon. Tesfaye says they may have booked another appointment to sing the same morning. He advises that covering ten places a day is not ministry. At times, young people just do not want to be advised or disciplined. He questions if this conduct is truly a ministry of love and suggests they should listen to and receive advice. but those who have an advisor and yet turn a deaf ear are in a critical condition. (Tesfaye, #7).

---

24. Interview with Tesfaye Gabbiso, Hawassa, January 9, 2015.

Tesfaye, having relinquished the lead-pastor position, is at present responsible to other leaders in his home church, Mulu Wongel, in Hawassa. He is involved full-time in preaching, teaching and singing ministries and purposely writes semi-annual written reports detailing his schedule and activities to his leadership team, even though this is not required of him. He feels that this discipline aids him in keeping on course and being faithful and responsible in his various activities.[25]

Financial Profit Considered

Tesfaye has consistently refused personal profit in the sale of his songs and CDs. He states that the gift is not of ourselves but belongs to the body of Christ. "There is little difference between singing from the pulpit and handing out songs on tapes. Both should have the element of giving." He therefore turns over his songs and whole cassette ministry to the church for management and he makes no personal gain. He says that if making cassettes is to get one out of poverty, then that is a wrong motive. He suggests that private singers should function in close consultation with their churches if they want to carry out a healthy ministry (Tesfaye, #4).

Tesfaye maintains that: "My primary purpose is to get songs to the people. Money is secondary. If possible I would distribute my songs free of any charge" (Tesfaye, #4).

SUMMARY

In summary, this chapter has helped us understand Tesfaye as a singer and pastor who is in the public domain. I have seen how Tesfaye expresses his thoughts through his self-composed songs, as well as through writing, interviews and speaking. He is a very public figure in Ethiopia and the subject of numerous articles and interviews. He insists that prayer and saturation in the Word are paramount. The life of the singer cannot be divided from the song he sings. The singer should be strongly connected to a local church. Tesfaye can be quite stern in admonishing singers about some of the issues they face. But he rebukes and suggests with grace and humility. The church has a great responsibility to its singers to encourage, correct, lead, and teach. In the following chapter, I turn to discover what Tesfaye sings about.

25. Interview with Tesfaye Gabbiso, Hawassa, January 9, 2015.

6

Song Themes Discovered

Let me compose a song of praise and sing it for Him. (V–9)

THE MAIN PURPOSE OF this chapter is to discover what Tesfaye is saying in his songs. Firstly, I present my methods of content analysis. Then I proceed to make inquiry into the actual content of the 104 song texts as found in the English-Amharic diglot songbook: *Yetesfayé Gabbiso Mezmuroch: The Songs of Tesfaye Gabbiso*. To whom does Tesfaye direct his songs? What does he believe about God? What does it mean to be a disciple? There is much he says to the unbelieving, the wayward. He is always pleading for people to return to God. In this chapter I inquire into these various topics. I trust that I exhibit reasonable objectivity in this writing—even in the choice of topics to study in the lyrics. Who am I, as a westerner, to place a template over the songs?

The process of analyzing another person's songs that have been "received from God" has puzzled me for many years since I first started working with Tesfaye's songs. What right did I have to enter into another person's "holy of holies?" I was reluctant to take on the writing of the article, "Theology in Song: Ethiopia's Tesfaye Gabbiso."[1] But in a conversation with Nathan Corbitt about this anxiety, he assured me with words something like "Just do it; that's what a scholar does." Since then, I have taken courage from him and others and have discussed the very issue at length with Tesfaye himself.

---

1. Balisky, "Theology in Song," 447–56.

In addition, translation of Amharic songs into English is challenge enough. Again, what right have I, as a foreigner to the country, to presume to interpret the songs? I read, write, speak and teach in Amharic, but even after forty years, I often feel like a child when communicating in Amharic. Throughout many years, translator Haile Jenai, who is proficient in both Amharic and English, did contract work in translating the songs to English. Then we would send the songs to Tesfaye himself, who graciously corrected errors or changed meanings to best fit his original lyrics. Both the translator, Haile Jenai, and Tesfaye are very proficient in use of the English language. Thus, I believe the result quite accurately expresses the Amharic meaning. However, in my reading of the English translation, it often seems to lack the power and glory and metaphorical beauty of the original language.

I found Lakoff and Johnson's writing on metaphor helpful in regards to the study of Tesfaye's songs. For example, "The primary function of metaphor is to provide a partial understanding of one kind of experience in terms of another kind of experience."[2] We speak and live in metaphor, so we are also free to interpret each other's writing in a somewhat subjective way and extend the ideas. Life is open-ended and we use metaphors as "systematic devices for further defining a concept and for changing its range of applicability."[3]

METHODOLOGY FOR CONTENT ANALYSIS

In pilot-testing coding, Margrit Schreier suggests that pilot testing should take place on the actual text that will be further studied, not on a separate text.[4] I began my pilot-test coding with actual songs of Tesfaye Gabbiso and using *in vivo* codes (actual words from text) as per Creswell.[5] I initially marked a suitable unit for pilot testing of the coding process by taking a body of twenty-one songs which comprised the first three songs of each of the cassettes.[6] This was already 20 percent of the songs, and I soon discerned the key points repeated so that I did not really need to code all the songs in detail. I could already see themes developing. "Local

---

2. Lakoff and Johnson, *Metaphors We Live By*, 154.
3. Lakoff and Johnson, *Metaphors We Live By*, 125.
4. Schreier, *Qualitative Content Analysis*, 91, 148.
5. Creswell, *Qualitative Inquiry*, 153.
6. Schreier, *Qualitative Content Analysis*, 142.

common-sense constructs . . . and personal experience with the subject matter" are valid sources of discovering themes.[7]

Both concept-driven and data-driven research methods are employed. I used certain "concept-driven coding frames"[8] based on my earlier inductive, rather intuitive research in 1997 in which I wrote that there is a large theme, unexplored, which I described as being "hit with a stick" (Song III–3).[9] However, Schreier points out that data-driven research assists in assuring "face validity" because it provides "exact description of your material."[10] Thus the value of coding specific words. Data-driven method allows "the categories to emerge from" the material.[11]

Another useful method may be a Compare and Contrast approach or "constant comparison method" which is used in the investigation of data.[12] I have also employed a "concept-driven" or deductive method.[13] Molyneux suggests that it is "probably more instructive to consider these broader patterns than to attempt close verbal analysis which would not only require an intimate knowledge of [Amharic] but also strain the limitations of oral expression."[14]

Gery Ryan and H. Russell Bernard also speak of metaphors and analogies and the "observation that people often represent their thoughts, behaviors, and experiences with analogies."[15] For example, one area of suffering which is very prominent in the Tesfaye songs is the situation of the back-slider who rejects the faith and needs to be restored. Who is the back-slider? He is suffering and fails to endure. I have not really grappled with this problem in the songs except to say that Tesfaye has a heart of compassion for all who are away from God. A model for such a study is found in Krabill's discussion of sin, suffering and salvation as found in the Harrist hymn texts.[16] Some subjects, such as ecstasy and pain, or hope deferred correlate with themes I have discovered.[17] A linguistic metaphor may be

7. Ryan and Bernard, "Techniques to Identify Themes," 2.

8. Schreier, *Qualitative Content Analysis*, 189.

9. Balisky, "Theology in Song," 453–55.

10. Schreier, *Qualitative Content Analysis*, 186.

11. Schreier, *Qualitative Content Analysis*, 84.

12. Ryan and Bernard, "Techniques to Identify Themes," 5.

13. Schreier, *Qualitative Analysis*, 60.

14. Molyneux, *African Christian Theology*, 173.

15. Ryan and Bernard, "Techniques to Identify Themes," 8.

16. Krabill, *Hymnody of the Harrist Church*, 349.

17. Molyneux, *African Christian Theology*, 189–97.

described as "something else" which contrasts or redescribes what is being talked about.[18] "Metaphors do provide rich information about a speaker's conceptualizations of a given topic and within a given situation."[19] Is the whole song a metaphor? Is the whole song movement itself a metaphor? Or what powerful metaphors are within the text?

The concept of "itinerary of a song" is being employed on several of the songs.[20] Tesfaye's Song I–14 appears in its entirety in *Sorrow and Blood*.[21] It speaks of suffering and endurance in the form of a Nebuchadnezzar story and ends with a strong deep *ïmbe, ïmbe, ïmbe* ("I refuse, I refuse, I refuse") at the end of chorus.

Others have inspired my thinking with their studies of song. Irene Sun, in describing China's "Songs of Canaan" discusses such aspects as the imagery and theology. She also relates the song to its context, discusses its use, talks about relationship with the divine, suffering and Christ's passion.[22] Hawn's categories and questions in analyzing global song have challenged me, especially the question, "What does this musical experience really mean in its original setting? Am I translating the experience accurately into my own terms and by so doing comprising the meaning of the original situation?"[23] This has been a question for my work. Who am I to dissect and interpret another's work and meaning?

Further, I know that "Quantitative content analysis focuses on a quantitative-spatial metaphor, which assumes that whatever "means" takes up more space and/or time."[24] Therefore, a direct count in "quantitative content analysis of song texts can be helpful to us in determining significance."[25] However, I am aware of her advice that with content analysis I am apt to "create an 'etic' construct" and must guard against that in favor of an emic approach that endeavors to appreciate how the other person really thinks."[26] I have adapted these approaches as observed below.

What is Tesfaye Gabbiso actually singing about? This was my question for many years. Why did the people sit weeping as they did during

---

18. Cameron and Maslen, *Metaphor Analysis*, 3–4.

19. Armstrong, Davis, and Paulson, "Subjectivity Problem," 156–62.

20. Krabill, *Hymnody of the Harrist Church*, 308.

21. Balisky, "I Refuse, I Refrain," 350.

22. Sun, "Songs of Canaan," 2–6.

23. Hawn, *Gather Into One*, 28.

24. King, *Pathways in Christian Music*, 125.

25. King, *Pathways in Christian Music*, 125.

26. King, *Pathways in Christian Music*, 125.

the revolution? Why were his songs played over radio on the public buses? Why did I hear his songs blaring from Muslim shops? Hours of discovery have followed. I used such methods as simple coding, grammatical study to determine to and for whom he sings, and purposeful sampling strategy.[27] What follows is only an initial first attempt at discovering the depth of Tesfaye's lyrics.

PERSON AND DIRECTION OF LYRICS

In beginning the content analysis, I first grouped the songs in terms of person and direction. The following chart gives an overall idea of the nature of Tesfaye's songs. In order to organize and control the corpus of 104 songs, I copied each song onto the left side of an 8 ½ by 11 sheet of paper, with the right side available for notes. Color pencils were used to mark various themes and individual word coding.

The following chart is calculated on the 104 songs that are the subject of study. The various characteristics overlap, so there is no exact number percentage, but I can see some general trends. For example, about one third of the songs are directed to both believers and unbelievers. About 40 percent of the songs are directed to God. The ratio is six-to-one of prayers in first person in contrast to the corporate prayer of "we." About 20 percent of the songs are general information about God in third person to an anonymous audience.

Table 2: Classification of Songs in 1st, 2nd, 3rd Person

Song direction	Number of songs
Song by Jesus as in 1st person	2
Song to Tesfaye's own soul in 1st person	1
Song directed to the enemy in 1st person	1
Song statement/affirmations in 1st person	6

Songs directed to God:
    Songs directed to God "I" singular – 30
    Songs directed to God "We" plural – 5
    Songs of affirmation to God   – 9
	44

Songs directed to both believers and wanderers	30
Songs in 3rd person on a variety of subjects	20
Total:	104

27. Creswell, *Qualitative Inquiry*, 125.

The first four songs in Table 2 are especially unique. Two are written as if Jesus were singing the songs himself. Song I–6 calls "my child" to come back. And in Song IV–3, God himself is pleading in the most beautiful language and longing that a fallen soul will return . . . "Let's be friends instead, for my mercy is full." Then, Tesfaye sings a song to his own soul (Song V–9) and one directly to his enemy (Song III–4). I found the contrast of direction interesting, both outward and inward. Both songs begin with a similar exclamation: "Oh, my enemy" and "Oh, my soul." To each one he tells what he knows about his God. He concludes, in both songs that he will rejoice again in God's goodness and forgiveness. There is always hope.

REFERENCE TO THE TRINITY

A study of the actual names used for the Trinity throughout the songs reveals words for God one hundred times, words for the Son 175 times, and for the Spirit eighteen times. The most common appellation used is various forms of "Lord" or *géta*, a word that is used culturally as a form of honor and respect. The chart below reflects only direct names for God.

Words relating to God the Father are used interchangeably in songs and prayers as ïgziabhér (a specific name for God) or *amlak* (a general word for god or deity). The appellation *géta* "lord, master or owner" is a reference of respect used in the culture but also referring to Our Lord. It is also used historically as a common appellation for a male of some distinction or higher position than the person speaking. (Note: This is a custom that, happily, has disappeared in recent years as missionaries always immensely disliked the title being constantly used for them.)

In Figure 3, I used only the specific names, as found in Amharic, that are used in theological vocabulary. I am not attempting to appraise his theological understanding, only to show the word usage. In addition to the definitive words, there are many other descriptive metaphors, names and attributes for the Lord. Examples include: Shield, Light, the Word, Good News, Mighty of the Mighties, King of kings, Comforter and Encourager, Firm Staff, Protector of the needy, Faithful Shepherd, Emmanuel, Redeemer, Healer, Alpha and Omega, Lamb of God, El Shaddai, King of Peace, Lion of Judah, Master. In Song IV–16, I see "Our sign is Jesus. Our wisdom is Christ. The King of Peace is our Commander." It was difficult in my study to determine apt categories for all of these colorful adjectives and metaphors.

Expressions of the Trinity

God (Ge'ez) - ïgziabhér (42 times)

God (Amharic) - amlak (49)

Father - ab (9)

Lord/O Lord/my Lord - géta/gétayé/géta hoi (179)

Jesus/Lord Jesus - yesus/géta yesus (75)

Christ - krïstos (10)

Savior - medhané (11)

Holy Spirit - menfïs (18)

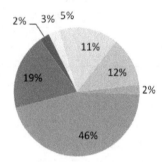

Figure 3: Expressions of the Trinity

Of special interest, as observable in Figure 3, is the detail that the third person of the Trinity, the Holy Spirit, is mentioned relatively few times. Though mentioned infrequently, the powerful work of the Holy Spirit is certainly presumed throughout the songs. Sometimes the absence of a subject or theme is evidence that it is simply taken for granted.[28] Certainly Tesfaye's personal life, ministry and writing are filled with the Spirit. It was during the prison years (1979 to 1987) in Yirgalem that God began to revive his people with the Spirit's power. It was there that Tesfaye began to experience "tangible spiritual transformation" in his life (Tesfaye, BG, 12). One evening, he "came to witness for the first time, the experience of praying in the Spirit and praying in other tongues while a visiting evangelist named Argaw Nida shared the Word of God and prayed for those present" (Tesfaye, BG, 13).

28. Ryan and Bernard, "Techniques to Identify Themes," 6–7.

We have observed that the Holy Spirit is mentioned by name only eighteen times. At other times in the songs, the work of the Spirit would certainly be implied, but Table 3 shows only the times the Spirit is actually mentioned. Mention of the Holy Spirit may be infrequent, but certainly the full person and work of the Spirit is covered in his thought and writing as indicated in Table 3.

Table 3: Person and Work of the Holy Spirit

Description or function:	Song numbers:	Total:
God is Spirit	II-12 (2xs), IV-12	3
Fruit of Spirit	II-1, II-4	2
Heeding the Spirit or not	I-2, III-13	2
Work of the Spirit	II-3, VI-6, VII-12	3
Spirit as dwelling place	VII-7, VII-8	2
Quickening/empowering	V-15, VI-5	2
Battle for a life	III-6, V-2, VI-3	3
Filling of Spirit	V-7	1
Total:		18

Tesfaye prays for the Holy Spirit to be active. Several illustrations are given about the "Work of the Spirit" in Table 3. He wants his life "sealed" by the Spirit (Song II–3). He prays to be given the "fire of your Spirit" (Song VI–6). In Song VII–12, he acknowledges the searching of the "Spirit and his examining word." This is a fascinating study in and of itself. However, one of the challenges in this text analysis is to remember that the person and work of the Holy Spirit is included in the larger scope of the Trinity, and I am ill-equipped to dissect the exact work of the "three-in-one."

RESURRECTION OF JESUS

The "resurrection" of Jesus or of his people is mentioned only once using the actual commonly used terminology *tïnsaé*. Stanza 2 of the Song IV–5 reads:

> He (God) prepares for battle and girds with power.
> Those who were positioned at the top, he casts them down.
> By his *resurrected* authority, he directs the war.
> He chases his enemies and says, "Gather the spoil."

There are other instances when resurrection is implied. "You who announced our freedom in your blood, you are at the right hand of the Father" (Song IV–8) and "Victoriously, he lives forever" (Song IV–9). Song II–12 tells us "Jesus lives, making known his existence and that he will reign as "Alpha and Omega." Songs V–2 and V–8 speak of Jesus who "raised the dead" and ordered "Get up and rise" by the power of the Holy Spirit. Ghanian theologian Kwesi Dickson has suggested that Western theology sometimes tends to "put the Cross in the shadow of the Resurrection . . . the Cross gets to be overshadowed in significance, it becomes a disaster, a regrettable prelude to Easter."[29] Perhaps the lack of references to resurrection in Tesfaye's songs reflects Dickson's idea that Africa concentrates more on the cross of Christ in her theology.

To a westerner, this minimal reference to the resurrection might seem like a "missing theme" that Ryan and Bernard suggest sometimes occurs.[30] As was mentioned about the Holy Spirit, so also the resurrection may be taken for granted in the songs. In the context of war and trouble, the death and suffering that is being experienced at the time of songwriting may predominate as the larger, more urgent theme over any fore-shadowing of resurrection praise. As a final word, however, one may conclude that the entire phenomenon of singer and song in this dissertation is a unified and significant symbol of the power of the resurrection of Jesus Christ.

Discipleship

As a result of dealing with the themes of "enemy" and "strength" and becoming aware of the larger theme of conflict between two sides in life, I continued on with a more thematic study of what he sings about the general subject of discipleship and aspects of the spiritual life that involve growth or bearing fruit. Approximately one quarter, or twenty-five of the songs express thoughts on this subject of discipleship. I may discuss this subject from several angles.

Much of Tesfaye's desire for himself is to be a true disciple, and this is stated mainly in prayer form. His first and main prayer in the songbook is that God would break, use and teach him, that he would be humble and obedient (Song I–1). One image he uses to express his longing is that of being broken.

29. Dickson, *Theology in Africa*, 190.
30. Ryan and Bernard, "Techniques to Identify Themes," Point 6.

Breaking and Crying

The word "to break" (*sebere*) is observed eighteen times in the songs and is used in four ways. The fact that God breaks the bondage is implied six times. A question as to who will help to repair the broken is asked once (Song VII–9). The fact that the enemy wants to break us is expressed once: "My enemy knew of my weakness and dreamed of breaking me" (Song II–3). We are broken by sin in Song IV–13: "I was found in a valley, broken." Our personal need for brokenness occurs at least ten times, one example being: "When the pot breaks the hidden light shines . . . my Lord, my God, I need a broken heart . . . lest I fall and break" (Song VI–9). And Song I–1 reads as follows:

> Dear Father, *break* my heart too
>
> So that the self may be crushed and grace may abound to me. . .
>
> . . .Making the children of your house humble (*broken*)
>
> I'm always *moaning*, seeking that meekness. . .
>
> Before my deep desire for *brokenness* declines,
>
> Why don't you rend the heavens open and come down.
>
> Consider my wish; please *break* me.
>
> Teach me humbleness and obedience.

In parsing this concept, I included the following Amharic words as having the meaning of crying, tears, moaning: *çohe* (v.) "shout out": *leḵese* (v.) "cry"; *ïnba* (n.) "tears"; *marere* (v.) "taste sour or bitter"; *weye* (exclamation) "telling one's sorrows or woes"; *musho* (n.) dirge. These words are found in twenty-nine of the songs.

First, I consider God's weeping but also his wiping of tears. His eyes shed tears of love for the lost child in the song written as by God in first person (Song I–6) and it is we who have caused God to weep (Song I–2). The kind Lord weeps for the wanderer even before we do (Song III–9). We learn that God hears and responds to our wailing (Songs IV–9 and VII–4). And in at least six songs, God wipes the tears from the eyes of his people (Songs III–3, 11, 12; V–11; VII–4,5) and comes as the God of comfort.

Secondly, to whom does the Lord listen? He listens to all who are wailing, the backslider, the one crying in sin, the poor, for those who weep as Hagar in bitterness, the one with problems, with regrets, the one who groans "Oh, my Lord," our secrets, the one who is fearful, those broken and weeping in the dark. He knows our secrets and hears our moaning.

Thirdly, the singer weeps in first person about his own dried up life, wretchedness and need and knows that the lord sees his tears and hears his cry (Song I–1, I–4). Very applicable to own life, he laments the vain running "if I sing you a song while I am not made right inside, or if I preach without knowing my defect, what fruit will there be?" (Song I–3).

One song that could be applied to his own experience of suffering is Song II–14 where he cried out with *weye*, a serious exclamation of alarm and woe. Then he affirms victory using images of the colony of bees after him, Goliath's falling, and the victory of Christ on the cross.

Growth and Building Up

First, there is a longing to move beyond the crying and brokenness. Tesfaye cries tears that he should be "built" to be mature (Song I–4). There is a sorrow for "not bearing fruit" (Song I–5). He would not want to sing without understanding the problem, or having a defect of his own, otherwise, what fruit could there be (Song I–3)? The title of Song I–7 admits that "My infancy is not yet over" and he wants to be "full-grown" and "see his life developed." He prays for God to teach him and be "seen in [his] daily walk" (Songs VI–11 and VII–3).

Secondly, the source of growth and true discipleship is not in himself. He has no strength in himself and cannot win the battle (Song I–9). He sees it as a battle and, (in Song II–15), while fighting the "good fight" he asks God to give him victory. In Song IV–15, he expresses his desire to "reach that stage" of maturity in his strength and struggle.

Thirdly, ways in which he joins others as part of the Christian community and prays for them are expressed in the plural connoting "we" or "you." He prays that other Christians will develop in their discipleship. He urges that the lives of Christians will be strengthened and shine by allowing the power of the Holy Spirit to lead them (Song V–2). The Spirit will equip and give power and grace. Songs V–2 and I–2 express these concepts.

Further, in seven of the songs, he uses the vivid image of fruit-bearing. He weeps in Songs I–3, I–5, V–7, and VII–9 for the sorrow of running fruitlessly or with a hand empty of fruit. He apologizes for his "lukewarmness" in not bearing fruit and acknowledges that "an ambassador of Christ" is identified by his fruit-bearing (Songs II–4 and II–1). Aligned with fruit-bearing is the larger idea of "growth". He desires Christians to be "full-grown" and developed in the Word and in truth and love (Songs I–7, VI–6 and V–6).

In Song III–10, I see a combined use of growth and fruit-bearing in his desire that he might remain firm and grow where he is placed. He learned to bear fruit after observing the sprouts which grew quickly in a stony place withered, without bearing fruit, when the hot sun shone. And he continues by comparing Saul's haste and decline in contrast to David's life which "was anointed and became great". He prays, "Open my eyes that I may know my place. Shorten not my life; instead make me grow."

Therefore, I see the actions or desired qualities expressed in his prayers are that he will fight effectively, rise up, be beneficial, learn before racing for power, be free of laziness, be quickened, be purposefully active, qualified, equipped, covered with charisma, be developed, steadfast and diligent.

ANTITHESIS: BACKSLIDER AND WANDERER

The antithesis of the whole subject of discipleship, growth and fruit-bearing is described in another oft-expressed situation or position of the back-slider or wanderer. This is a major theme in Tesfaye's songs. I propose that this whole theme is the antithesis of everything that is Godward. It is a sorrowful state of the world gone wrong, the individual person gone wrong. But for the grace of God, the song of the singer could ring hollow and the singer himself fall into the position of a backslider. That is another reason why Tesfaye wrote such challenging songs to the backslider. He could be one himself. In at least twenty-five songs, five of which were written in prison, Tesfaye speaks about the wanderer or wayward one. In four songs, he speaks directly to himself in first person about the actuality of his falling back, which is labeled "Personal Wandering" below. I may study this theme by looking at it under three different headings which describe what I identify as three kinds of wanderers:

LUKEWARM WANDERING

One of the themes observable in Tesfaye's songs is the problem of straying or laziness as a Christian. Tesfaye describes this dilemma in such songs as II–4 and III–2. He uses the colorful Amharic word *leb biyé* (like lukewarm water) even to describe his own wandering at times. He finds himself in a dilemma, near the gates of death. Instead of climbing up, "Down I went." Rebuked, he is trembling and realizes he is not an atheist, but neither is he a strong Christian. This kind of wandering is also characterized by various personal weaknesses. He is rebuked by the Word and appeals to God to raise him up. He is so ashamed of himself and his brokenness. He asks the Lord to examine, forgive and pardon him because he knows God is gracious. In so doing, he quietly waits for pardon and renewal.

There is always the enemy who gloats over the weak one. Song III–4 is actually a song addressed to this enemy. Tesfaye acknowledges he has sinned but will be patient until God brings him into the light again. This business between God and him will be settled because Jesus loves forgiveness, disrupts the enemy's wiles and will tear off the coarse clothes of disgrace and give him garments to wear. He will eventually sing for Him again, leaning on the arm of the Lord.

The whole of Song IV–12 "After Tasting Your Glory" deals with how he forgot his commitment after tasting the power and glory of the Lord. This happened because he looked at the world. How could he ever flee away from God's presence and Spirit? He misses his target and lets his eyes wander, and becomes jealous of the sinner's success and prosperity. But in the end, he gains his balance and realizes that the world's way is just a vacuum. How could he be so deceived when Jesus has promised never to leave him? Again, he speaks to the enemy, telling him to despair because he is powerless to make Tesfaye fall down.

Strangers in the Desert

In at least nine more songs he speaks to believers warning them of waywardness. He speaks of the wayward as becoming fearful and moving from life back into death. They deny their Savior (Song I–5). In Song I–6, he writes as the voice of Jesus, longing to stretch out his hand of mercy to those who have fallen back into depression and sin. Why would they wander? Both Jesus and the wanderer are in tears and Jesus pleads with them. Let the homesick come back to the grace and beauty of the Lord. In Song II–13, Tesfaye pleads with his friends not to doubt and deny Jesus. It is a beautiful listing of all the Lord will do for us. God never lies or reneges on his promises. The wanderer must believe in God's Word and recognize all God has done for him or her. Then in

Song III–6 he challenges the wayward one who is ashamed in believing. He began well with the Spirit, but then his heart melted and he began to "chat with the enemy." Some pretended to be Christians but did not have the right "passport." God's hand is not short to restore the prodigal. Song III–7 is a reminder to himself and others that flesh can so easily revive and sin sprout. We can freeze love, murmur and desire to stone our brothers. Lord, deliver, lest we be ridiculed and covered in shame.

Song III–9 rejoices that the deserter, who had been deceived by various obstacles and denied his Lord, has been pitied by God, brought back from the trap and restored. Song V–3 speaks of a "street man" who has been puffed up by his work and become proud in his visibility so that the Lord is not seen. He should examine his life, start praying again and lay his fleshly desires at the feet of Jesus. Then the light of Christ will again be visible through him to the world. The proud are reminded that "life increases when the seed of wheat dies." To the one who took off his Christianity and threw it away, running ahead of God's will, thus becoming a "stranger of the desert," Tesfaye pleads in VI–12 that such a one cut off his carnal racing, stop the useless consumption and come back to obedience and the advice of the word. Song VII–9 is a plea to those who would bring restoration. Why should we seek our own charming life without God? Our hands are empty of fruit while the other sheep become prey for wild beasts because we haven't been shepherds. Why do we bury our talents? Why are we lazy? The person who proclaims the Good News, who is compassionate and kind and gathers souls, will receive the reward and shine forever.

Unbelieving

Tesfaye is very concerned about the unbelievers and sings to them directly in many of his songs. He has the heart of an evangelist. They should not wait until tomorrow (Song II–2) and live deceived all their lives. Hesitation will bring death. Only Jesus gives life. The world lures and deceives us. It makes God's way seem foolishness, so one should believe, be saved and sealed forever because the Lord is the only one who will satisfy. In Song II–15, the unbelieving toss and turn in the world of the dead. They have scoffed as atheists and met their death with other atheists. They are all making noises in hell, all separated from God. It is difficult to decipher whether some songs are written to the unbeliever or the wandering Christian. Songs such as IV–2,

IV–3, IV–4 and VI–13 are examples of this uncertainty. The sinner, or whoever the wanderer, is challenged to come home and rejoice in God's salvation and strength.

SUMMARY

Many other subjects in the songs could have been addressed, but the main ideas have been considered as representative of Tesfaye Gabbiso's basic theology in terms of his writing and his own life narrative. We have discussed his concept of the Trinity, the death and resurrection of Jesus. His emphasis on discipleship included ideas of brokenness but also being built up. There is a stark contrast to the believer in his large concern for the lukewarm, the backsliders and the wanderers. His heart for the wayward, including his own weaknesses, is a great concern both in his life and in his songs. But in God there is always hope and salvation. I now move on to what may be the most significant themes in the songs, those of suffering and endurance.

7

Suffering and Endurance

By the rivers of Babylon as we sadly sat down,
we thought of Zion and bitterly cried.
But the God of comfort, looking at us from above,
wiped our tears and fixed our broken hearts. (Song IV–10)

AT THE CENTER OF Tesfaye's story lies the constant connection with the persecution he personally endured as a prisoner for seven years from 1979 to 1987. He was about twenty-four years old when he was put in prison. In a sense, he is an icon of suffering for the people of Ethiopia, one of the main reasons that he is taken so seriously. The Marxist revolution lasting from 1974 to 1991 was a time of unrest, fear, and difficulty in the Christian churches. Tesfaye was a young man at this time. Perhaps because he was well known and becoming quite a public figure, he was singled out by the revolutionary officials with other active Christian young people. His story of imprisonment and suffering is included in a series of testimonies collected into a volume on the persecuted church by the SIM director at that time.[1] Tesfaye tells his own story of the prison years in *Beziyan Gizé* or "Those Days" which is published in Amharic.

---

1. Cumbers, *Count It All Joy*, 66–67.

THE PRISON EXPERIENCE AND SONGS

While in prison from 1979 to 1987, Tesfaye composed forty songs.[2] Twenty of these songs are included in the songbook under study.[3] One of the favorite songs (Song V–11), even until today, has an actual prison experience behind it.

Tesfaye relates how they were mistreated in prison so many times. Infestations of bugs, wrapping themselves in their bedsheets when their only pair of clothes was being washed, enduring heavy labor, all were a part of daily life. Then the prison officials would challenge and deride them for their faith. One of the Christian brothers challenged the officials saying, "We know God will come down from heaven to help us. Please don't speak to us so disrespectfully." So Tesfaye and friends pondered those words. It was while he was still in jail, that the song came to Tesfaye, words and music included. One of the most well-known of the prison songs is "When God Assists" (Song V–11). They sang it in prison for the first time when they later settled in the Yirgalem prison. They accepted that song as an uplifting message that was truly a gift from God (Tesfaye, #2). The chorus goes:

> When God assists, descending from the heavens,
>
> When He wipes out all offences by His justice,
>
> Haven't you seen the trap broken,
>
> The captive freed and telling about His redemption? (V–11)

Verse 1 (Song V–11) speaks of many temptations on life's path, but the righteous who call on the Lord will never perish. God hears the cry "hold my hand" and pulls the distressed one out of the swamp leading him along in victory. Verse 2 speaks of the enemy defying God and attempting to devour the poor and helpless with prideful terrifying words. It is only God who can reach down and save. Trusting in man is pure vanity of vanities. Verse 3 describes the Christian brother and/or sister as deprived of everything. He has only the Lord standing by his side. The only foundation for hope is the Lord when one is shoved aside in a "foreign" land. Verse 4 concludes with the promise that the Lord will return after the ages are past when praise and glory will be given to the One who wipes away the tears from his children's eyes.

---

2. Email from Tesfaye Gabbiso, December 23, 2013.

3. These prison songs are marked with an asterisk in the songbook index at back.

As for actual singing while in prison, Tesfaye had to deal with rumours because of his stature as a singer. One rumour in the public was that he was asked to "sing for the revolution" at the central Revolution Square in Addis Ababa. That was not true. But in prison there were rare convenient times when they could sing. One time, a man in authority under the Marxist government, asked Tesfaye, "Would you sing at my child's wedding ceremony?" Tesfaye told him something like this: "I couldn't serve two masters and I didn't want to be a worldly and a spiritual singer at the same time. We did sing, when possible, in prison. The wardens would comment, 'They are singing!' We heard this was reported to the authorities." (Tesfaye, #8). In spite of restrictions, songs were written and sung during the prison years.

Song V–4, "When Will I Hear Your Voice?" written while in prison, illustrates the times of discouragement—truly a song from within Babylon. He pleads for his Savior to remember him in his moaning because his soul is weak. How can he continue? When will he be comforted or ever made happy? When will the appointed time come when sadness is completed and he is strengthened to stand on his feet again? He begs to hear the voice of the Lord so that he can be healed.

Tesfaye could create a song like VI-6 "Oh, Lord, Bless Us with a Blessing" in the prison. Ethiopia sings the song now as a blessing for the nation, but Tesfaye of could also sing it with full meaning within the prison cell. That was his total world. "Oh, Lord, bless us with a blessing, enlarge our spiritual territory. May your hand be upon us; You are our hope." Six meaningful stanzas follow, ending with "until the earth fills up by knowing God, our pleading continues without our strength being weakened."

PRISON SPACE

In Tesfaye's songs there is no place for compromise. It must be a total allegiance or nothing. "As for myself, I have chosen to carry Your cross. This Lord is the decision of my soul" (VI–8). Therefore, the Singer, the Preacher, the Prisoner, may be identified all in one persona, ringing true as a unity.

We look now at some aspects of this truth as the singer is confined in prison and anti-religious space. What impact does the place or space have? In the "world/community" quadrant of our Matrix in Figure 1, he is moved into a confined space. The song is still the same. And song is received, to a degree, in the confined space much more powerfully than just "word" would be received. Under persecution and in a confined space, it is a case of a "faith community" operating in the larger prison cell with many anti-Christian close neighbors, different than among friends. In order for this to be genuine, the life-styles of the prisoners should be above reproach. It was a confining situation. When we worship in a free space and perform our liturgies, the world around us is not involved or watching that much. But the world is demanding a correlation of life and song texts in the prison space. Ponder the wonder that prison officials and other prisoners were treated to live music and Christian choral expression in that confined and anti-religious space—a modern version of the Paul and Silas story recorded in Acts.

Another striking parallel to Tesfaye's life, worth mentioning here, comes from Eritrea in the experience of Helen Berhane, called the "nightingale." She needed nothing else but her total being to produce song in prison. She and fellow prisoners were kept in metal containers which were unbearably hot in the desert sun. Words, music, voice, all combined, revealed the power of her song in an Eritrean prison. This is different from art forms which require materials. The guards could not take her song away. She was ordered never to sing again. When ordered never to sing again, she replied, "I am a singer, and so I cannot give it up. I will sing quietly so as not to disturb the people in other containers, but I will not stop."[4] Gradually, other women did become afraid or worn down by the torture, and they agreed to stop singing. A song she composed is called "Who is singing?"[5]

We need to appreciate the liturgical act, that liturgy and worship in a given community, be it even in prison, is "capacitated by the Holy Spirit in baptism to speak to and about God, that is, to theologize."[6] Music in the Christian ritual in prison was core to the fellowship of the prisoners. McGann continues: "The musical action may be understood as a means of . . . offering praise, thanksgiving, intercession . . . of receiving power, love or nourishment."[7] Even prison was a place where there were working

---

4. Helen Berhane and Newrick, *Song of the Nightingale*, 28–40.

5. Helen Berhane and Newrick, *Song of the Nightingale*, 60.

6. McGann, *Exploring Music*, 19.

7. McGann, *Exploring Music*, 27.

strategies "to create a sense of 'world,' a redemptive order of existence within which participants are empowered."[8]

Prison Mission

What about the singer and/or the song in prison from a "missional" point of view? The prison dynamic, where he is within confines, removes him from the expected religious place or personal private space. The very act of singing was a very strong aspect of mission. This would seem to put an extra "burden" of carefulness on the singer and the meaning of the text. They were singing in Babylon. One inclination was to sit down and cry bitterly by the rivers of Babylon (Song IV–10). But the song moves on to say God "wiped our tears and fixed our broken hearts." Then follows beautiful poetry as to how God saves, disperses the enemies (and the enemy is listening!), and rewards the faithful who will find joy in the Lord their refuge and will do beautiful things like sparkle, ascend, run, be precious as God's jewels. Imagine the prison guards hearing them sing: "He (God) won't give us to the vultures but will take us home, carrying us on His wings." We may say that the music "in all its performativity"[9] is especially powerful in an opposing space, an unusual place.

Suffering and Glory

Pertinent to this is Sunquist's understanding of suffering and glory as the main story in mission. "Suffering is the path; glory with great joy is the end."[10] Surely Tesfaye's life and song illustrate this truth. Sunquist also points out the lesson "often neglected" that youth have been and are so vital in the story of missions.[11] These are lessons for young Christian singers worldwide. It is amazing to think that Tesfaye was only a teenager when his songs started blessing the nation in a time of persecution. Sunquist writes in conclusion on suffering and mission: "When the poor are fed and when criminals become a blessing, we are beginning to see a glimpse of God's glorious Kingdom on earth, as it is in heaven."[12] Tesfaye's song "Greater than This" almost echoes these words exactly: "When

8. McGann, *Exploring Music*, 33.

9. McGann, *Exploring Music*, 37–38.

10. Sunquist, *Understanding Christian Mission*, 399.

11. Sunquist, *Understanding Christian Mission*, 398.

12. Sunquist, *Understanding Christian Mission*, 399.

the hungry are fed, when the Most High gives His word, then the earth shakes with the joy cries of the righteous" (VII–12).

On June 8, 2013, three days after my husband and I had arrived back in Ethiopia, we had an unexpected welcome visit from Tesfaye and his wife, Hanna, at SIM Headquarters in Addis Ababa. I discussed with Tesfaye the recently narrowed subject for a dissertation topic, that of suffering and endurance. He quickly commented that suffering goes on through life, though in different forms, some deeper and far more difficult than incarceration. The former group of prisoners (he among them) recently celebrated the 27th anniversary of release from prison and actually discussed suffering as a topic on that occasion. The majority testified that their lives have been full of suffering since then in different ways. It is a normal and expected part of life.

Hof speaks of lament that is "voiced from concrete bodily experiences." It is not just "primarily a delicate and sophisticated theological undertaking, but arises in a far more direct way from the experience of pain."[13] Tesfaye's physical suffering described in his autobiographical writing *Beziyan Gizé*[14] is illustrated below.

Power of the Scriptures

Tesfaye is a biblicist in that he takes the Word of God literally. In the harrowing circumstances of prison life, often a verse from the Old Testament would be his strength or promise for the day. For example, he tells of the afternoon in 1977 when the preacher was speaking on Habbakuk 3, and in the midst of the sermon a local area soldier arrived at the meeting carrying a gun. This was only the beginning of persecutions (Tesfaye, BG, 20). In 1979, as they waited in Yirgalem for imprisonment that was soon to come, the verse in Tesfaye's mind was Luke 22:31: "Satan has asked to sift you as wheat. But I have prayed for you. . .that your faith may not fail. And when you have turned back, strengthen your brothers" (Tesfaye, BG, 30–31).

One can only imagine the power of the scripture on such an occasion. In 1978, at a revival conference in Yirgalem, a doctor friend, Alemayehu Mekonnen from Bale Goba, ministered in Biblical teaching. Tesfaye and his friends were refreshed through such conferences (Tesfaye, BG, 19).

13. Hof, "Missiology of Lament," 335.

14. *Beziyan Gizé*, yet to be released in English, will be entitled *Those Days*. The book is referred to as "Tesfaye, BG" in the List of Abbreviations.

Tesfaye records that when they were first incarcerated, none of them was allowed to have a Bible. They comforted each other by "exchanging Bible verses we retained in our memory" (Tesfaye, BG, 34). As they moved through the various prison experiences, God's word to Tesfaye was the verse: "I will give you every place where you set your foot" (Joshua 1:3). "Through the years, we witnessed God confirming his Word as He let us subdue and gradually put under our control all the sites where we stayed" (Tesfaye, BG, 36–37).

What to the general reader of the Bible might seem obscure and strange, Tesfaye found that the Old Testament stories became "the basis of sharing" on many an evening during their time of suffering. Isa 7:4–7; I Chr 12:33; I Kgs 20:7–8; Job 39:27,30; Gen 28:20-22; Ps 105:18: these passages became God's explicit and direct word to them for a particular moment in time (Tesfaye, BG, 77–78). Within the prison, they strictly maintained their worship, Bible studies, prayer and fellowship as much as possible. During one Bible study, they were meditating on II Corinthians 11 and were beginning to discuss verse 24: "Five times I received from the Jews the forty lashes minus one." At that moment of reading, the women prisoners were taken out to an adjacent room, and the whipping they received was heard as the lashes fell (Tesfaye, BG, 35). Tesfaye and his fellow prisoners took God literally at his word.

Even before they were put in prison, their Bibles were confiscated in Yirgalem, put on a pile sprinkled with gas oil and set alight, then the Christians were told to inhale the smoke. This sort of activity only caused the Christians to become more zealous and dedicated to the scriptures. One may conclude with the affirmation of Tesfaye that it was the power of the Scriptures, the Word of God, that had prepared them for prison. Right up until imprisonment, they maintained regular programs of prayer, communion and solid Bible teaching (Tesfaye, BG, 25–26). In 1979, they waited in Yirgalem for confined imprisonment that was soon to come. The verse in Tesfaye's mind was Luke 22:31: "Satan has asked to sift you as wheat. But I have prayed for you . . . that your faith may not fail. And when you have turned back, strengthen your brothers."

There were also moments of humor connected with the Bible and Tesfaye's use of it to good advantage. I relate several incidents:

Tesfaye records that when they were first put in prison, none of them had a Bible. When a Bible was smuggled in for them, they kissed it in traditional Orthodox custom (Tesfaye, BG, 34). On September 12, Revolution Day (1978/1979), the slogan was mass-produced "Forward with the Campaign of Promoting Production and Culture." This slogan had a positive twist, since there was the intention in the Marxist government to eradicate illiteracy through a campaign and in the process to promote industriousness. Tesfaye writes, "Since the Bible, the basis of our faith, encouraged such an undertaking, fellow Christians believed that God had placed us in different sites so that we could whole-heartedly participate in the promotion of this campaign" (Tesfaye, BG, 21–22). A twinkle was in their eyes.

On September 16, 1979, one New Testament was found discovered in the prison. The guard asked, "Who does this New Testament belong to?" The three Christians responded, "It belongs to the three of us!" A long harassment followed, and in the midst of the conversation, the guards were blinded to several larger complete Bibles lying in the rooms (Tesfaye, BG, 47). On another New Year's Day in September (Ethiopian calendar), he thought he would have a bit of fun. The prisoners had their own pillows, all of which had Bible texts embroidered on them in true Ethiopian evangelical fashion. He lined the pillows up against a wall in a logical order, then read the pillow texts aloud to the guards, thus creating a small celebrative witness for the prison personnel (Tesfaye, BG, 47).

All through his prison experience, he continuously refers to scriptures, cross-references them, between Old Testament stories, Psalms and New Testament truths, proof of saturation in scripture day by day. Unusual images and strange stories from the Old Testament gave them courage and confidence, stories we would pass by, for example: Job 39:27–30. The stench coming from the slain is of no concern to the eagle because amid the stench it finds food to sustain life. "We, too are staying in an inconvenient environment, but God's grace supplies us the patience to keep on living" (Tesfaye, BG, 78). They took God literally at his word. And thus, Tesfaye and his friends spent seven years of their young adult lives in prison for the sake of their testimony. We do not ask for Babylons. But they somehow enrich our spiritual journey and we learn to live in the meantime.

ENEMIES AND THE STRENGTH TO ENDURE

In the prison experience, the battle to endure was intense. I realized that if I were to study themes of suffering and endurance, there must first be elements for a cause of suffering. What was the cause of the suffering? How did Tesfaye deal with the constant persecution? Who was God to him in this situation? How did he encourage his fellow prisoners? He was dealing with this situation for seven years in the prime of his life.

Concept of Enemy

Upon scanning the songs, words like "enemy" plus additional concepts of "enemy" came into view. Therefore, I probed that word first. This is an example of quantitative content analysis which means a study of words that "takes up more space and/or time."[15] I had a question whether the actual word "enemy" was used frequently and discovered it was used forty-seven times. "Satan" was used eight times. Were there other words connoting the same meaning? Table 4 shows the results of the search using eight other descriptive Amharic words used in the songs.

Table 4: The Enemy and Synonyms

TOTAL WORDS FOR ENEMY AND SYNONYMS	TOTAL: 64 times	Song Numbers
enemy—ṭelat	47	Individual songs not listed because of large number
Satan—seyïṭan	8	I-10, II-5. III-8, IV-4, IV-10, IV-15, VI-3, VII-5
devil—diabïlos	3	III-14, IV-2, VII-4
evil army—kïfatïm serawit	1	I-13
rascal—gulbetenya	1	IV-9
dragon—zendo	1	V-13
demons—aganïnt	1	VI-4
destroyer—aṭïfiyu	1	VI-4
evil spirits, ïrkus menafïst	1	VII-12

The power of evil is vividly described in many songs. Because of all the metaphor and color in the verbs, I have made the choice to let the following lists stand in this thesis. It is a literary journey just reading through the descriptions.

Satan:
I–10   he protected me from Satan
II–5   a captive of Satan and pressed by his load
III–8   even the wise become fools and deceived by Satan
IV–4   he bade farewell to Satan, the world, and the flesh

15. King, *Pathways in Christian Music*, 125.

IV–10   he will keep us from Satan's snare
IV–15   compete with Satan, your rival, and victory is ours
VI–3   he who smote and crushed the power of Satan
VI–5   Satan wished to winnow us as wheat
VII–12   by his power, he casts out evil spirits

Diabilos:
III–14   the devil is roaring to swallow you (adversary as in a
         lawsuit)
IV–2   victim of the devil who is ruler of darkness
VII–4   the city of sin, the work of the devil

Other terms for the evil:
I–13   over the rule of this world and over the evil army
IV–9   the rascal came and stamped on it so it would not grow
V–13   were not you the one who wounded the dragon
VI–4   they were not destroyed by the destroyer
VI–4   the demons were ashamed, those who ambushed to
         attack us

To acquire a deeper understanding of the descriptions, I looked at the verb indicators of the enemy's activity using only the word ṭelat. The following is an alphabetized list of the enemy's specific nasty actions:

As shown in Table 5, the action verbs and imagery connected with the work of the "enemy" are richly varied and picturesque. These are all active verbs. Only once each is the verb "to be" or the verb "to have" used: The enemy "is angry" and "has arrow and sword." This list is related only to the usage of the word "enemy" and does not include the other terms for enemy and his actions.

Table 5: Action Verbs of the Enemy

Accuses VI-13	Defies God V-11	Scares I-10
Advances again II-7	Dreams of breaking II-3	Scoffs I-10
Asks where God is I-10	Hits with a stick III-15	Sees I have a helper II-14
Attempts to devour V-11	Increases in battlefield II-14	Sets a trap I-10
Blows whirlwind I-5	Laughs at us I-2	Shows strength III-15
Boasts I-11	Nags I-5	Snatches freedom I-10
Burns with jealousy I-5	Numbs I-5	Spreads a net I-5

Casts into fire I-14	Oppresses I-5	Stamping on Jesus' blood II-3
Causes to be sad II-3	Overpowers VII-3	Steals health I-5
Challenges I-5	Puts an obstacle in the way VII-5	Surrounds III-14
Comes like a colony of bees II-14	Ridicules VII-1	Ties up and casts into fire I-14
Cuts off the vine I-5	Roars I-5	Tries to cluck(snort/neigh) III-12

In the process of coding on that subject I discovered one song which is sung directly to the enemy and is the only one of its kind in the collection. Song III–4 is based on the prayer in Micah 7:8–9:

Chorus:

O, my Enemy, if I fall I will also rise
Even if I sit in the dark, God becomes my light.
So, so, don't gloat over me.

1. I am like one who gathers summer fruit at the gleaning of the vineyard
I stand dry beyond the blessings.
My lamentation of sorrow, my cry of bitterness
I leave before my God so He can see my life.

2. For I have sinned against God,
His anger fell upon me like thunder for my punishment
I will be patient until He takes me out to the light.
I will wait for Him until He redeems me.

3. The business between God and me will be finalized,
Completed by Jesus, the cornerstone.
So, my enemy, get away! May the Lord rebuke you!
Even now I am His child. Be clear about that in your heart.

4. He loves forgiveness; He is not angry forever.
He disrupts my enemies' wishes and stops their joy-cries
Tearing off my coarse clothes of disgrace and wearing white garments
I will sing for Him again, leaning on His arm.

One discovers that this song is being sung by someone who has sinned against God. It indicates another very strong theme in the song which is the backslidden condition, the wayward one, the wanderer, the sinner, the lukewarm, all needing restoration of some kind. In short, the subject of suffering and endurance is much larger in the song corpus than just the matter of persecution. It is very much a matter of one's personal experience of God.

Further, if there is an enemy, who defeats the enemy? What is the opposition to the enemy? Who will help us to stand? It is a kind of suffering and lack of endurance. There is perhaps a clue to this in Molyneux's discussion of "ecstasy and pain" as a mixture of joy, anguish and vulnerability.[16] Who will deliver us?

GOD'S SPECIFIC ACTIVITY IN THE BATTLE

The first task was to see what God himself says in first person in the songs. I mentioned two distinct songs above where God is actually speaking in the first person. In Song I-6 God says: "If you would come back to me, asking for pardon, if you would come to me, my hand of mercy is stretched out, and my eyes are shedding tears of love." In Song IV-3, again He invites us: "Retreat from the rough road. Don't step on my blood; that won't do you any good. Let's be friends instead, for my mercy is full."

Names of the God who defeats the enemy are beautiful: He is the Lord, the famous hero who fought and was crucified for one going astray; he is a Shield, the Light, the Word, Good News, Mighty of the mightiest, King of kings, Father of love, comforter and encourager, firm staff, protector of the needy, faithful Shepherd, Emmanuel. He is the Redeemer.

I then combed the songs to find attributes of God who defeats the enemy. This is listed in Table 6 with comments and synthesis following the listing. This list may not be exhaustive because it is such a large subject. Also, various grammar constructions and translations may limit complete listing. Now the activity of God in the battle is seen. There are so many metaphors and images, but I have attempted to categorize the phrases.

A first impression from Table 6 is that God's activity dealing with the enemy is diverse, intense, and effective. Two verbs are repeated; the enemy is badly bruised, and we are delivered from the enemy's strong mouth and jaws. One pictures being rescued from a crocodile. The enemy is thoroughly defeated by all those strong verbs. The enemy is cosmic as the powers of nature are involved with thunder and lightning. Two images that stand out immediately in stark contrast are the soothing "anointing" with oil for "his own" versus the "bruising" of the enemy.

16. Molyneux, *African Christian Theology*, 189–96.

These two verbs are complete opposites in the effect on the human body. God's hope and hospitality are given to his people. As in Psalm 23, His people are promised a feast at the king's table versus being fed to the enemy. God, the faithful one, does so many beautiful things for us and kills Goliath on our behalf. All the verbs of hope are encouraging and life-sustaining. Of whom, then, should anyone be afraid?

Table 6: What God Does in the Battle

Shows mercy	Calls his people to a feast VII-5 Calls to sit at the king's table VII-5 Changes the judgment VI-13 Loves I-8 Puts away reproach VII-5 Redeemer VII-3 Reigns in the praises of his people VII-5 Releases the bondage VI-13 Tolerates I-8 Turns the curse into blessing VI-14 Wipes away tears VII-5 Wipes out accusations VI-13
Deals with the enemy	Bruises the enemy's head I-8, VII-3 Casts out the enemy VI-13 Chases enemies IV-5 Contests the enemy III-15 Crushes the enemy IV-11 Defeats the enemy II-9 Destroys enemy VII-5 Disperses enemy with arrows I-10, III-4 Disrupts enemies' wishes III-4 Disturbs enemy with lightning I-10 Locks enemy's jaws III-14 Overpowers the enemy VII-3 Snatches him out of enemy's jaws I-8 Snatches out of enemy's mouth III-14 Tells enemy He is light III-4
Faithful	Becomes my light III-4 Comforts I-8, VII-1 Confirms that he will not abandon IV-12 Equips with armor I-2 Gives advice I-8 Makes crooked place straight VII-5 Pours out his Spirit IV-11 Protects VII-1 Sheds his holy blood I-8

Gives hope	Causes his own to reach home I-8 Covers with charisma I-2 Encourages VII-2 Gives full hope I-10 Gives life to his dead child I-8 Opens closed doors VII-5 Passes in front of me like a shield II-14 Prepares for battle IV-5 Sustains by His name I-8
Gives victory	Enables one to see Goliath falling II-4 Gives power and victory I-2 Honors his own before the enemy III-1 Rescues when the enemy ridicules VII-1 Saves when the enemy defies God I-10 Says, "Gather the spoil" IV-5 Snatches him out of the enemy's jaws I-8 Snatches out of the enemy's mouth, jaws III- 4, 14
Anoints	Anoints their heads VII-5 Anoints with oil IV-4
Does Battle	Assists reaching down and saving I-8, VII-3 Delivers from arrow and sword II-13 Descends in vengeance I-10 Directs the war IV-5 Flashes His thunder IV-10 Girds with power IV-5 Thunders down from heaven I-10

Song I–10, psalmic in nature and based on Psalm 34:6, Psalm 61, Proverbs 18:10 and Psalm 116, illustrates even more of the activity of God:

Chorus:

I will call on God who deserves praise.

And I will be saved from my enemies.

I will call on God who deserves praise.

1. When the flood of cruelty makes me scared,

And when the agony of hell encircles me,

When he asks me where my God is,

When my enemy scoffs at me,

When he scares me saying "Just wait"

I will call on the name of the Lord.

And I will be saved from my enemy.

2. The name of the Lord Jesus for me is a strong tower
Until this day whoever called on Him
Has not been embarrassed.
Because the One who lives in the cherubim
Gave me full hope.
I will in faith call upon His name
And I will be saved from my enemy

3. Whenever I am troubled I call upon God
Crying bitterly and brokenly in tears
I told Him the problems of my heart
Then he descended in vengeance;
He came thundering down from heaven
He disturbed them with His lightening
He dispersed them with His arrows.

4. He did not put me into the clamp of their teeth
He always saved me from the trap which was set for me.
He protected me from Satan
Who would snatch away my freedom.
Praise be to His name, Hallelujah.
May I live in His bosom, the secret place.

This song seems to capture the real heart of Tesfaye during his years of persecution. God is everything to him. Prayer, waiting on God, is crucial. Tesfaye admits his own weakness and fear. He witnesses to his only hope being in God. He lives with the memory of God's goodness in the past. The "just wait" of the evil one is such a threat, but Tesfaye's secret place in God's heart is where he is kept through all the trauma of seven years when from one day to the next, he did not know what was going to happen. The word *guya* has been translated by Haile Jenai as "in his bosom, the secret place," a precious and holy closeness to God. Perhaps the idea is suggested in older English hymn phrases like "Under his wings I am safely abiding" or "In the secret of his presence how my soul delights to hide."[17]

Another beautifully descriptive poem (Song II–14) describes God's work plus metaphors of the enemy. Stanzas 1 and 2 read thus:

17. During stressful and sometimes tearful moments in the process of accomplishing this writing project, it was the song lyrics themselves that often comforted and sustained me.

1. If my enemies increase in the battlefield,
    If I tremble in fear with melted strength,
    When I cry "Woe unto me, Lord, I am lost"
    Jesus, my shield, passes in front of me.

2. If my enemy comes like a colony of bees
    I will not go out, leaving my fort.
    In the name of God I shall win.
    I shall see Goliath falling with my own eyes.

In other songs, one learns that Tesfaye believes that men of prayer may disperse the enemy in the name of the Lord. David is referred to as meeting the enemy. We were enemies but God made us friends through his death and our accusation is wiped out.

In concluding this section, I suggest that the enemy is not just the revolutionary guard in the prison. All people are the enemies of God until their hearts are won through knowing Christ who died for them. Thus they move from enemy territory into God's camp. The contrast, the battle, is evident in many areas of life. The epitome of enemy and friend relationships is when David had the opportunity to "do Saul in" but he chose to let Saul live. Human as we are, who would show such a mercy? Tesfaye says about David in VII–10 above. How I love my enemies is the crucial test of how much I believe and love God. God is the great defender and will have the final word against all enemies and enemy territory, be they physical or spiritual.

Concept of Strength

Following a study of the enemy, I moved on in a natural sequence to coding the concept of strength as a method of starting to investigate the whole subject of endurance. Haile Jenai and I began with just the Amharic word which is usually descriptive of God's strength and power. It is also the general word for physical and moral strength of a man. For example, the royal name for the former emperor was Haile Selassie, the power of the trinity. A person very strong in character (sometimes negatively) is called *haïlenya*. Battles are won; evil spirits are cast out by the power of God. The word *haïl* is found twenty-three times in his songs.

But Haile and I found four other Amharic words were usually translated in English as "strength": *bïrtat, gulbet, şena, ţenker*. The word *bïrtat*, found thirteen times in the songs, is a gentler word suggesting, vigor, industriousness, usually with a sense of being an encouragement or strength in weakness. *Gulbet*, appearing twelve times, has to do with physical strength and energy of a person. Şena is a verb meaning to be firm, constant, to endure and occurs ten times. The word ţenker, stable, sturdy, consolidating, appeared only once. Taking all the words together, a few comments may be made in general by looking at three songs where there is a tripling of words for strength:

In three of the songs, there are three different words for strength used in the same song.

> I-13: *gulbeţé*; *atenkeré*; and *abïrtïché*
>
>> strengthening my power, and my arms strengthened. . ...
>
> III-15: şïnu; ţenker; haïlun
>
>> let your heart be firm. . ...don't be soft, be strong. . ...
>>
>> when the enemy shows his strength angrily
>
> V-2: *haïl*; *gulbetïh*; *teţenakïro*
>
>> by the power of the Holy Spirit, rise up again. . .your weak hands and
>>
>> feeble strength will again be strengthened.

This triple usage of the idea of strength summarizes all he says in the songs. Christians are prone to weakness, but they must strengthen their present forces, be bold in their hearts and bodies. This is also metaphorical. The enemy also has great strength and works against us. But, by the power of the Holy Spirit a person can rise up and be strengthened both in heart and hand, even if she/he has lost strength. Tesfaye and the other prisoners had no strength at all to get out of their situation, except to trust in God. They had no idea if they would ever be released. They often had death threats or saw others around them die. Tesfaye relied on the power of God for his strength and he emphasized the battle that we are in with the enemy.

In Figure 4 below, the word "strength" appears in over forty of the 104 songs, but sometimes multiple times in one song so that the word is actually used about seventy times. Similarly, "enemy" appears in almost forty songs but appears nearly fifty times in those songs. Column 4 indicates that in approximately twenty songs both "strength" and "enemy" are used a total of over forty times. In all, about sixty of 104 songs hold the combined concepts of "strength" and "enemy" approximately 115 times.

I conclude from this information that the battle is a heavy one and an important topic in Tesfaye's songs. There is no neutral middle; it is one side or the other.

In a practical illustration, I remember an event in Kamba in Gamo Gofa, southwestern Ethiopia where we lived from 1986 to 1989. There was a funeral one day for a prominent man in the village. The hollowed-out tree trunk that served as the casket was carried down the middle of the airstrip. Christian believers walked on one side of the airstrip singing their songs, while the unbelievers danced and screamed wildly down the other side. A guard in the middle zone kept people from crossing over the line. Everyone knew where everyone else stood in their loyalty. Westerners do not appreciate that kind of commitment or loyalty, nor do they really know their neighbor's position. They generally live in a very fuzzy neutral ground. In prison, Tesfaye and his friends had to show their colors constantly, all of which leads me on to the next story.

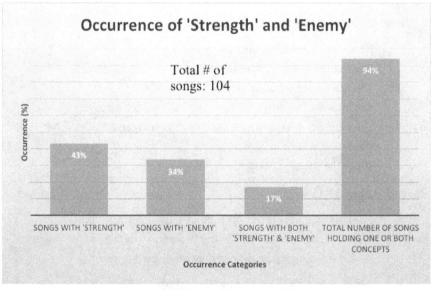

Figure 4: Usage of Words 'Strength' and 'Enemy'

Nebuchadnezzar Story

The Nebuchadnezzar story would obviously be one of special meaning to Tesfaye as it portrays the experience of persecution in the lives of Shadrach, Meschach and Abednego. The story is directly referred to in Songs I–14 and V–10 and is alluded to in two others songs (III–16 and

IV–15) as illustrated below. Tesfaye and his comrades identified themselves with the Old Testament story told in Daniel. During the Revolution, the youth, especially, were to support the banners of government leaders, and hold high their right hands in allegiance as they chanted a rather meaningless slogan, "Ethiopia First." This slogan could be interpreted in many ways depending on the current mood or campaign of the *Dergue* which was the group in power. Christian youth refused to participate in this activity.

In Song III–16, the Christian is mentioned as he observes the story of the three in the fiery furnace:

> Christian crossed over, passing through the flame. . ..
> The Father on His throne; the Son on His right hand.
> To meet, the One who is pushed aside on earth, in glory
> When Christian saw them inviting him out of his agony
> He came out of the furnace saying, "It is finished!"

There are further allusions in Song IV–15:

> Furnace of tribulation, fire of purging,
> Fire was the measure, coals of testing,
> These two were methods used by past warriors
> The owners of victory, wherever they had trodden through. . .
> The standard was the fire for the former generations. . .
> We, too, are called to be like them
> To see the terrible fire exactly as it is.

And in Song V–12 we read:

> All those who wish to live in Godliness through Christ Jesus
> Will be persecuted for the sake of His name and will be tested as gold.
> When, at last, they pass the test they will inherit eternal life.

The entire song of V–10 tells the story vividly:

> Other than their God, not to worship anyone,
> Not to bow down before the golden image
> Those who submitted their bodies—
> Let the God of Shadrach, Meschach and Abednego be praised forever. . .
> Who saved His faithful friends.

1. There is no God like Him Who can save.
He only could save them from the fiery furnace.
Salvation is from Him.

2. The Lord spoke and I heard only His voice.
I realize that power was God's only.
I saw Him putting out the fire.

3. If you give yourselves unselfishly,
Fire does not burn, because God acts.
Glorify His name and be strong.

I-14
I refuse, I refrain.
I will not worship the image.
Nor kneel down before a man-made thing
From the burning anger of Nebuchadnezzar
My Lord, whom I serve, will surely deliver me.

The refusal to worship the image is a powerful triplet of *"ïmbe, ïmbe, ïmbe"* at the end of the chorus. It is a word meaning absolute refusal, and Tesfaye repeats it in a strong base voice.

Tibebe Eshete, Ethiopian scholar writing on the evangelical movement, related a conversation he had with Tesfaye some years ago.[18] In earlier years, Tesfaye had been very shy and reluctant to admit that his songs were blessing the nation. Tibebe recalls persuading Tesfaye that when he sings the story of Nebuchadnezzar, Tesfaye's own life experience is, in fact, that story. The song and the experience were inseparable. Tibebe therefore encouraged Tesfaye not to be so timid about singing. He might as well sing boldly since it was the truth being directly expressed in Tesfaye's life.

SUMMARY

This chapter has illustrated that a battle of great proportions rages between the enemy and the Almighty. Tesfaye lived and sang in the heat of the battle that is manifested in many different ways. It is impossible for a person to pay allegiance to two sides at once. There is no room for compromise or dancing around on the edges of the warfare. It is all or nothing. The power of God far surpasses the wiles of the enemy, but keeping

18. Conversation with Tibebe Eshete, Addis Ababa, July 11, 2013.

the faith is not an easy matter. Tesfaye has the ability to sing metaphors about both the enemy's tactics as well as God's power and keeping. That "colony of bees" will never be able to destroy Tesfaye and his friends who are under the wings of God.

Moving into Chapter 8, I will consider some of the more poetic aspects of Tesfaye's songs, how he appreciates the Psalms and uses metaphor so effectively in his writing.

8

Psalms, Metaphor, and Deeper Meaning

Metaphors: words that have concrete reference but which are
open
to remarkable stretching in many directions
in order to touch our experience.[1]

THE TITLE OF THIS study, *The Songs of Tesfaye Gabbiso*, includes sing-
ing in Babylon, the Meantime, and Zion. I entitled it thus, using these
images, for several reasons. Tesfaye himself speaks of sitting down in
Babylon (Song V–4) and crying, thus using that image for trouble and
persecution. In the same song, Zion suggests a good ending, the city of
God, better days. In the meantime, however, people live life in various
situations: struggling, working, living, loving, and dying. That is why I
have chosen to use the word "meantime."[2] The title does not suggest a
chronology of time, but rather life in its various, many times overlapping,
experiences.

There are many ways in which songs may be probed for style and
meaning. Upon opening *The Songs of Tesfaye Gabbiso*, one senses that
many of his songs are like Psalms. But what, exactly are those psalmic
qualities? In this chapter I draw on the insights of two theologians, Walter
Brueggemann and Jeremy Begbie, in studying Tesfaye's songs. Firstly, I
consider Walter Brueggemann's illuminating concepts to compare with

---

1. Brueggemann, *Praying the Psalms*, 30.

2. Begbie, *Theology, Music and Time*, 103–4. "Meantime" is a phrase suggesting
"enjoying tension," as expounded upon by Begbie referring to Kathleen Higgins.

Tesfaye's psalmic style. Secondly, I discuss some ideas of Jeremy Begbie regarding music, "delayed gratification," the idea that constraints enhance art, and the connection between resolution and salvation. Both scholars have richly enhanced my appreciation and understanding of the songs.

PSALMIC QUALITIES IN TESFAYE'S SONGS

In the first stages of content analysis, I became aware of many metaphors that sounded like Psalm 23, and the following exercise came to my mind one day while I was attempting to pile-sort some of God's actions as described in the songs. In the illustration that follows, I do not attempt to note each song that is referred to.[3]

> *The Lord is my Shepherd*
>
> Those who trusted their Shepherd.
>
> *I shall not want*
>
> He has clothed us with his grace; covered us with charisma; given us full hope, taken care of me like the pupils of his own eyes.
>
> *He makes me to lie down in green pastures*
>
> He turns the desert green; made us lie down in his pasture.
>
> *He leads me beside still waters for his name's sake*
>
> He quenches thirst from his springs; he stretches out his blessed hand.
>
> *He restores my soul*
>
> He quietens the storm and gives peace; he sees our hopelessness and depression; he builds by his grace; helps me when about to be defeated; gives us rest fills us with joy.
>
> *He leads me in the paths of righteousness for his name's sake*
>
> Increases strength to the life that is weak; stood at my side and strengthened me; redeemed my life.
>
> *Yea, though I walk through the valley of the shadow of death, I will fear no evil*
>
> He protects from death in time of famine; is with me in the valley of life; took me across the river. He directs the war by his resurrection authority.
>
> Confirmed he won't leave me; causes life to flow in the desert; makes the crooked ways straight; will help me stand until the end; equips with armor; He chases the enemies.
>
> *For you are with me*

---

3. For this exercise only, the original Psalm is printed in italics and Tesfaye's words from various songs are in regular print.

He arrives on time for us. He comes close; supported me by his grace; hides me from darts. He is coming to rescue you; protects the needy; visited us in your generosity; grabbed my hand in his; listens when I am in trouble; listens to our secrets we tell him.

Your rod and staff they comfort me

He calms the storm; places my feet on a road; pulls us out, grace makes us stand. He does not let me go; loves his children; holds them in his bosom.

You prepare a table before me in the presence of my enemies

Crushed and bruised the enemy; broke our yoke; your hand is stronger than those who are stronger than we are; sustains by his holy name; showered the Hebrews with manna.

You anoint my head with oil

Came to rescue the destitute; graciously anoints their heads with oil; shares the burden, encourages; increases strength to the life that is weak; wipes my tears with his hand; says, "I am your healer."

My cup runs over

He reigns in their praises; calls us with honor; will satisfy you; fills us with joy; filled me with the Holy Spirit; gave grace in abundance; blessed my soul.

Surely goodness and mercy shall follow me all the days of my life

Will come to comfort and relieve us in Zion; he said, "May there be life and peace." You gave us life by your love on the cross; leads me to my country; quietens the storm and gives peace; prepares everything, a crown after fighting well; he will satisfy you; accomplished your good work in my life.

And I will dwell in the house of the Lord forever.

Causes us to sit at the King's table; made us your temple; fulfills what he says; will not deny what he promises; will appear soon.

What may we ascertain from looking at the abundance of psalmic imagery and metaphor in Tesfaye's writing? Brueggemann's writing on the Psalms offers further consideration of Tesfaye's experience, especially of suffering and endurance. He suggests that the Psalms of David are not just God speaking to His people, but human experience is interacting with God. It is a two-way dialogic communication, and often it is at the extreme "edge of our humanness" that we call to God.[4] When we are living in dislocation or disorientation, "It is the experiences of life that lie beyond our conventional copings that make us eloquent and passionate

---

4. Brueggemann, *Praying the Psalms*, 4.

and that drive us to address ourselves to the Holy One."[5] Also, at a time when one is experiencing the extremities of life, the greatest poetry and metaphor usually issues forth from the mind and soul. I believe this accounts for the power of Tesfaye's songs during the seventeen long years of the revolution (1974 to 1991) in Ethiopia. The song, in its metaphor and power, is a "threat" to the authorities. "It is for that reason that totalitarian regimes, even when they control all the hardware, are most fearful of the poet."[6]

As an illustration, one can imagine the frustration of the authorities with the content of Tesfaye's Song V-11 written in prison. "When God comes down" is enough to frighten any prison keeper. What will mere humans do "when God assists, descending from the heavens . . . wiping out all offences by His justice"? One senses the concern of the prison guards as they hear these lines sung in the cell: "When the enemy defies God and attempts to devour the poor and helpless by terrifying words which he speaks in pride, it is only God Who can reach down and save."

The language of the Psalms is also creative in that the utterances, often spoken in situations of extremity, as well as Tesfaye's songs, are "calling into being that which does not yet exist."[7] Tesfaye's song (VII–12), "Greater Things Than This," suggests what the people of God will see in the future "when the Lord's power is revealed" and "when the earth is filled with the clouds of His glory." It has not happened yet.

A further consideration suggested by Brueggemann concerns "language appropriate to a place" and speaks of the metaphors powerful to the "pit" or displacements, the Babylons of life.[8] In the Tesfaye songs, there were examples of distress in phrases like the enemy's coals burning seven times hotter (Song I-14), the arrows and swords of the battlefield (Songs II–13, 14), dealing with the enemy's fence (Song III-5) and such images as net, trap and jaws.

In contrast to the "pit" there are beautiful images of what it means to be safe in the care of Christ, "under safe wings."[9] Tesfaye sings of both "I" and "we" living under the shelter of God's wings under his care and watchfulness and being held in God's hands (Songs VII–6 and

5. Brueggemann, *Praying the Psalms*, 6.

6. Brueggemann, *Praying the Psalms*, 19.

7. Brueggemann, *Praying the Psalms*, 18.

8. Brueggemann, *Praying the Psalms*, 29–42.

9. Brueggemann, *Praying the Psalms*, 37.

VII–11). "Holding all my breath and my ways in Your hand, taking care of me like the pupils of Your own eyes, You have hidden and veiled me from that which could harm me" (Song II–10). Song I–10 speaks of Christ being a strong wall for refuge and that the One who lives "in the cherubim" gives hope. Then there is the honor and intimacy of being at the King's table itself in Song VII–5. Furthermore, in Amharic there are two descriptive words ïk̲if and *guya* which suggest an intimate place, or the bosom of Jesus (Songs I–10, I–12, VII–6 and VII–11) where one may live and be kept safe. Never is it an easy escapism, but there is always a sense of getting through the difficulty, of reaching the end victoriously.

CONSIDERATIONS IN THE MEANTIME

In combing through the songs, I marked many of them simply with the word "endurance" but had not come to any definitive way of thinking about the subject. Begbie's concepts of lament, interval, delay and resolution in music were most illuminating.[10] I discovered examples in Tesfaye's songs, a few of which are diagrammed below in Table 7:

Table 7: Elongation in the Meantime

LAMENT	MEANTIME	RESOLUTION
I-9: I am facing a great battle. . . I am about to be defeated	I am waiting, watching for your victory. I'll keep quiet. You fight for me	I have seen the successful fight of those who extol You. Now I know that the battle is not mine
II-14: Woe is me, Lord, I am lost	I will drink the cup of the cross	I shall cross over and victory will be proclaimed
III-4: My lamentation of sorrow, my cry of bitterness, I leave before my God so he can see my life	I will wait for him until he redeems me	In the future I shall sing for Him again, leaning on his arm.

In Table 7, take note of the passing of time that is indicated between columns 1 and 3. In the middle, the meantime, Tesfaye acknowledges what he will do: he will wait, watch, keep quiet, drink the cup of the cross. This was the prison experience.

The signature song for this schema could be Song V–11, "When God Assists," one of the most famous of the prison songs, the creation of

10. Begbie, *Theology, Music and Time*, 71–126.

which Tesfaye gives the story (Tesfaye, #2). The lament, interval of meaning and eschaton are all vividly described in this song as follows.

The lament: He speaks of lying in a soaking wet soccer field with people gathered all around. On the nearby gravel road, the prisoners were made to walk on their knees, and the bystanders shouted, "Let's see if God can deliver you from this." As he was lying there, he was reminded of the words shouted to Jesus on the cross that if he was the son of God, why didn't he come down off the cross? Tesfaye writes, "But God was silent, and in Isaiah 53:10 we learn that it pleased the Lord to bruise him. Jesus said, "My God, my God, why have you forsaken me?" Tesfaye realizes that it did not mean God had left them (Tesfaye, #2).

There was an interval of meaning: "We were true; he was with us. We felt that in our distress he would honor us as we passed through the trial" (Tesfaye, #2). In such times, the prisoners really felt and knew that God came down and rescued them. They kept thinking about that, then started singing. They knew this was a message from God, and God made something beautiful out of this bitter experience. He now realizes that the song was given not only for them in prison, but also for believers on the outside (Tesfaye, #2).

The eschaton or resolution is when the help of the saints will come from heaven. After the ages are past, the Lord will return. He will wipe away the tears from his children's eyes. Glory and praise will be given to His name (Song V–11).

The prisoners had no idea how long the interim, the meantime, might be. They were quite helpless to try to effect a physical solution.

CONSTRAINTS ENHANCE THE ART

The idea of constraints enhancing the art was a useful concept to me as I read about the making of art. One is always restricted by certain physical factors or other restraints, but great art is released as one is able to break through the limitations. Somehow the restraints or having to work within limits "yields intensity."[11] This relates to the creation of song. Is it then possible that Tesfaye's songs have a certain power and influence because they were composed in times of stress and uncertainty? It seems that Tesfaye was composing many of his songs in a context of restraint. "Composition refers to all the activity which precedes the sounding of the entire piece of music, everything which is involved in conceiving and

11. Nachmanovitch, *Free Play*, 78.

organizing the parts of elements which make up the pattern or design of the musical whole."[12] The whole phenomenon of a song from beginning to end was a whole, created under pressure and therefore refined.

"The word of promise. . .always creates an interval of tension between the uttering and the redeeming of the promise. In so doing it provides man [*sic*] with a peculiar area of freedom to obey or disobey, to be hopeful or resigned."[13] Is it possible that the persecution and extreme tension of the revolution, and especially the prison, years, created this interval of tension between the uttering and redeeming? During his prison years, it appears that Tesfaye was living in a space where he had the freedom either to hope and obey or waver and disobey. This creates a distinct intensity in living and in songwriting that is missing in a culture where things are just rolling along comfortably, and everything is short-term or immediate. In the final analysis, "There is a patience proper to Christian faith in which something new is learned of incalculable value, which cannot be learned in any other way."[14] It is a process, a path and a journey which is not easy.[15] I contend that this is what one senses in Tesfaye's songs.

In the writing of Tesfaye's life, there were constraints which enhanced his songs. This added to the strength and deep meaning which was, and still is, so appreciated by the people.

SUMMARY

In this chapter I considered some of the art forms which Tesfaye uses in his song composition, mostly unconsciously, but inspired by the Spirit. There is beautiful imagery and metaphor that speaks to the mind and heart. With insights from Brueggemann and Begbie, I observed ways in which he is psalmic in his poetry. Art speaks powerfully to people, and Tesfaye's songs are loved, for one reason, because they speak both to minds, emotions, and unconscious aesthetic longings of the Ethiopian people. In many outward ways, he was restricted and limited with plenty of reason for lament. He was forced by circumstances into a difficult space. But no outward constraint could deny or control the creation of song. In fact, the constraints enriched the song.

12. Begbie, *Theology, Music and Time*, 183.

13. Begbie, *Theology, Music and Time*, 98, quoting Jurgen Moltmann.

14. Begbie, *Theology, Music and Time*, 105.

15. Begbie, *Theology, Music and Time*, 106.

A challenge for the present generation of singers and writers is to understand that the offering of songs is demanding upon the total person and asks for a deep commitment of time and spiritual energy. Because Tesfaye was writing from a place of constraint, his songs reach deeply into all the areas of human experience in our Babylons, Zions, and the Meantime. It is the Holy Spirit who inspires the creation of the contemplation behind the lyrics, the lyrics themselves, and then the mental and bodily activity in the singing of the song.

In the next chapter, I look at Tesfaye's life and song through an expanded missiological lens. It is a useful way to examine the extent of his subject matter and his own interaction within the quadrants of the Global Church Music Matrix.

9

Life and Song through an
Expanded Missiological Lens

The very dynamism of African Christianity provides invaluable resources for world Christianity.[1] *(Stinton 2004, 107)*

IN THIS CHAPTER I provide a missiological lens through which to probe Tesfaye's songs. Using the Global Church Music Matrix, we have a tool to process the effectiveness or wholeness of his song career. Thus far I have examined the life of Tesfaye through ethnographic study. The content of his songs has been studied through textual analysis. How does this all mesh together into a missiological framework? I now employ the Matrix as a tool to determine how Tesfaye and his songs fit into these four quadrants of music in culture. What I learn about Tesfaye through this grid will also become a mirror that the reader may look into to assess his/her own life and ministry.

In addition to utilizing the matrix or grid, I will suggest a larger view of the universe which has as its throbbing foundation a sense of the *missio Dei*, God's great surging purpose for the world. Overarching the diagram and thinking is the aesthetic of God, the beauty of God in which human song is a high and holy calling. The book of Revelation pictures all of the world's people singing gloriously in the eternal day.

---

1. Stinton, "Africa," 107.

PROBING THE SONGS AND LIFE OF TESFAYE GABBISO

The tool being used for this research is a four-arena diagram or Global Church Music Matrix as illustrated in Figure 4. We will ask if Tesfaye's contribution to hymnody is full-orbed in terms of this schema. If my conclusion is in the affirmative, I have a model that will assist potential Ethiopian songwriters in their understanding of theological constructs of personal life, Scripture, church community and witness in the larger world. Most songwriters have never had the opportunity to see into such a mirror before. It will provide a way of thinking about the contexts in which they compose and into which they sing and serve. This will be an interpretive inquiry using textual analysis. An element of ethnographic research is also employed as I also refer to life events and written documents to support my evidence.

First of all, I invite my readers into the middle of the four arenas to see Tesfaye standing there as the singer.[2] I will discuss his songs and also look at what he says or lives in each of the four arenas. This is following King's thesis that there is an "interplay between the Christian faith, music, and culture" and these four "arenas of study serve as a framework for the church that is seeking to know God in worship and witness within its local setting."[3]

As research for this chapter, I analyzed Tesfaye's songs as pertains to each of the four arenas. I also used material from his autobiographical account of life in prison plus information from interviews and articles recorded in Ethiopian magazines. Again, in this entire chapter, if exact words are not already in quotation marks, I will identify Tesfaye's "voice," if not perfectly evident, with the special font used elsewhere. This is especially necessary when I am connecting various phrases that contain his ideas. The abbreviations I use for each source of information are the following: 1) his own prison biography identified as (Tesfaye, BG); 2) the ten articles either about him or interviewing him (Tesfaye, #1–10)); and 3) his own songs indicated with cassette (Roman numeral) and song (Arabic numeral) numbers.[4]

2. This is an expansion on Figure 1 in chapter 2.

3. King, "Beginnings," 11–16.

4. See List of Abbreviations in front matter.

GLOBAL CHURCH
MUSIC MATRIX

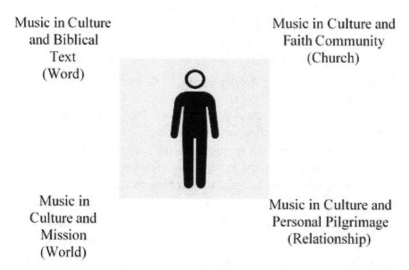

Music in Culture
and Biblical
Text
(Word)

Music in Culture and
Faith Community
(Church)

Music in
Culture and
Mission
(World)

Music in Culture and
Personal Pilgrimage
(Relationship)

Figure 5: Global Church Music Matrix
(Adapted from King, "Beginnings: Music in the African Church," 13)

In the following discussion, the movement around the matrix begins with Personal Pilgrimage as Arena 1 and moves diagonally to Word as Arena 2. I then move to the Faith Community in Arena 3 and, finally, move diagonally down to the World in Arena 4. What will be discovered as I view Tesfaye's life through this grid?

Personal Pilgrimage, Relational: Arena 1

Who is Tesfaye as a person? How does he tend to his own life? What was/is his spiritual journey? These are some of the questions explored in this section. While in Yirgalem high school, Tesfaye says that his spiritual growth began to expand as a result of the influence of fellow believers (Tesfaye, BG, 11–12). Addisu Amdie was one of those who had great influence in Tesfaye's young life. Addisu was a ridiculed *"pente"* (derogatory term for "pentecostal" or evangelical), and denounced by the local community cooperative (*idir*). Therefore, Addisu was persecuted but continued gathering believers into his home in the evenings. Tesfaye attended the meeting one night. "That evening I witnessed, for the first time, the experience of praying in the Spirit and praying in other tongues while a visiting evangelist called Argaw Nida shared the Word of God and prayed for those present . . . This love, genuine attitude, and spiritual dynamism . . . had a role in introducing most of us, including myself, to engage in prayerful self-examination (introspection) of our position in life" (Tesfaye, BG, 12). They had precious worship times and shared the word of God. In Yirgalem, he was in the midst of a group of younger Christians who were zealous for their faith when the heat of persecution was building up. It was a group of young zealous Christians who formed themselves into the Full Gospel Believers Chapel.

A choir was organized in 1976 that consisted of a few choir members who used to practice with hushed voices at Pastor Teshome Worku's rented lodging. It continued until 1977 and was conducted at worship times in private homes. Tesfaye writes, "The Lord was providing the choir new songs and new hymns with 'meaningful content'" (Tesfaye, BG, 18). Songs were in Amharic so it suited all the ethnic groups among them. They were writing out of their own life experience.

In his growing spiritual experience, Tesfaye knew periods of heaviness (Tesfaye, BG, 98). Isaiah 59:19 was a comfort. Fear that others from their midst might forsake the Lord gripped him, and Tesfaye's prayer for them was Psalm 107:30 that they would "reach their desired haven" (Tesfaye, BG, 104). He spoke often from the Old Testament, for example, about restoring the vineyards from Hosea 2:15. These young Christians in prison knew their Bibles in a deep way and found many lessons in unusual Scripture passages to trust in, lean on, and obey.

When Tesfaye sang honestly and personally of his own life, he was, of course, encouraging the entire Ethiopian church. He witnessed boldly in prison, and peoples' lives were transformed. Prayer fellowships were formed in the different prison rooms (Tesfaye, BG, 109).

He speaks of an unusual experience in prison when a song mightily blessed him. On October 7, 1979, Pastor Teshome and Tesfaye slept in the same room where some aged Christians, just apprehended, had been allowed to bring their radios. Revolution day celebrations were in progress. They were able to tune in to Christian transmission in Amharic and, with very low volume, listened to sermons and Christian songs transmitted from Seychelles broadcasting station. The radio speaker preached on Ephesians 6:10, "Why should you feel distressed? The Lord Jesus has come to your aid and will hold you up in your weakness." Then they heard the Addis Ababa Full Believers Gospel Church choir sing a song about the presence of God in time of dread. This was such an encouragement to them (Tesfaye, BG, 47).

Tesfaye is very honest about himself in many of his songs, especially on cassettes I-III. In at least thirty-five of the songs he expresses aspects of his own personal pilgrimage with God and in relation to others. The following illustrations are only a sampling of a very substantial and rich personal testimony.

His own brokenness and insufficiency is admitted in many songs. Song I-1 is a prayer that God would break his heart, for him to cancel self and pride. He asks for grace and meekness to abound. He uses first-person singular pronouns eighteen times in this song. His lack of meekness keeps him moaning, crying a lot, with "lushness dried up." He pleads for God to break him and teach him humility. Then he will know for sure who he really is, when his internal eyes get bright. He admits that his infancy is not over and he would like to reach "adulthood" (Song I-7). In a very strong song (II-3), he admits his weakness and temptation; he does not want to be lazy as in "instead of climbing up, down I went" (Song II-4).

What Christ has done for him is his strong testimony. Tesfaye wants to share his testimony in Song III-5: "Let me tell you the wonderful story of what He's done for me. You all, please do listen. Let it be a lesson to you. Let your hearts trust. Be comforted in the Lord." In Song II-6, Jesus his Savior and lord brought him light, took his faults, snatched him from uncleanness, came to find him, died for him. "His salvation is wonderful" and the love of God has no end. In Song III-3 Jesus is the cure of his soul. Many other songs such as Songs II-5, 6, and 9; III-2 and VII-3 spell out his own testimony.

He also expresses the kind of a Christian he desires to be. For example, in Song III-7, he asks for renewal lest he lack humility. In all moods, seasons and stages, he wants to see God's face and complete his race well. In Song III-10, he longs to live faithfully like David did. He wants to encourage others to endure (III-11). In Song V-7 he conveys a personal longing to please God stating that he is blessed because he is filled by the Holy Spirit. He also conveys that the decision of his soul is to submit his whole being (Song VI-8). He is thirsty for God and has chosen to carry the cross. He expresses submissiveness in his need for wholeness and health in all parts of his body, to have a broken heart, open ear, healthy eye and walking feet for God's glory. "When the pot breaks, the hidden light comes to shine; when the wheat seed rots, the plant bears much fruit . . ." (Song VI-9). Encouraging others is an important theme. In Song III-1 he desires to be a witness effectively to the world. Song VII-1 is also a song of encouragement to others in that Jesus "sees you" and is coming to rescue those who are in the wilderness, or those who weep, those whose life is messed up and everything is scattered, those who have sad and sorrowful hearts, those who are being ridiculed by the enemy. For all of those, he assures them that their comforter and encourager is none but the Lord, protector of the needy, a faithful shepherd, Emmanuel who is for us. In Song IV–15, he encourages the "patriot of the Gospel" to struggle. "Compete with Satan, your rival, and victory is ours."

Personal endurance is a daily discipline. He says we are called to be like those who were persecuted. They competed with Satan and won; likewise, we patriots of the Gospel should compete with Satan, our rival, and our victory is sure. Song V–7 expresses his personal longing to please God. He loves Jesus and knows Jesus loves him. He is blessed because he is filled by the Holy Spirit. But at times he is sorry for "disappearing anywhere" and not bearing much fruit. In two songs he expresses his desire to be strengthened and to finish his race well (Songs I–8 and I–9). In III–13, he admires those who have endured and have challenged him (think of his own family), but in verse 4: "I found a better friend than father, mother and relatives." Song IV–7 speaks of a literal and figurative endurance in prison.

Who the Lord is to him reveals a deep spirituality. In Songs I–10, I–12, and VII–11 God is very personal to him, his *guya* (secret place) and hiding place, under God's wings. In IV–14, he gives a strong testimony that he lives by faith; there is no one else to go to; Jesus is alive and is his shelter, his clothes and his bread. His soul is satisfied by his dignity and glory. Song II–10 is also full of beautiful images of the Lord of all comfort in his life. "My soul knows you, I cannot live without your fatherhood." In Song IV–1, he is realizing what Christ suffered for him and in Jesus' death struggle, "my life he redeemed." The day of suffering for Jesus was a day of healing for him. To whom else can he go? God is his help (Songs IV–12, IV–13).

Descriptions of prison life reveal his times of personal distress and questioning of God. In Song V–4 he asks, "When will I hear your voice? When will God's power, descending from on high, fill me? When will I ever be made happy? When will I be comforted? When will I be strengthened and stand on my feet?" On the other hand, he wrote Song VI–11 in prison and prays to do the will of God as a "stranger in the land" (perhaps as a prisoner in a foreign space). Whatever might come, he acknowledges that God's will is marvelous, and he asks under-standing for today, tomorrow and the rest of his life. "Show me the way I should walk. Let me know your will."

Two songs of special interest in this area of "personal pilgrimage" are the following: (1) Song V–9 is a song to his own soul, speaking of personal relationships and pilgrimage. He is telling himself his own testimony and longing. May he live for the Lord of mercy and "let me compose a song of praise and sing it for him." (2) Song V–15 took on a life of its own for me when it was sung at the memorial service for Dr. Steve Strauss[5] on June 25, 2013, in Addis Ababa. It was the only Amharic song in the midst of an otherwise English service. I played the piano for the English hymns, but this Amharic song was sung *a capella* with great gusto by the Ethiopian majority attending the funeral.

As I pondered the words, I wondered what song in English could possibly encompass the longings of any soul "before it returns to her God" better than this one? I could think of none. Tesfaye sings, "Let me hurry up and do my job quickly before my soul returns to her God, my body to the ground".[6] Those active for God will be rewarded for using their talents. He prays that the Spirit would always quicken him and let him stand for God's glory. He knows his life is like a vapor, but prays to be purposefully active and running without complaint for his Lord. The song ends with a verse that was such a fitting theme for the Steve Strauss memorial: "Now I have fought the good fight; I have kept the faith and finished the race. May I say this, as Paul and as Jesus, 'It is finished.' That I may present my praises to the King of hosts."

Interestingly, I had planned a chapel program for the SIM Ethiopian co-workers two days following the memorial service for Steve Strauss. The chapel was designed to illustrate the evolution of Ethiopian evangeli-cal church hymnody, so I began with antiphonal singing in a vernacular, followed by a translated hymn from the Swedish which represented the old hymnbooks. In bringing the chapel group up to the present with the popular Christian music, I had them sing Tesfaye's song that had been sung at the Steve Strauss memorial, something from very recent memory. All of them lustily sang the entire four verses with chorus (Song V–15) completely from memory.

5. Dr. Steve Strauss was an SIM theological educator in Ethiopia, later the direc-tor of SIM USA, and eventually professor at Dallas Theological Seminary where he passed away.

6. The concept of "soul" is feminine as expressed in Amharic.

In summary, Tesfaye's life is molded by prayer and the Word. This is evident throughout the four quadrants as he deals with himself, serves in the church and the world around, be it in a church or a prison. He quickly acknowledges all his own faults and weaknesses. One of his most public and graphic statements was in an interview with Kebede Mergia on the The Day of Salvation program, (*yemedan ḳen*), in 2011. On that TV program, he insisted very forcefully that prayer and the Word are absolutely foundational to a person's life if they are to be fruitful in service.[7]

Word, Biblical Text: Arena 2

Biblical Text or Word should be foundational in our creation of song texts. We have the opportunity to voice what we know of God, and putting it into song makes it all the more influential. Roberta King writes, "The biblical text serves to teach, correct, and nourish in the daily lives of people; a major means of doing so is through song. The singing of the biblical text is central to the spiritual life of the church in Africa." [8]

Tesfaye's songs are steeped in Scripture. As we have seen earlier, his knowledge of the Bible was basically formed earlier through the influences of family, the local church, his friends and Christian leaders with whom he was connected. Many of his songs were written when he was a young man in his twenties and early thirties. This is long before he later in life had opportunity, after release from prison, to attend Daystar, a Christian university at in Kenya, and later, the Evangelical Graduate School of Theology in Addis Ababa.

In at least fifteen of Tesfaye's songs, direct reference to the Word of God as scripture is mentioned. But all the songs are soaked in biblical images, quotations and biblical truth. What does one see in the songs of Tesfaye Gabbiso that may yield insights as to his knowledge and use of the Word? How do these discoveries fit into the schema of this four-arena paradigm?

Tesfaye's songs refer to usage of the scriptures as his own school teacher. He prayed to be strengthened in the Word (Song I–4) and Song II–15 speaks of Biblical characters that he saw, Abraham, apostles, martyrs such as Stephen, all from stories and history in scripture. He prays that "all that is written" will be for a lesson. He also

---

7. See Tesfaye Gabbiso, "Day of Salvation."

8. King, "Beginnings," 15.

speaks of the "Word of life" and necessity of "preaching the word" in Song V–3 to one who is tending to fall away.

The song "It's Wonderful to Be at Your Feet" (V–5), written long years previously, was sung by Tesfaye recently at the inauguration of Phase II of the structure of the Ethiopian Graduate School of Theology on March 15, 2014.[9] This song emphasizes the goodness of studying God's Word and the necessity of learning before "racing for service." He advises to sit still and hear from God's mouth. He admits the weakness of talking too much and not listening to God through his Word. What an appropriate message for the current students of a graduate school of theology. Having been a student there himself, he knows the mind and inclinations and temptations of theology students.

Tesfaye sings of the fact that weakness and strength of soul depend on our knowledge and use of the Word. if we are "rejecting His decree and despising his Word" we will be weak and ill-equipped if we are in the battle (Song I–2). He banks on "It is written" as he speaks of the inheritance of God for his people who were rescued from Egypt and slavery (Song VI–14).

Tesfaye admits his personal weakness at times (Song II–3) when he "lost a desire to read God's Word, felt drowsy to pray, was wretched." He longs to be "strengthening myself in your word" (Song I–4). In a particular time of personal trouble, he realized that he was known in the "Book of Life," and the comfort of the Word kept him (Song VI–1).

When singing to other believers, he advises "Contest the enemies by the Word of Good News, the Gospel" (Song III–15) In the "Word of His cross is healing for life" (Song IV–5). Tesfaye advises that if we are burdened with problems beyond our ability, God the omnipotent will come to our rescue. As proof, he mentions various stories from the Bible such as the feeding of the five thousand, the manna in the wilderness, the healer of blind and lame, commander of winds and storms, conquering king. This is a strong example of using the Biblical stories to teach the nature of El Shaddai (Song IV–11).

Tesfaye sings from Ephesians 6 (Song I–13) on aspects of the armor of God and expounds on I Corinthians 13 (in Song VII–10) asking who would actually put the truths of that chapter into practice? His answer is from the Old Testament where David displayed patience and kind love to Saul when he let Saul go rather than killing him. This is a strong lesson in the necessity to love all people. He obeyed as he saw truth

9. Email from Tesfaye Gabbiso, April 5, 2014.

in Bible narratives. Then in Song VII–11, Tesfaye thanks God himself for a litany of truths from the Word: Jesus Christ is the same, yesterday and today and forever, the Alpha and Omega, the One who never tires or weakens and whose hand is strong. In this same song he reiterates Scripture in that while we were yet sinners, Christ died, clothes us with his righteousness and shelters us under his wings. For Tesfaye, the Word of God is an essential part of his daily life and practice. His memory of it is part of his psyche and stored forever in the songs he sings.

Many additional references, imagery, and allusions to the Bible permeate his work. The Bible, the Word, is an innate part of his life and writing.

Faith Community, Church: Arena 3

Tesfaye solidly committed himself early in life to the local faith community and broader church denominations to which he belonged. He suffered together with the band of believers in the midst of persecution during the mid-1970s. In the midst of trouble, he notes that "there was a steady increase of people ushered into the kingdom of God through faith and repentance as well as the increasing number of ministries and minsters of the Gospel. In 1978, I committed my life to full-time ministry and became ordained" (Tesfaye, BG, 21) in Yirgalem. In what ways does Tesfaye demonstrate his dedication to the church and his beliefs about the faith community?

Tesfaye makes clear for the faith community that they will most certainly endure persecution. It is a norm for followers of Christ (Song V–12). Song V–11, written in prison, is a signature song in this regard. He covers the gamut of our salvation through Christ, the traps and enemy broken, our forgiveness and foundation in Christ, and the promise that the "help of the saints" will return after the ages are past, and the tears of his children "will be wiped away", a rather comprehensive theology of the church.

It is in this area of "faith community" that I have come to some clearer understanding of his constant plea to backsliders in his songs. Over and over Tesfaye emphasizes the necessity of clinging together in their predicament and taking time to worship while in prison. This included feeding on the scriptures and praying together. At one point they "grabbed each other's hands, made a circle and sang a song then hugged each other by the neck", committing themselves as a body of Christians (Tesfaye, BG, 80–81). It was absolutely essential to maintain the unity and guard against anyone falling back. It could be deadly if even one should deny the faith (Tesfaye, BG, 104). Tesfaye writes, "The other prospect that bore additional weight upon me . . . was the possibility that there be from among us some who, after having persisted so many years with us, should feel so weak in their lives that they might forsake us" (Tesfaye, BG, 107). One of the great themes in the songs concerns defection from the faith by professed believers, not only his great sorrow for those still outside the faith. Tesfaye's great longing is to see both groups return to God.

The fellowship of the faith community outside prison was manifest in many beautiful ways over the period of Tesfaye's imprisonment. Christians came, as was possible, to disinfect and wash the prisoners' clothes. They brought cooked food and other sundry items. Usually a fence secluded the prisoners, but often they were allowed some conversation with visitors. When the prisoners were being transported from Yirgalem to a distant southern prison in Borena Negelle, the free believers came out to wave, pray and encourage as the prisoners were whisked away in a truck (Tesfaye, BG, 83–85). Tesfaye says the letters from believers are "recorded in the memoirs of heaven" (Tesfaye, BG, 95). The unity of believers in prison and outside composed a united church fellowship that was alive and at work.

As was mentioned previously, within the prison, they maintained their worship, Bible studies, prayer and fellowship as strictly as possible. I repeat, as an example given earlier in the essay: During one Bible study on II Corinthians 11:24, just at the moment they were reading "Five times i received from the Jews the forty lashes minus one," the women prisoners were taken out and whipped. They could hear the whipping in an adjacent room as the lashes fell (Tesfaye, BG, 35). Prison life was real and earnest from one moment to the next. The church of Christ within the prison needed each other.

Tesfaye's songs have much to say and teach about the body of Christ, the Church. He includes himself in the Church with "we" as he encourages the people. Song IV–10 promises that God's mercy is everlasting. The pronouns "we" and "us" are used 13 times in one song. The God of comfort not only "wiped our tears and fixed our broken hearts" in prison, but it was true for the entire Ethiopian Christian community. "By the rivers of Babylon as we sadly sat down, we thought of Zion and bitterly cried." God is strong for us when "the enemy hits you with a stick and makes you drink vinegar" and we should not be ashamed following the way of the cross (Song II–15).

Rebuke and the call to repentance come through continually in Songs I-2 and I-3. He calls the church to weep for their pride and listen to the Spirit's rebuke. He goes on to ask for forgiveness in the first-person plural. "Cleanse and rearrange our inner being." He prays for power, grace, and charisma for the church. He rebukes the church that, in the past, they had wept for the lost and now their fervor is gone (Song I-6).

He recounts all that God is and does for the church by teaching the Bible in song. This is explicit in what he "sees" in Song II-5 as he recounts the victorious ones through the ages: Abraham, the apostles, martyrs. And then, as usual, he mentions the backsliders and prays a corporate prayer with the church that God would help them control themselves and be victorious.

In terms of the wandering ones, the church rejoices in their return (Song III-9). Backsliders are offered forgiveness through the grace of Christ (Song VI-13). In Song VII-7, God's house is to be a temple and place of prayer, not a "world market center." The final joy for the church is that we as believers are "set at the king's table, feasting on the bread of life" (Song VII-5).

Tesfaye's preaching and ability to give advice to the church in song is clearly represented, for example, by all the verbs in Song III-14: put on Jesus; pick up your armor; fight a good fight, do not doubt the victory; take care; study your surroundings; don't let strength be flimsy; fight vigorously; foresee the rewards; fight your best; don't surrender to the rule of darkness; be faithful to death; don't value your soul but give it over to the faithful creator; don't be scared by the Devil's noise; get up and fight; you will defeat in the war. This song is also an example of the theme of battle that runs through the great majority of his songs. Some other songs that give general advice to the church are I-11, III-12, V-6, and VI-7.

A gift given by Tesfaye to the entire faith community of Ethiopia was putting the Lord's Prayer, in the Amharic language, to tune (V-16). He was actually encouraged to consider doing this by a Catholic priest in the region of Sidama. All the church traditions, of course, use the prayer, either spoken or chanted, but the evangelical churches, especially, have tended to race through the spoken prayer, getting faster and faster as the prayer progressed so that one was almost breathless by the "Amen." Tesfaye solved that problem by putting the prayer to a very slow tune. Now there is plenty of time to ponder each phrase. The sung version quickly gained national popularity, even though the tune is quite ponderous in that many of the syllables are elongated and no tune phrases are repeated within the song. Here is an example about how putting the Lord's Prayer to tune has won the day.

In the Amharic Bible, the Lord's Prayer begins with "Our Father who art in heaven" (*abatachïn hoï be semaï yemïtïnor*). Tesfaye began his song with a different Amharic construction: "In heaven, the one who lives, our Father" (*be semaï yemïtïnor abatachïn hoï*). I noticed, following the appearance of the song in tune, that people began using his song construction, instead of the old written/read style, when speaking the prayer. In other words, the song overrode the traditional translation in the usage of the people, thus proving the power of a tune.

Song V–8 is a beautiful song that sounds like the disciples (or faith community) singing. They remember the time when Jesus of Nazareth called them. They saw His miracles and believed and surrendered to Him. He brought comfort in trouble, and His love is like the dew for the withered soul. They traveled with Him.

Another theme is that God never breaks his promises to his people (Song VII–11). This song was sung by Tesfaye at a building inauguration at the Ethiopian Graduate School of Theology (EGST) in 2014. Jesus Christ is the same yesterday, today and forever. In the plural, "we" have been released from death, seen the faithfulness of God and the fulfillment of His promises, all the goodness of God in delivering from powers of unrighteousness, and God's counsel in life as well as God's availability as a refuge and the safety of His shelter.

A signature song for this quadrant could be Song IV–9 with a history of what God has done for his people. This song is addressed to God, blessing Him for making His people more than a multitude, making a small mustard seed grow so that it is a tree of shade for the weak and tired. Who can compete with God for what He has done? He has planted His people in His courtyard and nourished them as palm trees. This is not exactly mentioning the church but it is one of the most beloved of Tesfaye's songs and sung publicly with great gusto. He multiplied a seed in this song. Then in Song VI–6, he prays that the spiritual territory of God's people may be expanded. He asks God directly to grow the seed, to multiply and enrich the seed's fruit and make His people grow until the whole "earth fills up by knowing God." He will keep praying this prayer without weakening. What great songs for a nation's churches to sing. The word "multiply" is used in both songs. Tesfaye demonstrates strong concern and prayer for the faith community in which he participates.

Context, Missional: Arena 4

Tesfaye is missional and challenging in all his preaching and singing. His singing has also been appreciated by the secular society in general. I remember his tapes being sung on public buses as we traveled the down-country highways back in the 1970s. In the market places of Addis Ababa, one might well hear his songs blaring from the loud speaker of a Muslim shop. Even in his late fifties he is still respected as a national singer, not only in the church but in more public spaces. To validate this, one needs only to watch online the celebration of Love Ethiopia crusade in late 2013.[10]

Tesfaye also spoke boldly into the context of Marxism and a Communist government. He spoke, during dark days, to a waiting and watching nation, to lukewarm Christians, and to those who needed to repent. In Song III–6 he spoke to deserters as "those without passports" and sang that "deserting Christ should be completely stopped." In Song II–12, he testifies to the one who has all power and calls "Come to the Lord . . . the Alpha and Omega . . . the one who "increases strength to the life that is weak."

This God "cannot be estimated by men. . .he strengthens his arm in in power." God controls nature and his eternal power is "revealed beautifully from the very beginning of his creation." But man ignores this, lives sinfully, folding his hands and saying, 'The Lord doesn't exist' (II–12). He sang to the nation about Jesus saying, "Don't doubt Jesus as a human being" (Song II–13).

During the revolution, Tesfaye had continual opportunities to interact with Marxist officials in the prison, witnessing to the Gospel, explaining Jesus Christ as Lord in skillful exchanges with self-proclaimed atheists (Tesfaye, BG, 38). Or, when he would be asked questions, the whippings would come. When he was ordered to talk with a political cadre, he would request to ask several questions before the discussion began, such as: "You have been talking to my friends (his fellow Christians in prison with him) turn by turn. How do you assess them?" And "What are your views about God?" He had clever ways of turning the whole conversation around (Tesfaye, BG, 86).

Shouting slogans against the imperialists, an important aspect of Marxist loyalty, was not what Christians thought they should do. Their reasoning was "How could we curse people with the very mouth with which we bless God?" from James 3:9–13.

10. Love Ethiopia Press Release at http://www.palau.org/news/media-resources/press-releases/item/love-ethiopia/press/release.

> None of us was in favor of the former political system which was denounced through the slogans, but it was only because we preferred to contend with the evil in objective practical ways that we were subjected to suffering. This was evident to all. However, although the outward allegation was that we refused to shout slogans, the basic problem was that we were believers in an era of atheistic ideology. (Tesfaye, BG, 20)

He further explains his use of I Samuel 17:41–45 as a reason for not cursing. When Goliath came cursing David, the young man David did not respond with a curse. Instead, he called upon God for wisdom in his response. Though not a direct answer to the problem of reciting slogans, he presented "a text that I took as a principle" (Tesfaye, BG, 110).

In at least 25 percent of the songs he writes directly to the world that needs salvation because "God would never want the sinner to perish . . . none should perish; the Savior has died for us. Christ Jesus has become a ransom for us" (Song VII–2). He gives a strong challenge that we need to be diligent in gathering the harvest. God's time and the Lord's appearance will soon be here. He asks in Song III–8: "Who bewitched us that we do not observe the times?" In other words, he challenged fellow Christians, in first person plural, to join him in missional witness by saying, "Think of the responsibility that has been put on us" (Song III–8).

Tesfaye himself has pointed out that he creates songs stressing the Gospel and discipleship. But discipleship is a large subject, and the songs often refer to societal situations or may be understood to have several meanings. This is illustrated with a few songs. In Song I–5, Tesfaye speaks of the atheist who denies that God exists. He reminds us in Song III–14 that we live in a time of war and need to study our surroundings and keep our armor on. We are not to be proud of our experience (Song V–6). This song about growing in truth could well be applied to an entire nation's churches. In Song VII–7, he warns lest God's temple become a "world market center, a profit-making place." Instead it should be a place of healing.

Regarding witness, in Song IV–16, he "proudly preaches" that "Jesus is Lord" and that his "friend of Calvary" is the answer for all people: Jews, Greeks, those who do not understand, those who think the message is foolishness or feel "ashamed by the word of the cross". He never proclaims an "empty hope" but insists that Christ "the king of peace" is the commander of salvation, the one who bought us by his blood. He says he is not afraid to preach this Word because the Lord is with him (Song IV–16). He challenges us in Song V–13 that the same one who "called Moses out of his shepherd life . . ." is the same God "who overcomes the dragon, who heals cripples and casts out demons?" (V–13).

Perhaps VI–5 "According to the Mercy I've Received" could be the signature song in this missional quadrant of the Four-Arena diagram. Because of the mercy he has received, he wants to serve the world by the Spirit's power. Because all the chains of sin and bondage have been removed and he has been called to be Christ's own, he prays to bless those who have stumbled, to help the weak. In order to do this he prays to be quickened, to wake up early, to be faithful, to be rid of laziness, to work hard under his grace that "I am witness saying, 'Jesus saves'!" He pleads that the love of the cross should fill his life. He prays for those who are not wise, for the educated who only think they know the truth, that he will be able to tell them the Gospel. He sings that the Gospel is "not reserved or limited by any boundaries;" it must reach "the end of the earth without being restricted . . . righteousness distributed far and near" so that all of creation proclaims "hurrah" in finding Jesus." The word translated "hurrah" is *iseï,* an exclamation of joy.

In every context and with every sort of person, Tesfaye always takes the opportunity to witness boldly about Jesus Christ. One may ask if there is a world-wide, evangelistic theme in his missiology. If not specifically stated, it is presumed. He is always pushing, encouraging and challenging his listeners to have a missional vision. Tesfaye himself has traveled world-wide in his singing and preaching ministry. In at least thirty of the songs, his missional heart is clearly expressed. In synthesizing what the songs themselves tell us of mission, we may propose the following:

The Gospel of salvation is for all the earth and the singer's plea is that this gospel and God's greatness be proclaimed and widely known (See Songs V–15, V–14, VI–15, and VII–12). He prays in Song VII–8 that "millions who lack satisfaction" will hear of God's fame and come into His house.

"The One Who Died for Us" (Song IV–16) is a proclamation of the Gospel. "But to the One Who died for us and who bought us by His blood, his salvation and His kingship of all creatures. We shall preach, yes, we shall preach." The answer to all who ask is "our friend of Calvary." "Jesus is Lord," we proudly preach. In Songs I–1, II–1, and VI–5, the desire is to proclaim and tell the Gospel with great boldness to those who thirst for life so that they may believe and be saved.

The God of mission is the King of the Ages, active through the Old Testament in such stories as Moses (Song V–13) when the dragon was wounded. From the Hebrew people to the present, He is El Shaddai (Song IV–11). Salvation came from God in the time of Nebuchadnezzar (V–10). Throughout history God gives victory and salvation over the rulers of this world and the evil army to the saints who travel on in the faith putting on the Gospel of peace and the breastplate (Song I–13).

Tesfaye is humbled as a servant of this Gospel message and, with an allusion to John the Baptist, he must prepare and sweep the road. All human beings shall see God. In Song III-1, he feels himself to be a stumbling block or mountain in the face of what God wants to do and prays for humility as God's servant.

As is evident throughout his songs, he is also very concerned for the wanderers who have sold their birthright and live in the agony of rejecting God's salvation (see Songs V–1, V–2). Those who are hesitating to choose, standing at a fork in the road, are admonished to make a choice before death casts its shadow and takes them blindfolded (Song II-2).

Regarding the Marxist years, he comments sometimes on the national state of affairs. "Man, in revolution and denial of God, folds his hands and says, "The Lord doesn't exist" (Song II–12). In Song II–13, Tesfaye issues a call to the general public not to doubt Jesus. Song III–8 challenges us that a season will come when time will be fulfilled and the Lord will come. "Who bewitched us that we do not observe the time" when the land labours in pain and when things change. Let us rise up and speak and struggle for souls. In times of trouble he gave the advice that Christians should "contest the enemies by the Word of Good News, the Gospel. . .fighting for their country for an inheritance that will not pass away" (Song III–15). While in prison he wrote: "Who would seek the lost, would treat the hurt, would repair the broken, would renew the ruins?" (Song VII–9). The one who gathers souls is compassionate and kind; the one who proclaims the Good News will receive the reward. In prison he wrote song VII-2 about the Lord's mercy, truth, love and kindness and that all should draw near in repentance and receive forgiveness. "None should perish; the Savior has died for us and Christ Jesus has become a ransom for us." In Song VI–3, also written in prison, he points out that surrender to Jesus is the answer to our own wisdom. In other prison songs, he sings that we are winners through faith (Song VI–7) and will continue living in Him and while we are alive we will manifest the work of the Lord (Song VI–2) we never deny in our mouths what we believe in our hearts (Song II–13).

In summary of this probing of the four arenas of the Global Church Music Matrix, I come to several important conclusions. (1) Tesfaye's songs reflect a full-orbed theology. (2) His life and songs complement each other. (3) His personal life is in line with the Word. (4) The Word is an absorbing part of his spiritual life. (5) Tesfaye lives in a healthy relationship and responsibility to the community of faith. (6) Tesfaye is concerned and vitally involved in the witness of the church in the world. According to the proposed schema, his total life and ministry are full-orbed.

EXPANDED MISSIOLOGICAL MODEL

In an attempt to capture all the considerations of this dissertation, I suggest a further developed diagram that seeks to add two more dimensions to encompass or hold the four arenas in the Global Church Music Matrix. This next diagram shows the model against a backdrop of under-pinnings and over-arching dimensions. It is impossible to express all that I wish in such a drawing, but it illustrates to some small degree what I want to convey as an overall thematic statement for this entire work.

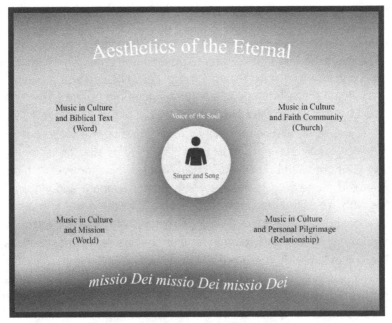

Figure 6: Missio Dei and Aesthetics
(My expansion of Matrix for Studies in Global Church Music)

Foundational Missional Impulse

In Figure 6, the basic Global Church Music Matrix remains as formerly presented in Figures 1 and 5. However, I now add two levels to the discussion. I have chosen to name the foundation the *missio Dei* to describe the surging mission of God in creation from the foundation of the world. The cohesive thought is what we read in Colossians 1, that all finds its meaning in the truth that "Jesus is Lord". I find the same foundation in Philippians Chapter 2. All Trinitarian churches would agree that this missionary nature and commitment of the church flows "from a deep conviction regarding the uniqueness and all-sufficiency of Christ's person and work."[11]

The singer-musician, standing in the middle of the four quadrants within a given culture, is transmitting a message through a form of performative knowledge. Vanhoozer speaks of a theodramatic understanding of the church's mission.[12] His "canonic principle" insists that Scripture is what our stories (songs) must follow, and further that "every fitting performance of the gospel must also take account of our present speech and action." A singer fits the definition of "improvisation" in Vanhoozer's terms as a form of "disciplined spontaneity." This leads me to suggest that a soloist singing his song in an appropriate manner is an example of continuing "the evangelical action by responding to the offerings of Word and Spirit in culturally (and intellectually) appropriate manners." To sum up this discussion, the gospel is "infinitely translatable" and "infinitely performable."[13] "Ordinary life is indeed the scene in which our speech and action demonstrate the understanding of faith."[14] This is demonstrated well through Tesfaye's melodies and lyrics.

God's Beauty as Overarching Aesthetic

At the top of Figure 6 is a layer above the singer which I name *Aesthetics of the Eternal*, a concept discussed by N. T. Wright. His view is one of a new creativity, based on Romans 8, which holds an "integrated worldview, and with a theology of both creation and new creation." [15] There is a delight in beauty which leads us to God and the new creation. Wright

11. Bevans and Schroeder, *Constants in Context*, 326.
12. Vanhoozer, "One Rule," 111–12.
13. Vanhoozer, "One Rule," 113–16.
14. Vanhoozer, "One Rule," 111–12.
15. Wright, *Surprised by Hope*, 222–24.

says, "When art comes to terms with *both* the wounds of the world *and* the promise of resurrection and learns how to express and respond to both at once, we will be on the way to a fresh vision, a fresh mission."[16] In Jesus' resurrection, the nail marks in his feet and hands were still present in his identity. This overarching aesthetic therefore also helps to illuminate the deep meaning of many of Tesfaye's songs as he lived and sang in a time of persecution.

Synthesis of Missio Dei and Beauty

The singer stands in the middle of the proposed illustration, living life and singing into all four arenas. Not only is the song from within (in whatever means we understand its origins) but the person himself is the musician and the instrument. This phenomenon represents a very profound theology-making in a given culture and space. Song penetrates all arenas, but its origins are deep in the missional impulses of God and are beautiful and aesthetic in the singer's unique culture, all of this adding to an eternal paean of worship. This is the power of a song such as Tesfaye's. The singer and the song are one totality, which I have indicated as "voice of the soul."

What is the dynamic and influence of a singer and his song? The singer and his song correspond. McLuhan's famous dictum, "The medium is the message," proposed that a medium affects the society in which it plays a role, not only by the content delivered over the medium, but also by the characteristics of the medium itself. He writes that language is the "medium of human extension" and that "the human voice may be compared to the radio transmitter in being able to translate sound into electromagnetic waves . . . furthermore, the voice has power to shape air and space."[17] I therefore propose that a singer is both the medium and the message in the total production of a song. Being "soaked" in the Word and prayer, the more prepared he or she is to receive songs from the Spirit. Disciplines of life style, innate creativity, the voice of the singer as the instrument, all combined transmit the message. The more the singer's total person is aligned with what he sings with his voice, the more he becomes the message itself.

---

16. Wright, *Surprised by Hope*, 224.

17. McLuhan, *Understanding Media*, 80.

SUMMARY

Who the singer is as a person and in relationship to every quadrant of life is impossible to put boundaries around. Especially in the case of Tesfaye's imprisonment, this is a powerful concept to consider because the prison cell becomes the entire "area" of the illustration I have proposed. All four arenas are contained in one prison room, the constraint being illustrated in Figure 6 above by the border around the Figure. There is no possibility of moving out. In fact, there may not even be a written "Word". Therefore, everything needful is contained within the prisoner. His entire world of mission, church and himself is strictly limited. He himself, as a person, is limited in space, permission, opportunity, conveniences (for example, instrument or holy book). The song comes purely from who he is in his person. As far as the body of believers, some in prison are believers being consoled and taught through the song if they are in the same cell or nearby. Others are a community forced into his space as unbelieving, perhaps anti-God, prison keepers. He is captive in their space. And likewise, they are captive in his space. Who he is *in toto* with his song is a complete message. No one can limit a singer from singing unless they actually throttle him. The Word penetrates in every situation. Revolutionaries hear his teaching. This is the power of the singer and his song.

10

Challenges and Possibilities in Leading for Change

WHAT ARE THE CHALLENGES and possibilities in leading for change which may result from this study? The original question to be answered was: What interpretations and insights may be discovered and modeled through this study of the life and songs of Tesfaye Gabbiso that will inspire and instruct Christian musicians in discipleship and creation of spiritual songs? There are several challenges inherent in this question. Here I want to take a look back into Ethiopian song with the use of the following beautiful piece of art with Ethiopian motif.

Figure 7: Ethiopian Singer and Child
(Drawing by Betty Warhanik; public domain)

This distinctive pen-and-ink drawing was created by Betty Warhanik, an early SIM missionary teacher and artist in Ethiopia.[1] The instrument is the *begena*, often referred to as "David's harp." It is my favorite of Ethiopian traditional cultural instrument. It is mainly used for religious purposes in the home, most often during Lenten season, with its soulful quality, to sing ancient stories or narratives from the Bible.

"The Ethiopian Singer and Child" in Figure 6, illustrates the power of music and Ethiopian spiritual song. I see it as a symbol of all that church singers and musicians represent and are responsible for. In the drawing, we see the passing on of song from one generation to another. Because it is a musical form, the memory of the experience or story being sung will be more forcefully imprinted on the child's memory. Firstly, this piece of art presents a mirror into which the Ethiopian church may gaze to observe their distinctively rich musical heritage of spiritual songs. Secondly, the drawing represents the responsibility of passing on the story from one generation to another. Not that the styles won't change. But the importance of song in each generation must be passed on in genuine life-giving ways, nurturing, reminding, teaching, by example. The medium is the message.[2]

ETHIOPIAN EVANGELICAL CHURCH LITURGY, WHAT IS IT?

The songs of the Ethiopian Trinitarian churches are wonderful. I very much appreciate the rich liturgical heritage in the Orthodox and Catholic churches. In the evangelical churches, I would hold that the song-singing is the one main liturgical aspect of their worship.[3] If there is little or no other liturgy like creeds, prayers, or formal statements, then the texts of the songs sung are all the more important.

McGann, who writes broadly on liturgy, suggests five points that may help guide in thinking about songwriters and their work into the future. Firstly, because song-texts are "integral and constitutive of liturgical

---

1. Betty Warhanik served with SIM in Ethiopia for about thirty years beginning in 1944.

2. McLuhan's famous phrase was discussed in the previous chapter.

3. EECMY, Ethiopian Evangelical Church Mekane Yesus, would be an exception, although they, too, are increasingly moving away from their historical liturgical tradition and hymnbook. The Seventh Day Adventist Church recently issued a new hymnal.

action," they should therefore be tested to discover the theology of the worship.[4]

Secondly, musical traditions may be studied and explored as to "how these traditions are being shaped and handed on to future generations."[5] Are the Ethiopian churches willing to nurture a future generation of singers? Are the theological schools willing to include the arts as a part of the curriculum? What will Ethiopia's future song be?

Thirdly, study of song-texts may "provide a way to bring our liturgical theory and theology into greater dialogue with practice."[6] Since song is so powerful, as illustrated in the testimony of Tesfaye, there must be a realization about how necessary it is to sing a correct theology that inspires discipleship in the church. This will demand a dedication to the value of the arts, plus the determination of the church to actively support and encourage its singers and musicians.

Fourthly, a question arises as to who is "'at the table' when liturgical theologizing is being carried on."[7] Do churches have any liturgical theologizing at all? Here again, the church and theological institutions need to become actively engaged in the process. Music and worship arts are presently almost non-existent in the curriculum of evangelical schools in Ethiopia.

Fifthly, and finally, questions arise "about how we imagine the future work of our disciplines at this time of massive cultural change and global consciousness. How will future generations of liturgical scholars and theologians be trained for their role in the churches?"[8] In Africa today, the cultural changes are massive, and the young people are growing ever more globally conscious. What is the future work of the church in these areas? The *zefen-mezmur* ("worldly" versus "spiritual" songs) issue needs to be addressed in this fast-paced and changing world, or the dichotomy will continue to divide Christians unnecessarily and alienate musicians of a younger generation.

4. McGann, *Exploring Music*, 79.

5. McGann, *Exploring Music*, 80.

6. McGann, *Exploring Music*, 80.

7. McGann, *Exploring Music*, 80.

8. McGann, *Exploring Music*, 81.

PRESENT ISSUES FOR CONSIDERATION

Thus far, I have studied the life narrative and songs of one singer, Tesfaye Gabbiso. He is of a previous or former school with roots back in the 1960s. Tibebe Eshete describes those times in the following way:

> Overall, apart from offering comfort and daring faith, the songs helped believers develop a consciousness of victory in a climate of terror and powerlessness. The songs also had catechetical values that provided guides to daily life much needed in those confusing times. In particular, Tesfaye Gabbiso, song composer, theologian, and soloist, greatly contributed to the expansion of gospel songs, both before and after his imprisonment.[9]

Song is always evolving. It must be remembered that Tesfaye, in his youth, was singing a new kind of song in contrast to what had been common in the churches up to that point. Today offers a period of new spaces and modernization in a fast-globalizing world. Fifty years from now, how will the present church singers and their songs be described by the historians?

A recent 2015 description of one large local church in Addis Ababa, the Old Airport Full Gospel Believers Church, reads thus:

> There are between five and ten worship teams in the one church. They take turns at leading the congregation in singing. On Sunday, the singing takes anywhere from 30 to 60 minutes. They welcome soloists, but we do not have people singing solos every Sunday. Somehow, we prefer singing as a group activity. Church members are composing songs all the time. New ones will be tested out at other meetings before they make it to Sunday worship. We no sooner get used to a song and it is replaced by another one! But many of our songs are "home-made."[10]

This sounds like a church that is alert to its music program and thoughtfully mentoring the singers, both choirs and soloists—a church taking responsibility for its musicians and song ministry. There are, however, several issues that beg for consideration in the present church music scene within Ethiopia. Here I mention three issues that have already received some earlier discussion from Tesfaye's point of view in Chapter 5.

---

9. Tibebe Eshete, *Evangelical Movement*, 282.

10. Printed interview by Brian Fargher with Bekele Wolde-Kidan entitled "Good News from Ethiopia" on October 10, 2014, in Calgary, Alberta.

INNOVATION ENCOURAGED AMONG MUSICIANS

In spite of some positive points and trends, critique of present-day sing-
ers is often heard. This section gives voice to the renewal that is being
called for on various fronts. In Chapter 5, I discussed Tesfaye's views and
philosophy on song and singers. He expressed some concerns, always
very carefully and kindly stated, on some of the innovation needed in the
areas of life style, spiritual disciplines, temptations and traps, and finan-
cial profit-making.

Now I consider what some other present musicians and critics are
saying about current Christian music. About Africa, in general, the fol-
lowing has been written, "They (Africans) seem to sing from birth to
death. Yet this blessing sometimes seems to lack depth. The simplicity
in song, while providing spontaneity, at times is devoid of sound biblical
worth."[11]

Recently two current Ethiopian singers, Ephrem Alemu and Te-
wodros Tadesse, were interviewed. In their discussion, the "spiritual
song" history of the past fifty years was divided into three approximate
time segments:

Era One (1960–1980): This era gave us the fathers of song like Tes-
faye Gabbiso, Tamrat Haile, Dereje Kebede and others. There were rela-
tively few singers compared to the plethora of song writers today.

Era Two (1980–2000): The "middle" singers were very creative and
prolific and sang well in a golden age.

Era Three (2000–present): The present is a time of *tïrmïs* or "great
confusion" and a mixture of positive and negative aspects. Singers con-
centrate on style, but the content is weak. A proliferation of communica-
tion techniques, a desire to strike it rich by singing, a lack of solid content
in the texts, disregard for rights and tendency to plagiarism have all con-
tributed to this confusing situation.[12]

One must, however, refrain from generalizing when speaking of
today's writers and singers of "spiritual songs". Each singer must be evalu-
ated individually. It is a very mixed phenomenon at present. These young
singers describe the present situation as one of great turmoil, mixing
globalization and burgeoning technology. The instrumentation and pro-
liferation of songs will change considerably, but the lyrical content should
remain constant in the hands of Christians who pray and proclaim the

11. Phiri, "Great Shift," 401.

12. Ephrem Alemu and Tewodros Tadesse, "Current Development," 4–5.

Biblical text and truths in their songs. This generation must reach out from the traditional solos and choirs and congregational songs of the church into the wider world and culture in which we are called to live as God's people.

There are positive efforts being made to encourage worship song writers. In this regard, a symposium was held in November 2008.[13] Gezahegn Mussie and Zelalem Mengistu were both presenters. Geza- hegn Mussie, a soloist himself, directs the Living Worship International Ministry in Ethiopia and has had a long career of serving the church in music and worship. He and Tesfaye Gabbiso are in the process of gaining permission to host a TV program within the country which will concen- trate on Worship and Music.[14]

The purpose of his ministry is to "exert effort to see Biblical, liv- ing worship prevail in Ethiopia and elsewhere for the glory of God, the edification of the body of Christ and the extension of his kingdom."[15] He expresses concern about current trends and how church leaders have left the preliminary worship entirely to the whim of the young people. Little attention is given to coaching and discipling worship teams and choirs. As a result, there is frustration and some church musicians have joined modern secular bands because they have not been encouraged and strengthened in the music ministries of their own churches.

In his teaching, Gezahegn urges singers to learn the discipline of appraising their song lyrics.[16] He speaks of the responsibility of the local congregational leaders to guide their singers. Gezahegn is strong on the kind of worship we should be offering to God. He emphasizes several significant points. He teaches that even though the song and delivery of a singer may be very pleasing, we are making a mistake if the life of the singer invited does not match the song.[17] The congregation is as guilty as the singer. The churches should be much firmer in what kind of sing- ers they invite. Songs have been losing their message which tends to be

---

13. This symposium was coordinated by EvaSUE (Evangelical Students Union of Ethiopia) and led by EvaSUE director, Zelalem Abebe and Paulos Fekadu.

14. Email from Gezahegn Mussie on May 10, 2014.

15. Gezahegn Mussie, "LivingWorship International Ministry" brochure, Addis Ababa, n.d.

16. Gezahegn Mussie, "Christian Worship and Music Syllabus."

17. Gezahegn Mussie audited the ethnomusicology course I taught at the Evan- gelical Graduate School of Theology (January–May 2008) and made many valuable contributions in the class.

self-centered and egotistical about a personal spiritual experience of the singer. To write a song that will pass the test of time, the Word of God and the filling of the Holy Spirit are necessary. Like David, the word of God must be in the mouth of the singer. Many of today's songs are very repetitious, poor in message and strong on the keyboard. If Christians realized what an impact their song can have, they would tend more carefully to the songs which are allowed to be sung.[18]

Gezahegn also speaks about how songs are often written very hurriedly. Everyone is in a rush to produce. Or, a chorus may perhaps be written well, but to lengthen the song, some stanzas suddenly need to be created so that the song can be sung. Sometimes the hurriedly written stanzas have nothing to do with the chorus.[19]

Zelalem Mengistu has written several significant articles and gave papers at the symposium in 2008. In exploring the quality of lyrics being written, he mentions a lack of depth in thought and content. But young writers and singers may be encouraged in positive ways to consider some of these ideas and work on them in their own songs. Songs are composed too quickly with emphasis on the accompanying sounds and the desire to produce a quick CD. He observes: "Many singers do not live an accountable life and have no meaningful relationship with a local church. They spend almost all weekends in other churches and away from family." Many are too busy to read the Word.[20] Songs are written too quickly with emphasis on the accompaniment and usually the desire to produce a quick CD.

Three further thoughts from Zelalem illustrate his views. Some young writers feel their lyrics are untouchable because they received them from the Lord. Older mature Christians may respond saying that "receiving it from the Lord" is not necessarily from the Bible. There is opportunity to work on shaping the lyrics. Zelalem also shared a saying: "Birthing a good song is the difference between a C-section and a natural delivery."[21]

Regarding life style and walk, Zelalem encourages singers that they are to be servants in the pulpit. They are to be careful in their composition, editing, serving and printing of their songs. They are to exhibit wisdom and skill in their work. They must scrutinize their work and consider

---

18. Gezahegn Mussie, "Worship Is Not a Fashionable Suit," 4–6.

19. Gezahegn Mussie, "Songs of Yesterday," 1–5.

20. Zelalem Mengistu, "To All Singers."

21. Interview with Zelalem Mengistu in Brooks, Alberta, May 31, 2014.

those who follow them.[22] Three major aspects should be considered in the creation of a song: literary quality (*sïne ṣïhufawi wubet*), linguistic content (*ḵwanḵwawi yïzet*), and Biblical doctrine (*meṣïhaf ḵïdusawi astemhïro nachewu*).[23]

Eyob Denio's book, *Yemezmurïna yemezemïran hïywet* ("Song and the Singer's Life"), has gone through several printings in Soddo, Wolaitta, where he teaches.[24] The book proved valuable in the Soddo Workshop which Eyob and I convened in early 2015.[25] Eyob's book could well serve as a springboard for future workshops. He is especially concerned about the life of the singer and speaks from Colossians 3:16–17 about letting the Word of Christ dwell in us richly. He insists on the necessity of keeping the main thought in the chorus; therefore, all that is in the stanzas should support or illustrate that main thought. Another sample of his advice is that songwriters should not use difficult words or allusions, even from the Bible, that people will not understand.[26]

The three critics cited above have little appreciation for weak texts and have quoted some lines, not without a dose of humor. Someone has said, "I compare contemporary Ethiopian gospel songs with a sandwich that has a small filling of egg between twelve slices of bread, six below and six above!" [27] Some samples of questionable texts are quoted below by writers concerned about appropriate lyrics:

> My sin stinks like muddy boots. *Haṭiaté gema ïndeboti çama,* or
> Jesus, you are my candy—*Iyesus yené kereméla.*[28]

> When my heart thinks of you it is satiated.
> My joy's spice is Jesus.
> Oh my, you are my sugar.[29]

One challenge is that many young people consider their compositions as divine inspirations and allow no room for "weeding" or editing.

22. Zelalem Mengistu, "Critique of Songs."

23. Zelalem Mengistu, "To All Singers."

24. Eyob Denio is director of the Wolaitta Evangelical Seminary, operating under the auspices of the Kale Heywet Church.

25. See Appendix B.

26. Eyob Denio, "Song and the Singer's Life," 27.

27. Zelalem Mengistu, "To All Singers."

28. Eyob Denio, "Song and the Singers' Life," 26.

29. Gezahegn Mussie, "Songs of Yesterday," 2

We need to appreciate trends. Tesfaye Gabbiso's songs have been described as "timeless."[30] But, we need to appreciate the passing of time and remember that in Tesfaye's younger years, he was very innovative, joining musicians in a new kind of music, both in lyrics and tunes. The older Christians weren't sure of the trend; they never are in any generation. In order to enhance Tesfaye's songs for a modern generation, a few young musicians are taking the original tunes and adapting them; for example, humming along at points, adding harmony, adjusting the beat and generally bringing the lyrics into newer musical styles. Tesfaye acknowledges that this is true and supports the trend.[31]

In two recent public events in Addis Ababa, Tesfaye asked Dawit Getachew to accompany him because of Dawit's more eclectic or integrated style. The first of these events was the inauguration of the second phase of development at the Ethiopian Graduate School of Theology.[32] The second event was the Luis Palau Crusade, "Love Ethiopia" in 2013 when Tesfaye sang "But I Know One Thing."

The Christian public, in general, needs to be encouraged to support the arts, not diminish their importance. The question is asked why the wealthy people in the churches do not feel a responsibility to support the arts like the broader population does?

RESPONSIBILITIES OF THE LOCAL CHURCH

The generation of church pastors and leaders today are young and have a short historical memory. The Ethiopian revolution is now just history, hardly remembered. Through an understanding of this study, they will gain a deeper understanding of the context of his Tesfaye's song creation and the challenges he faced. One goal would be to assist them in thinking through, or discovering for themselves this generation's challenges that need to be addressed in song. King suggests that such a process needs to begin at the national church level. "The development of culturally appropriate songs relevant to the felt needs and spiritual concerns of the people ultimately relies on the encouragement of the national church."[33]

Churches have the responsibility to develop their own music ministries and encourage their own people to work on creating songs for

---

30. Interview with Yohannes Girma, Addis Ababa, January 7, 2015.

31. Interview with Tesfaye Gabbiso, Hawassa, January 9, 2015.

32. Interview with Dawit Getachew, Addis Ababa, January 27, 2015.

33. King, *Pathways in Christian Music*, 195.

children, teaching at all levels, encouragement in small groups, special occasions and more. It only takes one or several church members with creativity to think of new ways of using song. Young musicians should be encouraged to form their own groups and work on creative music for the local churches under the supportive leadership of the elders. The churches should enfold rather than distance themselves from young songwriters. This also includes financial help from the local church if appropriate.

Local churches need to encourage and enable their member families to know the joy of creating songs together, even at home. Leaders as well as parents in the churches should be encouraging their musical children by grounding them in the Word and prayer as children, just like Tesfaye's mother did. Then they need to accept their musical children and encourage them rather than discouraging or judging them.

Young Artists—Finances and Support

Church singers rarely become wealthy. As seen in Chapter 5, Tesfaye gives all responsibility to the church for producing and selling his song cassettes and CDs. He never intended to make money in the process of being a solo singer. This is a downfall of singers today, of artists anywhere. They are not to blame in that they do need to make a living. If a singer is enfolded by the church, submits to the authority of the local church, and becomes a worthy singer, the church congregations should take responsibility for the artists in their midst.

A continuing issue in Ethiopia is the copyright and financial aspect of song makers. One writer suggests that if we say the song of Christians has weakened and declined, we really need to blame the church for not taking hold of the situation, because we are all in the Body of Christ. The "worldly" singers find patrons, but the church does not support the arts. It is reported that some church people think that even putting up a poster advertising a concert is worldly. Singers are always being blamed; therefore, the thinking of the evangelical Christian public needs to change. The market for Christian music is actually declining because many singers are out there singing without two things: (1) a genuine calling and (2) a filling of the grace of God. Because many of the songs are empty, they are not being appreciated by Christians.[34]

Ezra Chitando discusses this dilemma about young people who are into writing songs for financial reward, as an income generating project

---

34. Ephrem Alemu and Tewodros Tadesse, "Current Development," 4–5.

"undertaken by individuals in an oppressive economic environment."[35] For those who succeed in making money, it is considered God's blessing. Chitando aptly describes the cultural changes and suggests the notion of "hybridity" which opens a door to more freedom in the whole area of song creativity and production, beyond the bounded spaces of, for example, sacred and secular.[36] The storm of the sacred and secular, or *mezmur-zefen* (spiritual vs. worldly songs) still rages in Ethiopia. I now turn to that topic.

Spiritual vs. Worldly (mezmur-zefen) Debate

An ongoing tension in Ethiopia's churches is the *mezmur-zefen* debate. Its roots go back at least as far as the early centuries of the Orthodox Church and St. Yared who received special spiritual songs from heaven. Steinhovden assists in an understanding of the present dilemma through word studies and the comments of various musicians on both sides of the issue.[37] He explains how one of the main problems is the translation and interpretation of the word *zefen*, or dance, in the modern translations of the Amharic Bible. It is my contention that this issue needs deliberation so that evangelicals can look at the arts in a more wholesome, kingdom-vision way of seeing. Perhaps in the past, it was easier to have a Christ-against-culture mentality.

However, today, with the plethora of ways to make and reproduce music and the multitude of studios that create popular music accompaniments to "spiritual" words, there is a need to broaden our minds as Christians and allow exploration. Many young Christian musicians, discouraged or even denounced by their local congregations, make their way to the bars and drinking houses to make their music, there seemingly being no middle ground in which to move. A question might be why the church cannot be more open-minded, intent on enfolding its singers, and learning to move in a wider middle space? Holding tight to such a dichotomy suggests a Christ-against-culture and protectionist mentality rather than an open flow with the opportunities to sing with meaning into the culture. Jean Ngoya Kidula wisely explains the tensions

---

35. Chitando, *Singing Culture*, 86.

36. Chitando, *Singing Culture*, 91–93.

37. Steinhovden, "*Mäzmur* and *Zäfän*," 1–38.

between lyrics and music instrumentation. She maintains that the lyrics are the defining difference in a song, never mind the instrumentation.[38]

Historically, Tesfaye assuredly belongs in the traditional spiritual songs (*mezmur*) camp. I am not encouraging a falling away or dilution of truth; but as long as an "us" and "them" attitude is held, musicians will not move in creating church music for a future that holds faithful theology and is also musically appealing to a globalized younger generation. Ephrem Alemu contends that it is the Devil at work dividing the church and destroying the testimony of song.[39] He says the singers should not be blamed; rather, the church must take responsibility. This issue is pleading for teaching and guidance. Hansen writes that it is in worship, for example in creating new songs, that the church has "especially fertile soil for new living rituals" if it can break away from dualistic thinking.[40]

Dawit Getachew, connected to the Mekane Yesus Jazz Music School, is graciously leading a movement into a more eclectic view of music and song.[41] In a similar vein, Moges Berassa has suggested that we open our hearts to rap and pop music as means of Christian communication. So many aspiring singers are "scattered in their minds."[42]

Arts bring us closer than anything else to the eternal spirit of beauty, so it is in this area that we struggle as Christians. We must dig deeply into our worldview to appreciate and utilize the power and influence we may have as Christians in music and song-making.

MISSION

An orientation into the importance of the arts is crucial for current and future Ethiopian missionaries now being sent either within Ethiopia or internationally. Ethiopia is being used of God as a missional church in an amazing way at this time in history. The far reaches of the Ethiopian nation are being evangelized by their own missionaries. They have not received specific training in ethnomusicology or other church music, but being Ethiopians, they have unconsciously sung indigenous music in their local churches. How will they begin to promote indigenous textually rich spiritual songs in the mother tongues of their host areas and

---

38. Kidula, "Making and Managing," 110–11.
39. Ephrem Alemu and Tewodros Tadesse, "Current Development."
40. Hansen, "Transforming the Dualistic Worldview," 141.
41. Interview with Dawit Getachew, Addis Ababa, January 27, 2015.
42. Interview with Moges Berassa, Addis Ababa, June 19, 2013.

countries of ministry? The Wolaitta churches, for example, have sent out evangelists for eighty years to other ethnic groups in Ethiopia, but I have no knowledge of any musical instruction ever having been available to them as they crossed tribal boundaries.

Beyond the homeland, what song is being carried across boundaries by Ethiopian missionaries? Are those being setn as witnesses being trained to create and initiate songs appropriate to their new contexts? At the time of this writing, the Ethiopian Kale Heywet Church, for example, has sent missionaries to the following countries: Chad, India, China, Sudan, Bangladesh, Zambia, Kenya, Cambodia, Malawi, Thailand, Kuwait and Pakistan.

Roberta King's challenge to the western church now holds urgency and motivation for the newer missional sending nations such as Ethiopia. Their missionaries should be receiving specific training so that they can begin producing or encouraging "culturally appropriate songs for use in ways that function at deep cultural levels . . . and penetrate the thought process of a people."[43] Christian musicians in Ethiopia would benefit from studies in ethnomusicology and such models as King's "Model for Doing Christian Music Communication Research" that combines various disciplines to produce appropriate songs for both church and mission.[44]

DISCIPLESHIP

A currently very strong emphasis rising in Africa, through the efforts of combined church and mission leadership, is the thrust of active discipling. Many seminars and groups are involved. The impetus is spreading through various kinds of networks. A wonderful contribution to this ministry would be songwriting. Those being discipled as well as mentoring disciplers should be using song that they create together. What a powerful way to ignite cohesive oneness and learning. Sing the discipleship principles. Sing the scriptures. Teach through song. Songwriting is often included as an aspect of Bible translation and literacy, and this has been done effectively within Ethiopia in ethnic groups just receiving scripture in their own languages. Singing can carry the training far beyond an academic exercise.

43. King, "Toward a Discipline," 300–301.

44. King, *Pathways in Christian Music*, 194–95.

INFLUENCE IN SOCIETY

I believe it is possible for Christians in music to influence society at large. Recently, an Ethiopian theologian based in Canada, Girma Bekele, wrote a pastoral letter to the churches and ethnic groups of Ethiopia encouraging unity in the Trinitarian churches. He challenged them to relinquish the ethnic strife that is evident even in the churches.[45] This pastoral letter, in the first week online, had over 200,000 readers. It seems that it was very timely in the life of the Ethiopian nation. If skillfully crafted song could be added to this challenge by the "in-between" people (Ethiopia's Trinitarian churches), how might the impact be strengthened?[46] Finally, the internet world holds great power for influence through Christian music, with some Ethiopian groups already taking good advantage of that media form.

CREATIVITY IN THE PERFORMATIVE ARTS

Ethiopians are excellent dramatists. Sometimes at Christmas or Easter the most amazing plays will be almost spontaneously produced. I would encourage the churches to develop the performative arts and promote creativity. Appendix B describes a Workshop held for a local church area in Soddo, Wolaitta. Young people are eager to be creative and, with good leadership, may contribute much to the churches through creative performative arts.

SUMMARY

In this chapter I have explored the challenges and possibilities in leading for change in the Ethiopian church setting. An understanding and commitment to the value of the arts is being fostered by a few leaders, but the movement needs to expand. Local churches must take the responsibility to encourage, disciple and support their young musicians. There are several crucial arenas where song demands attention, among which are the mission movement outside of Ethiopia and the cross-cultural opportunities within the country. Song is vital in all local church teaching as well as in broader discipleship movements. The ongoing debate over "spiritual" versus "worldly" music is a challenge for theologians to work

---

45. Girma Bekele, "Pastoral Letter."
46. Girma Bekele, *In-Between People*, 1–2.

on in Ethiopia. Christian musicians have, literally, a great opportunity to impact the entire world far beyond the church walls.

Conclusion

DURING THIS PROJECT, I have dreamed. In considering the adaptive change component necessary to this work, it has come to me as an epiphany that the real conclusion and future vision is encompassed well in one of Tesfaye's songs: "Greater Things Than This" (Song VII–12). This significant song was selected by the SIM Publishing group in Addis Ababa as the artistic background for the Tesfaye songbook which is the subject of this project.[1]

Song VII–12 represents the four arenas of the Global Church Music Matrix and the comprehensiveness of what we have seen in Tesfaye's life and song. No wonder the churches of Ethiopia continue to sing this song with great gusto at many public occasions. I have seen crowds raise their hands to heaven, their bodies swaying, and singing "Greater Things Than This" from the depth of their hearts in loud decibels. The beat and rollicking tune in the chorus drive the church forward in an almost heavenly dance of hope and expectation.

Song VII–12 is a comprehensive illustration of the legacy Tesfaye has given to Ethiopia. Tesfaye was one of the forerunners or fathers of a bold new spiritual song movement in which lyrics and tunes, new to the Christian church, sprang from the hearts and minds of young songmakers. The songs were not translations of western hymns, and the tunes were indigenous. A country lad could become a popular public poet.

Tesfaye's life is consistent in Babylon, the Meantime and Zion. The circumstances of Tesfaye's pilgrimage took him to prison for seven years

---

1 See Appendix C for the entire songbook translated into English.

in his young manhood, but whatever the dimensions or confines of daily life might be, he sang. His songs appealed to a nation in a time of trouble because he had a message of comfort and strength. He knew his God, and the songs demonstrate his allegiance. Tesfaye did not have much earthly hope during the seven years of young manhood which he spent in prison. Nevertheless, he continued to sing with an eternal perspective. The songs exuded a balm and strength to the minds and spirits of Ethiopia's people during a time of great suffering. His loyalty and convictions were uncompromising. Life is a battle, and everyone must make ultimate decisions and then live by those decisions. Life is not always free from sorrow, but there is a way through. His singing, backed up by example, encourages a life of discipleship, consistency, and obedience. His songs also still appeal to a broad international spectrum in the Ethiopian diaspora.

For Tesfaye, the two foundational disciplines of the Christian life are the knowledge and imbibing of the Word and the practice of prayer. He saturates his lyrics with memorized scripture. Tesfaye consistently teaches and exhibits in life and song that the Word of God and prayer are the two foundational disciplines in one's personal life.

As a church leader, in addition to being a singer, Tesfaye expends energy on teaching the church about true worship and the song which the church should be singing with all their heart and mind. He adapts to the changing music scene in styles of accompaniment. Tesfaye is a poet whose appropriate words and metaphors resonate with people's thoughts and emotions, no matter what the culture of the listener.

Tesfaye does not fear battle, and he contends that we always live and struggle with sufferings and constraints of various kinds. In the power of God, He contests all the enemies. The tests and suffering of today's generation, perhaps more subtle and imprisoning than a physical prison, are just as great or greater than his prison experience. Tesfaye sings with understanding and a wide perspective on time and eternity, not just with feelings of the present moment. The cross and death of Christ are inextricably bound up with the resurrection and life. Tesfaye's songs magnify Jesus as Lord. Those who wander or live in denial and unbelief are of great concern in his songs.

Ethiopia's rapidly expanding church, being one of the most historic, blessed, and gifted in the world, holds a great legacy in the songs of Tesfaye Gabbiso. Singers of today and tomorrow have a weighty responsibility in how they will present their offering of songs into the future, not only within Ethiopia, but to the ends of the earth.

Tesfaye's songs rose out of an environment of social ferment, constraint and repression. His songs are universal for a world wearied by war and displacement, a world searching for peace and meaning. The central argument of this thesis may be summarized as follows: If the evidence presented is correct, then the soloist Tesfaye Gabbiso has made a significant contribution to Christian song in Ethiopia. Not the least significant feature of this contribution is the fact that his songs rose out of an environment of constraint and repression of the Christian church. Truly, he sings with understanding in Babylon, the Meantime, and Zion and proclaims a timely message for the entire world church.

I have been to the field and have told the story. I now challenge Ethiopian scholars and musicians to look into the mirror of this story and build on the findings for their own ministries in song.

When we are looking for African theology we should go first to the fields

. . .

We must look at the way in which Christianity is being planted
in Africa through music, drama, songs, dances, art, paintings

. . .

Can it be that all this is an empty show? It is impossible.
This then is African theology.[2]

2. Okullu, *Church and Politics*, 54.

Appendix A

Photographs

Tesfaye Gabbiso (left), as Paul and Lila Balisky first knew him in Aletta Wondo, Ethiopia, early 1970s. Here he is posing, in typical Ethiopian fashion, at a photo shop in Aletta Wondo with his singing companion, Estifanos Negash. Both young boys were compeers with our three sons. Tesfaye and Estifanos, at this young age, were beginning to sing "specials" in the Amharic church service in the Aletta Wondo local congregation about 1970. Tesfaye recalls that their voices blended in an amazing way at that stage of their lives (Tesfaye Gabbiso, Interview, January 9, 2015 in Hawassa, Ethiopia).

Tesfaye singing at the International Conference on the History of SIM in Africa, July 12, 2013. He was accompanied on the keyboard by Henoch Abaye (photo: LWB).

Tesfaye and family at their home in Hawassa, Ethiopia c.2000 (photo: LWB)

Choir with young girl drumming in Tesfaye's boyhood church in Sidama region (photo: LWB)

Appendix B

Song Writers' Workshop

Song Writers' Workshop at Wolaitta Evangelical Seminary in Soddo, Ethiopia, held from January 20–22, 2015. These young people are all presently singers and composers active in their local church music ministries.

I WAS PRIVILEGED TO lead a Song Writers' Workshop with Eyob Denio in Wollaita, Soddo, in January 2015. Twenty young singer/musicians from local Wolaitta Soddo churches were called to the Workshop, one representative from each of twenty-one local churches. They were all young adults who compose their own songs and have mucis responsibilities in the local churches. The leadership of the seminar was in the hands of the local theological seminary director, Eyob Denio, who is also a musician and has written a book in Amharic on *Yemezmurïna yemezemïran hïywet* ("Song and the Singer's Life"). We shared the teaching sessions together. He taught from his book, based on scriptural principles, using the traditional Ethiopian didactic method. I concentrated on introducing creative activities and ideas to challenge the participants in new ways of seeing their own songs and encouraging more deliberate thought and action in the singing life of their local churches. None of these young adults has had formal musical training, but history proves that they have the creative drive and ability to produce worthy indigenous songs for their churches and life situations. They mainly need encouragement and some helpful direction.

There were three dynamics of the workshop that lifted the workshop to a level beyond an ordinary atmosphere. The first was in the beginning session of the seminar where we sat in a circle, in silence, and we each one were invited to sing a song we had ourselves created sometime in the past (This was an exercise patterned after an experiment of Heifetz as found in Parks, 102ff). Their singing was unaccompanied, in random order. They could sing in whatever language they wished. Everyone gladly and skillfully participated, most in Wolaittinya (mother tongue) and several in Amharic (official language). I was the only one who sang in English. What holy moments transpired as we listened to each other's composition and heart language in a very reverent atmosphere.

The second dynamic was the availability of the Tesfaye songbook for each person. Somehow the fact that they saw his songs in print (both Amharic and English) made an impact, something entirely new to them - something to be treasured. Thirdly, on the second day, I told them I had a story to tell. My narrative began with how Tesfaye became intertwined in our lives as a lad of about twelve. I think they were astounded to consider the simple fact that he was once a boy, once younger than them when he began to sing. We took the opportunity to ask where songs come from. What is the human voice that sings? What inspires the lyrics? What is the imagination, the creative spirit in a human being? Where does the song originate? These were questions they had never thought about, and again, all these dynamics really added what might be considered a "holy glow" to the whole workshop.

The following are some of the main points, issuing from the workshop, which may be considered into future trainings, and which may be thoughtfully developed with singers.

1. We should know and appreciate the history of spiritual song in our churches and make use of this rich heritage. For example, the antiphonal style can still be used with great profit even in our large urban settings. This was illustrated in Addis Ababa at a recent city-wide Christmas program held at the Stadium when cyclical call and response was used. For example, where there are no songbooks, the congregation can sing the chorus (which they usually know) and a leader can read the stanzas in between so that the people hear the full text of a song. The group of singers in Soddo listened attentively to their own song history stretching back as far as St. Yared in the 6th century and moving into the present day when older mission-translated Swedish/western songs are sometimes incorporated in adaptive ways in the newer songs. (Dawit Getachew, at Mekane Yesus Jazz School of Music, has done some of this adaptive mixing, just as it is happening in our western praise song with older hymn lines being reinstated in creative ways.)

2. We must foster creativity and planning of our church music that involves the discipline of small groups working together to create and plan songs for worship. The keyboard and instruments tend to control the worship, whereas we should be concentrating on the actual song of the people. Perhaps the entrenched concepts of the "soloist" and "choir" need to be lessened in prominence to allow the gathered congregation to be more involved in creating and delivering song. (An example was the Soddo Kera Church ladies' choir that sang for a full thirty-five minutes during the service while the congregation sat listening.) "Let the people sing" should be the main thrust of the music ministry. Let them join in with a choir or solo at certain times. The development of worship teams, which are largely replacing choirs, is helping in this area. But whether choirs or worship teams, it is important that the church leadership insist that the people are enabled to sing.

3. We should foster the young singers and enfold them into groups that are mentored and taught the principles which will dispel the confusion which reigns today. We need to concentrate on encouragement of Word and Prayer, as Tesfaye emphasizes, in the lives of our young singers. That is a church responsibility to build them up in their most holy faith. The singing group in the church should be discipled and taught on a regular basis, either among themselves or by others in church leadership. The solo and choir concepts are worthy and do bless the congregation, but we need to see the value in other forms of song and in concentrating on helping the congregation to participate meaningfully in the song. That takes effort and planning.

4. We do not have to think "solo" or "choir" all the time. At the workshop, small groups prepared worship programs and actually wrote songs in small groups on a chosen theme. One group geared it to children on the subject of prayer. Some of the songs were acted out very dramatically. This was all new and very creative for them, and they were delighted with the results. We broke through a rigid style in the workshop, and they found it to be very constructive.

5. We experienced just a taste of what it is like to assess song-content. We considered how to collect a list of songs that the entire church sings over a period of several weeks and study the content of what one local church is actually singing about, whether in the kitchen or the choir, in the elders' meeting or the kid's club.

6. We used the Tesfaye book in various ways, to choose personal favorites and to test the value of singing songs on a certain topic. A book can help. One singer, Moges Berassa has suggested that a national church committee should produce a new songbook. The Mekane Yesus churches and Seventh Day Adventists, for example, do utilize their songbook tradition, but the other evangelical churches might benefit from something new that includes the best of today's songs.

7. The only instrument in the room was one guitar, used occasionally. We sang acapella for three days. A keyboard was not controlling the situation. They learned that it is possible to sing beautifully without instruments, that the flow can be much more easily directed. The electronic age (not only in Ethiopia, mind you) militates against the human voice, the ability to improvise or add flexible comments.

The actual singing of the people is secondary to the control of the instruments.

8. We need workshops where not only teaching is given, but small groups gather at the local level, learn and work together, creating drama and singing, acting, and speaking to each other on a variety of themes that they themselves have determined will bless their local churches and situations. At the end of the three-day workshop, the participants' main request was that more such instruction and encouragement could be made available more frequently in their local areas. The workshop closed with prayers and the singing of Tesfaye Gabbiso's "Greater Things Than This" (Song VII-12).

Appendix C

Songs of Tesfaye Gabbiso

as found in
Amharic-English Diglot publication
The Songs of Tesfaye Gabbiso

(Cassettes #1 to #7)

Translation by Haile Jenai
Compiled by Lila Balisky

Published and printed by SIM Press, Addis Ababa, Ethiopia
First Printing December 2011
Revised edition, May 2012

(English translation only included in this appendix)

Tesfaye Gabbiso Songbook

Table of Contents

(Songs composed in prison are followed by an asterisk*)

His Mercy Is Everlasting IV-10
What Is Heavy and Beyond Your Ability? IV-11
After Tasting Your Power IV-12
To Be in Need, To Have Plenty IV-13
I Live by Faith IV-14
Keeping That Grace in My Life for Me IV-15
The One Who Died for Us IV-16

Cassette V

Why Did You Sell Your Birthright? V-1*
You Who Fall Asleep V-2*
Oh, You Street Man V-3
When Will I Hear Your Voice? V-4*
It's Wonderful to Be at Your Feet V-5
Oh, Lord, Cause Us to Grow in Truth V-6
But I Know One Thing V-7
Jesus of Nazareth V-8
Oh, My Soul, He is the Lord; Worship Him V-9
Other Than Their God V-10*
When God Assists V-11*
All Those Who Wish to Live V-12*
Rise Up, Rise Up V-13
There's No One Who Can Challenge You V-14*
Before My Soul Returns to Her God V-15*
The Lord's Prayer V-16

Cassette VI

Oh, God of My Heart VI-1*
If His Hand Was not Stretched Out VI-2*
Let Not the Wise Be Proud in His Wisdom VI-3*
A New Song VI-4
According to the Mercy I've Received VI-5
Oh, Lord, Bless Us with a Blessing VI-6*
Winners Through Faith VI-7*
My God, My God VI-8
When the Pot Breaks VI-9
That They Serve Him VI-10
To Do Your Will VI-11*

CASSETTE 1

Song I-1: Dear Father

CHORUS:
Dear Father, break my heart, too,
So that the self may be crushed and grace may abound to me.
Cancel out my pride; give me meekness.

1. Seeing that they are humiliated, bless them,
making the children of Your house humble with pride destroyed and a
meek heart;
I saw them simply shedding their tears.

2. I'm always moaning, seeking that meekness.
I'm crying a lot, day and night.
For how long will my life stay dry like this?
I'm living, Lord, with the lushness of my life dried up.

3. Before my deep desire for brokenness declines,
Why don't You rend the heavens open and come down?
Consider my wish; please break me.
Teach me humbleness and obedience.

4. I will then know for sure who I am.
I will see clearly when my internal eyes get bright.
I will proclaim Your name with great boldness.
I will glorify You with full blessings.

SONG I-2: YOU WHO ARE IN THE HIGH PLACE

CHORUS:
You, Who are in the high place, in heaven,
There is nothing You cannot do;
You are omnipotent.
You who search the heart and kidneys,
O Lord,
Cleanse and rearrange our inner being.

1. Rejecting your decree and despising Your word
We always listen to Your Spirit rebuking us.
Being carnal (only flesh), we are engulfed in rebellion
We are completely unable to examine ourselves.

2. Like in former times when You sent us,
Equipping us with Your armor,
Giving us power upon power, covering us with charisma (grace),
We went out to the battlefield. You gave us victory.
But today woe unto us; the enemy has laughed at us.

3. If we go out to fight thinking it would be as before,
If we throw out the net to catch in quantity,
Where will the catch come from?
It will only be useless labor.
We are confused by this empty labor.

4. Now we have understood—we have sinned.
We have caused You to weep with a few darts of sinful pride,
Because of our accursedness, Your look has become heavy against us.
We ask You, "O Lord, reconcile us, forgive us."

SONG I-3: BEFORE SIN SENDS AND STRENGTHENS ITS ROOTS

CHORUS:
Before sin sends and strengthens its roots,
Before it has a chance to grow or death is born in me,
Stir me up in time to repent.

1. A cloak of theft, gold or silver,
Won't remain buried under my tent
While Your children strive to keep Your word
And bitterly cry, prostrate, due to hidden sin.

2. While embracing sin, if I call You,
"O Lord";
If I sing You a song while I am not made right inside,
Or if I preach without knowing my defect,
What fruit will there be? It is running in vain.

3. O Lord, I have none but You who is close to me,
Who deeply knows my weakness, my strength.
So examine me and tell me my error.
Let me repent, humbling myself.

SONG I-4: SEEING MY TEARS, LORD

CHORUS:
Seeing my tears, Lord,
Hearing my cry, Lord,
Give me my desire.
And I will praise You, Jesus.

1. Wishing one thing, I am patiently waiting on You.
If it is Your will, look at me with Your eyes.
Stretch out that blessed hand of Yours.

2. Putting my hope on You, strengthening myself in Your word,
I am waiting the answer, while in a trance,
Depending on Your faithfulness.

3. All the good gifts and perfect blessings –
They come down from the Father of light, above.
They pour down from Your throne.

4. May my bitterness and my thorniness be finished.
May my wreckage be stopped and may I be built by Your grace.
O Lord, just take away my wretchedness.

Song I-5: God Who Searches the Stray

CHORUS:
God who searches the stray,
Mount of mercy,
You who weep for the lost
Call back the one who went
From life unto death,
From rest into depression.
Please return him, Lord,
Back to the barn of your flocks.

1. Fearing to live in the likeness of his Lord and to struggle,
Forgetting the one who gave him promise and hope,
That person, who was the child of death
And who was delivered from destruction
Denied the one who delivered him from destruction and the one who
was crucified for him. That was Jesus his Savior, whom he'd denied.

2. The Lord, that famous hero, who fought and captured
That warrior who decisively stood to the enemy,
Standing at the other end,
Burning with jealousy,
Spreading his net before,
He captured my brother.

3. Inside his God's temple
Confidently roaring
As he proclaims the fame of Judah's lion.
A strange thing took him away by nagging
Shaving off his grace and honor
With great distress.

4. Oppressing in everything
Challenging his strength,
Stealing his health from him
Numbing him by disease,
That whirlwind of denial (atheism)

Blowing on his life –
It cut him off the vine
So that he won't bear any fruit.

Song I-6: Come Back, Come Back

CHORUS:
Come back, come back, come back,
Oh, My child.
Come back, come back, come back,
Oh, My child.

1. Seeing you hopeless
Sunk in depression and lost
I had saved you from that pain.
You felt happy by getting relief
But then what made you a wanderer today?

2. When you walked putting your trust in Me,
In tears and prayers your strength got restored.
But where is that grace and beauty now?
Come, come, be My friend while My grace is present.

3. You preached the gospel of love to others
You felt their burden and wept for the lost;
By your testimony you brought them to life
Oh, I am sorry but you have gone astray.

4. Being homesick for My house,
If you would come back to Me
Asking for pardon, if you would come to Me,
My hand of mercy is stretched out
And My eyes are shedding tears of love.

Song I-7: My Infancy Is Not Yet Over

CHORUS:
My infancy is not yet over;
I am still an infant.
Feed me Your word, Lord,
And make me a full-grown man.

1. Running in hypocrisy,
Getting diverted from Your truth,
Being pushed by my emotions,

Lacking the fullness of Your word,
Lest I perish, attacked by the enemy.

2. My youth exposes me
And misery withers me:
The whirlwind tosses me around,
The foundation of sand is sinking me.
Lest it knocks me down, help me.

3. Ceasing from drinking only milk
And also gnawing at bones;
And ceasing to think like a child,
Replaced by adulthood;
I would like to see my life developed.

Song I-8: In Season and Out of Season

CHORUS:
In season and out of season, standing strong in Your name,
I long to see Your face
After completing my race.
So may it be Your will, my dear Father,
Cause me to reach home in peace and health.

1. Bruising my enemy's head,
Snatching me out of his jaws,
Shedding Your holy blood,
Giving life to Your dead child -
I experienced the great salvation
And now I want to be strong.

2. When I was restless, You gave me advice.
When I was sad, You comforted me.
Even though I wounded You, You loved me.
And You have always been patient with me.
You tolerated me until this day,
Your holy name sustains me.

3. Always and at all places
Let me be like You and fear You.
Make me different from the world

Let them see You through me.
Let me crucify my body for the world;
Let me travel following You.

4. My life being loose because of fatigue
And my walk being spoiled,
Lest Your name be insulted,
I beseech You, think about Your child.
Until You come for me in glory,
May I live honoring You.

5. In height and depth, in sorrow and in happiness,
Without being confused,
But in calmness,
Not being defeated by temptations,
May I be steadfast and diligent in this world;
Let me see Your face in glory.

Song I-9: I Am Simply Standing

CHORUS:
I am simply standing;
I am leaving the battle to You.
I look by faith unto You;
O Lord, I am waiting, watching for Your victory.

1. On this earth I am facing a great battle;
I'll keep quiet; You fight for me.
I have seen the successful fight of those who Extol You.
And I have learned that from their Triumphant song.

2. Thinking the battle was mine and saying "I will win"
When I was fighting with my flesh, I was Faint and weary.
I am about to be defeated, Jesus, my Lord.
Oh, please come quickly, don't let my Troubles increase.

3. Chariots of fire, that divine army
The sound of thunder that panics my enemies
Let Him come and fight for me, for I have no strength;
Now I know that the battle is not mine.

SONG I-10: I WILL CALL ON GOD

CHORUS:
I will call on God Who deserves praise.
And I will be saved from my enemies.
I will call on God Who deserves praise.

1. When the flood of cruelty makes me scared,
And when the agony of hell encircles me,
When he asks me where my God is,
When my enemy scoffs at me,
When he scares me saying "Just wait,"
I will call on the name of the Lord.
And I will be saved from my enemy.

2. The name of the Lord Jesus for me
Is a strong wall.
Until this day whoever called on Him
Has not been embarrassed.
Because the One who lives in the cherubim
Gave me full hope,
I will in faith call upon His name,
And I will be saved from my enemy.

3. Whenever I am troubled
I call upon God.
Crying bitterly and brokenly in tears
I told Him the problems of my heart
Then He descended in vengeance;
He came thundering down from heaven.
He disturbed them with his lightening.
He dispersed them with His arrows.

4. He did not put me into the clamp of their teeth.
He always saved me from the trap which was set for me.
He protected me from Satan
Who would snatch away my freedom.
Praise be to His name, Hallelujah.
May I live in His bosom, the secret place.

Song I-11: God Is Mighty

CHORUS:
God is mighty.
He is mighty in battle, too.
By whom was He ever defeated?

1. Protecting His people, He fights;
He is not fearful of the enemies boasting.
He is the One, our God, Who takes revenge.
He defeats but never has been defeated. (2x)

2. The victorious in faith, without any regret
Believing in the Lord, without feeling ashamed of Him,
Wearing chains for His hope,
He gave away his life unreservedly. (2x)

3. You, too, may win in His power.
Being tested and purified in/by the furnace,
You will be fit for His kingdom.
May the Lord help you. (2x)

4. The one who fought and defeated,
Who loosened his enemy's tendon
Who strikes a hard hit,
The omnipotent, victorious Lord. (2x)

Song I-12: My Unshakable Foundation

CHORUS:
My unshakable foundation,
Lord Jesus, my protection,
Healer of my pains, my Savior.

1. That valley, the place where I was sad –
Jesus, You did not leave me there lest I wander.
You are my life, my joy and my protection,
Jesus, Your love is my shield.

2. When the world's storm tends to beat me
The Lord did not let me go out of His hand.

The Lord loves His children
And, holding them in His bosom, He will watch them.

3. How can I estimate the amount of Your suffering?
And how can I understand the extent of Your favor?
May I never forget Your coming for me
The healer of my sickness and my Savior.

SONG I-13: I WILL STRUGGLE

CHORUS:
I will struggle, I will struggle
I will struggle until the end.
I believe the God of Israel
Will give me victory.

1. Strengthening my power
And my arms strengthened,
I will travel along happily
Not depressed, but encouraged.

2. Putting on my feet
The gospel of peace
Trusting in His shelter
And covered by His blood.

3. I will put on the breastplate
Which arrows cannot penetrate.
I will not let my life be intimidated;
I will stand alert.

4. If the saints travel
Making faith their shield
If their lives go well
And they gain the victory.

5. If defeat and triumph
Is gained by being patient,

Over the rule of this world
And over the evil army.

6. All that which has been
Prepared for me by Jesus my Lord
I will receive—and my crown,
After I fight well.

Song I-14: I Refuse, I Refrain

CHORUS:
I refuse, I refrain.
I will not worship the image.
I will not kneel down before a man-made thing.
From the burning anger of Nebuchadnezzar,
My Lord, whom I serve, will certainly deliver me.

1. A friend of the dead
A sinner was I.
Believing the Lord, I was saved from loss.
Though I'm forced to deny now
This life of mine,
I will not deny my Jesus
And worship an idol.

2. I can see the furnace. I can feel the heat.
I'll not hate it because of fear;
It will purge and cleanse me;
It will make me fit for His heavenly kingdom;
It would never bring hurt to me as people might think.

3. Those who were in the fire,
Even the smoke hasn't affected them.
But to those who tied them up and cast them into the fire
The flame of the fire consumed them.
Since I have such a powerful Lord
Let the fire burn seven times hotter.
What does it matter to me?

CASSETTE 2

SONG II-1: TELL THE GOOD TIDINGS

CHORUS:
Tell the good tidings to those who thirst for life.
If they gratefully accept such a life, Jesus saves.
He is preached even this day.
A satisfying fountain is flowing for all.

1. If brothers in fellowship would sit closer
Having the Word of Grace useful for edification;
If they would open their mouths in a Christian language,
What a joy it would be when gossip would be absent.

2. Bearing the fruits of the Spirit in his life
The ambassador of God is identified.
If he reflects the Lord till the day of his death,
From glory to glory shall his face be changed.

3. To unload his burden at the foot of the cross
When a Christian kneels down with a broken heart
Telling his secrets to the Lord in tears –
He will rise comforted, filled with faith.

4. Strengthening fellowship with God
When life is made straight by successful relationships,
Life with Jesus is preferred to the world;
It has a flavor, is tasty; it is worth choosing.

Song II-2: Think About It Today

CHORUS:
Think about it today; don't wait till tomorrow.
Do not let your years go by in deceiving yourself.
Jesus is life. You won't find someone else.
Believing, be saved and sealed forevermore.

1. Before the time of grace and mercy is over
The light having disappeared, the day of invitation darkened,
Before heaven lets loose, the earth will tremble,
Before the Lord appears with the flame of fire...

2. "Let's rejoice together, just wait a moment"
The world says to you deceivingly.
The joy replaced by distress and sorrow,
Don't enter into Sheol unexpectedly.

3. God's way for the natural man
Is sheer foolishness. He can't understand it.
When the spirit is released from the natural body,
You'll understand then. His way is wisdom.

4. While you hesitate to choose,
Standing at a fork in the road,
While you change roads with no satisfaction,
Before death casts its shadow and takes you blindfolded,
Accept the Lord for He is the One who will satisfy you.

Song II-3: Lord Jesus, Do Not Leave Me

CHORUS:
Lord Jesus, do not leave me.
Oh, my God, do not let me go.
While I am tied down in distress,
Do not ignore me; come, pull me out.

1. Sin was too much with me and my strength was weakened.
I could not walk and my way was darkened.
My enemy, knowing, dreamed of breaking me.

2. Causing You to be sad, stamping on Your blood
And being an obstacle to Your children,
I am perplexed, I am confused.

3. I lost a desire to read Your word
And I felt drowsy to pray.
I am very exhausted; I am wretched.

4. My life being sealed by Your Holy Spirit,
My presence being beneficial among Your children -
Qualify me to meet You after all is completed.

5. Falling and dying is caused by small things;
Thus, I have realized this; keep me from falling
Lest the storm throw me down and the flood carries me away.

SONG II-4: I WAS NOT LIKE THIS

CHORUS:
I was not like this but today I am;
I am desiring the previous better life.

1. I have carried Your name as a simple thing
And yet I am called a Christian.
But if inside me were to be examined,
This isn't true.
The fruit of the Spirit is not in me at all.

2. I haven't become a true atheist;
Nor am I strong as a Christian.
In fact, being lukewarm, I am in a dilemma.
But today, in repentance, I prostrate myself.

3. The love I had for the Christians and You
When I served You, glorifying Your name;
The steadfastness of prayer I had –
All declined and I'm trembling in weakness.

4. Instead of climbing up, down I went.
I am very near to the gate of death;
Now I am rebuked by Your word.
I have appealed to You to raise me up again.

SONG II-5: Hanging on the Cross

CHORUS:
Hanging on the cross, by my distress He was distressed.
He was afflicted like that for his wretched son;
Compelled by His love, He shed his blood.
Humiliated on behalf of me, He saved my life. (2x)

1. Lord of hosts, my powerful Savior,
When judgment and damnation awaited me,
When I was crying in sin, living bound,
He untied me from my binding and led me to my country. (2x)

2. Completely useless and dull was I,
One who knew not his Savior, awaiting judgment,
A captive of Satan and pressed by his load;
I was such a person before the Lord found me. (2x)

3. Let fear, doubt, evil and uncleanness,
Jealousy and envy be eliminated from now on.
Mischief, lies, gossip, evil wishes –
Let them be destroyed by the rock of Zion.
(2x)

4. Let them altogether fall, be ground down, changed to powder.
The yoke is broken; I want no more slavery.
My debt being paid, freedom is proclaimed.
Death does not frighten me. Life is given to me. (2x)

Song II-6: I Was Created in God's Likeness

1. I was created in God's likeness.
To do good in His presence, but
When I was living in sin, it almost made me useless.
Losing my dignity, I forgot my God
And I became like the animals that perish.

2. Though I didn't see the Lord,
From above He came to find me.
He snatched and pulled me out from uncleanness.
Wretched He was in the world, yet He took my burden.
He died for me, wiped away my countless errors.

3. He is my Jesus, my Savior, my Lord, my God.
For His kindness may I kneel and praise Him.
His mercy is plenteous, His salvation wonderful.
The love of God has no end.

4. While I was in the shadow of death in absolute darkness,
Jesus my light came.
He saved me for He is merciful.
I was given to judgment, engaged to Sheol.
While I was naturally a child of wrath
He took my faults, Jesus my help. (Repeat).

Song II-7: The One Who Saw Me Tied Up

CHORUS:
The One who saw me tied up against my will,
The One who gave me freedom, You my friend and my hope.
Who is the One that did this favor except You?
What else can I say except, "Praise my Lord!"

1. When I was strong and untouched
When I was tied in the street, at the doorway,
I was a colt which didn't have freedom.
Before I knew You, You knew me and untied me.

2. I ran for your honor with this strength of mine.
I stamped on snakes and scorpions in Your name.
Hearing of my prize, the enemy advanced on me,
But when he saw You over me, he was put to shame.

3. You released me from prison to dwell in me,
To offer this great opportunity to the poor.
Well, I, yes, who am I?
Ought I to be chosen for this by You?

4. What though they shout Hosanna in the highest,
What though they spread out their clothes and leaves,
Though my feet stamp on them, You are over me;
Glory is yours. Live forever glorified.
The untied colt has become an object of honor.
Giving it freedom, the Lord is honored by it.
Leave alone the untied; honor the One who untied him.
Say Hosanna to Him and declare His reign.

Song II-8: Sing for Our God

CHORUS:
Sing for our God.
Sing, sing for our King
For God is the King of all the earth;
Sing to Him with understanding.

We will sing, we will sing
In season and out of season.
The whole of our life, we will glorify the Lord (2x)
We will glorify the Lord. (2x)

Song II-9: Be Praised, My Lord

CHORUS:
Be praised, my Lord.
Honor and fame be to Your name. (4x)

1. That I may stay warm without getting weak,
You girded me with Your strength from above, my Savior.
Though the strong stormy rain overflowed in flood,
All the enemies are defeated in Your name.

2. Shelter of my life, my honor, my shield,
My strength will be renewed, You are my joy.
When the storm rises attempting to drown me,
I can clearly see my helper's arrival.

3. The extent of God's kindness cannot be estimated.
Though "Nineveh" does sin frequently.
God, wanting to advise them,
He ordered Jonah to talk to them.

Song II-10: Let Me Thank You Today

CHORUS:
Let me thank You today, my Lord,
For Your unspeakable gift,
For Your countless favors;
You are faithful truly.
May Your great name be praised and glorified forever.

1. Holding all my breath and my ways in Your hand,
Taking care of me like the pupils of Your own eyes,
You have hidden and veiled me from that which could harm me.
What can I pay You except to say thank you?

2. When I am hit by sorrow and am sometimes sad,
When I am oppressed and depression is added on top of it,
Lord of comfort, whoever came just in time for me but You
To share my burden and to encourage me?

3. I know myself that I was so ugly;
I was poor, aimless, and restless in sin.
But You took me as I was, and I am
Made somebody because of You.
I have no words to explain Your numerous kind deeds.

4. Gentiles don't know you, but my soul does.
It daily longs for Your face of love.
And I cannot live without Your fatherhood.
All imitators, deceivers, can't separate my soul from you.

Song II-11: My Lord Was Concerned About Me

CHORUS:
My Lord was concerned about me
And my sin worried Him.
Being silent, like a lamb,
When false witness was given against Him and was biased,
He paid my debt, crucified to death.

1. Lord Jesus, my Lord, my ransom,
When my wretchedness was great,
He was dishonored for me;
He was slaughtered on my behalf. (2x)

2. He is not a hypocrite as we are;
Custom never touched Him;
What was seen at Golgotha
Was truly love. (2x)

3. All who accompanied Him fled
Giving Him up to the swords and clubs.
He perspired that night.
Moaning, He rescued my soul. (2x)

4. The skin of His back peeled off by whipping,
Expressing His love in pain,
Paying His pure blood for me,
He spent the day drying up on Golgotha. (2x)

5. His love, submerging into my life,
Performing the work of salvation,
Changed my filthiness.
I have seen a beautiful life. (2x)

SONG II-12: HE WHO HAS ALL POWER

CHORUS:
He who has all power in heaven and earth
The One who calls, "Come to the Lord,"
Who cannot be changed but who causes change,
The Alpha and Omega is the Lord Jesus.

1. God is a spirit and cannot be perceived by flesh.
He is so great and cannot be estimated by men.
Today, like before, He strengthens His arms in power.
Liked or disliked, Jesus will reign.

2. He draws near when called by those trusting His name.
He increases strength to the life that is weak.
He quietens the storm and gives peace.
He quenches thirst from His springs and turns the desert green.

3. If we could realize it, by the power of the Holy Spirit indeed,
His unseen nature and eternal power
Is revealed beautifully from the very beginning of His creation.
And Jesus lives, making known His existence.

4. The God of miracles, when was His hand ever shortened?
Man, thinking he knew, did a lot of searching.
Loving sin, and living for judgment,
Man folded his hands and said, "The Lord doesn't exist."

SONG II-13: DO NOT DOUBT JESUS

CHORUS:
Don't doubt Jesus as a human being.
He does not know lying, so keep your promise.
He won't forsake you in time of trouble.
Believing with your mouth, don't deny Him in your heart.

1. He will deliver you from the enemy's arrow and sword.
He also will protect you from death in time of famine.
He will make His name honored, and the matter He knows well.
Because he is not an infant, He fulfils what He says.

2. For His faithfulness, don't set limits.
Don't let your doubtful soul hold back in being firm.
The everlasting God does not lie.
What He has promised you He never will deny.

3. As long as you are with Him, He is with you.
Lest He would completely leave you, don't you leave Him.
Stop for a while; think about the days you have wastefully spent.
Even today, believe and call on the One who saved you.

4. As you have called on His name,
How many things have you escaped from?
From how many dangers, how many times have you been saved?
The Lord will be disappointed when His favor is forgotten.
But if you believe in His word, all will be possible to you.

SONG II-14: THE RULE AND CONTROLLER OF NATURE

CHORUS:
Compared to the one who confronts me in the world,
The One Who is in me is much greater.
The ruler and controller of nature,
The Lord Jesus is with me.

1. If my enemies increase in the battlefield,
If I tremble in fear with melted strength,
When I cry, "Woe unto me, Lord, I am lost"
Jesus, my shield, passes in front of me.

2. If my enemy comes like a colony of bees
I will not go out, leaving my fort.
In the name of God I shall win.
I shall see Goliath falling with my own eyes.

3. Firm and strong, warrior of God.
He is one for a thousand, the patriot of faith
Sprinkling his blood at the hands of the sinner,
He multiplies his fruit, trusting in his God.

4. My enemy sees that I have a helper.
He will not continue boasting.
I shall also drink the cup of the cross.
I shall cross over and victory will be proclaimed.

Song II-15: I Saw

CHORUS:
I saw, I saw, I saw
I saw, over across the way,
Those who died believing.
I coveted to be like them.

1. I saw Abraham, the friend of God
Who prepares the sword
To sacrifice Isaac.
He keeps his word, a nobleman.
He is decisive about his thoughts.
He is a patriot of faith.
He does not have a hidden idol
Which separates him from his God,
Or which, in time of crisis
Snatches his faith.

2. I saw the apostles,
The soldiers of love, the enemies of sin,
The leaders of faith.
By their united prayers they shook the earth,
In victory, in the Gospel light
They flooded the world.
They had permission from
The Lord of Lords.
Authorities could never stop them with threats.
3. I saw the martyrs such as Stephen.
They believed in Jesus.
The world hated them.
The blood-thirsty
Gave them hardship.

Their faces shone, and they resisted all hardship
While they interceded for the world
Just as their Master.
Alas. The way they died—makes one to covet it.

4. I saw the backsliders entering into the darkness.
They said that neither hell, Satan or the Lord exist.
They scorned at His name.
They scoffed at His blood.
They met death with those who said He didn't exist.
My spirit saw them all
Making noises together.
They were tossing and turning painfully
In the world of the dead.

5. Therefore, my Lord, control my being
That I not forsake my covenant, lest I purchase death.
When the light becomes dim
And when the fog surrounds me,
You lead me and help me to get to the top.
May all that is written be for a lesson.
I'll fight vigorously.
You help me to be victorious.
May all that is written be for a lesson.
I'll fight the good fight;
You help me to be victorious.

CASSETTE 3

Song III-1: I Am the Mountain

CHORUS:
I am the mountain that great stumbling block,
The cause of wretchedness and weakness of Your people.
Oh, how bitter is the cup of my pride
O Lord, make me humble before its fruit kills me.

1. The voice of the wilderness, the word of the spokesman says,
Prepare and sweep the road.
Let the hill be made low.
All human beings shall see God.

2. The Lord greatly opposes the proud
But to the humble He gives His grace.
For formality, I am a servant but I lack Your grace.
My prestige shows up but Yours is hidden.

3. Oh, what's the best thing for me?
O Lord, come quickly.
People could not see You through me.
Break the top mountain of my heart.
Kill the small seed to multiply the fruit.

Song III-2: My Brokenness Seems Non-repairable

CHORUS:
My brokenness seems non-repairable,
But my Savior, what is difficult for You?
Since Your mercy is available, what's the use of murmuring?
Oh, it's much better for me to fall into Your hands.

1. I have no feet to stand in Your presence
Nor do I have eyes with which to see You.
O God, the One who called me, look at my shame,
Pull me out of the marsh by Your mercy.

2. What's hidden from You, O Lord?
What remains hidden and not made plain?
You are the examiner of my heart,
Capitalize "K'nower of my interior,
Forgive my scandal, the keeper of my soul.

3. Though You are gracious, You are not to be scorned.
I will not give an excuse to cover up my sin.
With all my transgression, I submit myself to You.
Pardon me and accept me.
I have violated Your word.

4. Even though today shame covers me
And though it is hard for me to see Your face,
I quietly and hopefully wait for Your word;
I believe You can renew me with victory.

Song III-3: Jesus, Cure of My Soul

CHORUS:
Jesus, Jesus, cure of my soul, the king of peace,
Jesus, Jesus, come, and cure my life.

1. "Call unto Me and I will answer
And I will show you great things."
Because You told me in Your word, I thus am calling.
I am calling Your name that You may cure me.

2. My life pushed around by storms of weakness,
It was badly hit by a hard stick.
The repressed pain, getting an outlet from my heart
And followed by tears, has reached You.

3. You said, "I will not cast you out and I will never leave you."
I have not forgotten what You promised me.
You said, "I am your healer" and You healed me.
Come, and save me today from my wretchedness.

4. Fixer of the broken, repairer of the torn down,
You are my healer, and You wipe my tears away.
You saw my wounds which other people could not see.
Of course, You are the only one Whom I have today.

Song III-4: Oh, My Enemy, If I Fall

CHORUS:
Oh, my enemy, if I fall, I will also rise.
Even if I sit in the dark, God becomes my light.
So, so, don't gloat over me.

1. I am like one who gathers summer fruit at the gleaning of the vineyard.
I stand dry beyond the blessings.
My lamentation of sorrow, my cry of bitterness
I leave before my God so He can see my life.

2. For I have sinned against God,
His anger fell upon me like thunder for my punishment.
I will be patient until He takes me out to the light.
I will wait for Him until He redeems me.

3. The business between God and me
Will be finalized, completed by Jesus, the cornerstone.
So, my enemy, get away! May the Lord rebuke you.
Even now I am His child. Be clear about that in your heart.

4. He loves forgiveness; He is not angry forever.
He disrupts my enemies' wishes and stops their joy-cries.
Tearing off my coarse clothes of disgrace and wearing white garments
I will sing for Him again, leaning on His arm.

Song III-5: Let Me Tell You the Wonderful Story

CHORUS:
Let me tell you the wonderful story of what He's done for me.
You all, please do listen.
Let it be a lesson to you.
Let your hearts trust. Be comforted in the Lord.

1. Jesus, walking before me in my daily life.
Increases His mercy and His miracles also.
My God showed me a great and noble thing
To lead me like this to the country of the righteous.

2. From my left and right, ambushing and ambushing,
Spreading his deceitful and deadly net -
But when the Lord saved me by His compassionate love,
The devil was prepared to attack me, yes, was prepared.

3. Jumping over the fence of my enemy
As he spreads the snare, I continue to escape.
Not by my might but by trusting the Lord,
I'll continue racing, defeating all—defeating all.

4. By the eternal Savior, I narrowly escaped.
I found a better friend than father, mother and relatives.
I will sing to Him in the midst of the unbelievers.
I will give thanks to His honored name—I will give thanks.

Song III-6: Afraid of Criticism

CHORUS:
Afraid of criticism, ashamed of believing,
Deserting his dear God, breaking His promises –
Oh, how many, many, got drowned into the sea?
Lord, reach him quickly if he stretches out his hand and says, "Help me"
in regret.

1. Beginning with the Spirit, he ran and ran
He chose the cross rather than being appointed by the world.
He wasn't appointed to a top-ranking position.
But today his heart melted with rumors
And he began to chat with the enemy.

2. To be belittled is not a curse.
Be assured, it is honorable to be criticized.
By being friends of this present world
Deserting Christ should be completely stopped.

3. For those who dropped off the cross from their shoulders
And for those who say, "We, too, are Christians,"
For those travelers who do not have passports,
Let us pray for these deserters.

4. If his eyes could open and see that he is drowned
If he could repent and begin to have zeal again
Is Your saving hand short at all
When Your prodigal son calls from the deep?

Song III-7: Flesh Is Reviving

CHORUS:
Flesh is reviving and sin is sprouting.
Humility forgotten, the proud eye stared
Throwing love to the cliff to give power to hatred.
People began to sharpen their teeth to bite each other.
But You, dear Lord, pour out Your mercy. (2x)

1. By stretched out arms and by the strong hands of God
He is saved by the Lord from the gates of death and hell.
How can man forget and start to murmur?
He stretches his hands to stone his brother.

2. Leaving his place, hurrying to failure
Putting off humility, getting restless only to die,
Look at that forgetful man breaking his promises?
By the attack that he brought, he froze love.

3. Let me live all my days fearing You –
Lest I lack humility and fail to honor You,
Lest Your hand strike me for my rudeness.
Lest I be ridiculed and covered in shame.

Song III-8: The Season Speeded

CHORUS:
The season speeded, ran and hurried on.
The coming of our Lord has approached.
You people, hurry up and gather the harvest.
Think of the responsibility that has been put on us.

1. The time will soon be fulfilled.
The trumpet is to be blown soon.
The matter is to come to an end soon.
The Lord is to appear soon.

2. When the sky gets heavy and the clouds get dark
When our land labors in pain and when things change
Who bewitched us that we do not observe the times?
Please, let us be awake and let us not sleep.

3. When people get too busy to salute death,
When they get sick in sin because of their departure from God,
When even the wise become fools and deceived by Satan,
Let us rise up and speak; let us struggle for souls.

4. One, not dead himself, who had not denied himself.
The Lord doesn't control him; he is not restrained from sin.
What helps him to testify? His heart is trembling.
He denies and flees when asked to pay the price.

SONG III-9: THAT WANDERER

CHORUS:
That wanderer, deserter, member of ours
Has come again, hurrah, let us rejoice.
That wanderer, deserter, member of ours
Has come again, hurrah, let us rejoice.

1. Because he was saved the angels rejoiced.
And by his service many people were satisfied
When people were edified by him, an obstacle got him
Yes, the one who denied his Savior and fell.

2. People who heard this bad news wept for him.
They prayed from the heart so the Lord might raise him.
By their bitter cry they mediated for him unto God.
God has pitied him and brought him back.

3. He told him the reason for his failure and cautioned him
The Lord wept for him even before his brothers did.
Though he enters the trap ignoring reprimand
The Lord is so kind; He has not been harsh with him.

4. Putting that fierce lion to shame publicly
Crashing his jaw with His strong rod –
Praise God, He has restored him back.
Wailing is changed to joy, hurrah, let's rejoice!

Song III-10: That I May Stay Firmly

CHORUS:
That I may stay firmly where You placed me
That You may be pleased when You come to visit me,
Oh, Lord, multiply Your grace towards me.

1. Making the paradise, my dwelling place, so beautiful
That I may eat my food without any hardship
When talk deceives me while You placed me here
Don't watch me negligently while it is stripping me to nakedness.

2. My heart hastens; my feet incline to run.
My eyes long to see shame.
Crossing the borderland, spending the day with sin,
Eventually, at last my weight was made light.

3. The sprouts on the stony soil which rapidly grew up
When the sun rose, which got dried and burned.
It taught me to bear fruit.
Don't let me down after raising me up, oh, my Lord.

4. That hasty Saul was despised in your sight.
The young David was anointed and became great.
Open my eyes that I may know my place.
Shorten not my life; instead make me grow.

Song III-11: In Patient Quietness

CHORUS:
In patient quietness, in prayerful diligence
Victory comes from the Lord.
In patient quietness, in prayerful diligence,
The answer comes from the Lord.

1. When a hard battle surrounded me
I patiently waited on God.
And He leaned to the side to hear me.
Wiping my tears with His hand, giving me His word, He comforted me.

2. When your soul is naked and completely empty.
After you have sown all you have, you would see yourself.
Think of your past victories; let your hope revive.
If you wait on your knees, you shall certainly be visited.

3. Those who were weak and recovered their strength passed into victory.
Those who lined up, on the right hand of Jesus,
They defeated kings, then knocked the fort down.
They are men of prayer who dispersed the enemies.

Song III-12: You Who Watched Over Us Until Today

CHORUS:
You who watched over us until today,
You who covered us from arrows,
You who broadened our borders,
Come and also wipe our tears away.

1. By Your irreproachable honor
By Your immeasurable strength
You who revealed Your being,
You have become our protection.

2. When we saw the anger of the enemy
When we measured our strength
When in despair we wailed "Oh, dear!"
You, Emmanuel, arrived on time for us.

3. Flattering us to persuade
If he fails to threaten us,
The enemy tried to cluck on us.
You foiled his conspiracy against us.

4. One who lives a straight (non-mixed up) life
Who has learned from God,
Though he gets weak, he will win,
He will make the name of his God
well-known.

Song III-13: Seeing You and You First

CHORUS:
Seeking You and You first
I will put myself last.
I will cross over by faith.
I will see Your face in victory.

1. I have learned from those who went before.
I am waiting for Your promise.
Look at me by Your mercy
Add to me more faith.

2. Clothed in goat skins
Leaning on Your cross,
There are many who wandered
Who left their own honor for You.

3. They called Your name by faith.
They told You everything in prayer.
You heard them from above;
You listened to all the words they said.

4. By faith they dried up the sea
They escaped from the hands of the enemy.
I want to be like them;
I will call, by faith, on Your name.

5. They heard messages from the Spirit
Lord, they saluted You.
I'm asking You, give me faith,
I, too, am begging of You.

Song III-14: Putting on Jesus

CHORUS:
Putting on Jesus, pick up your armor,
Fight a good fight in Him.
Jesus will win. Do not doubt about the victory.

1. The one who bruises has risen against you.
Christian, take care; you are surrounded by the enemy.
Study your surroundings; let not your strength be flimsy.
Fight vigorously; see the rewards you will have; fight your best.

2. It is obvious that one gets wounded in battle.
Even death is your benefit.
Don't surrender to the ruler of darkness.
Be faithful until death. Don't give value to your soul.
Give it over to the faithful Creator.

3. Your enemy the devil is roaring to swallow you.
Don't be scared by his noise.
Your Father is with you; He will snatch you out of the enemy's mouth
And will lock his jaws.
He will show him clearly that He will never leave you.

4. The time of war is now, brother.
Get up and fight him; you will defeat him.
Fight him vigorously; the God of Abraham will be your shield.
After He has brought you to your country,
He will give you a crown.

Song III-15: Let Your Heart Be Firm

CHORUS:
Let your heart be firm; don't be soft, be strong.
Don't be ashamed of the Lord in Whom you trust.

1. Happiness and joy, comfort and blessing
Always a luxurious comfortable life –
It isn't like this; don't expect it all to be easy.
Christianity sometimes has hardships.

2. When the power of darkness casts its shadow,
When the enemy shows his strength very angrily,
When he hits you with a stick and makes you drink vinegar,
Brothers, don't be disappointed on the way of the cross.

3. When you seek an escape, searching for an outlet,
Even when the least hope of light is hindered and lost,
When all men forget you and you are thrown in prison,
Don't think that the Lord of your life will ever forget you.

4. Contest the enemies by the Word of Good News, the Gospel.
Be patient and look at the future,
Fighting for your country for an inheritance that won't pass away,
Let us meet the above overflowing with Your blood.

Song III-16: After Suffering and Languishing

CHORUS:
After suffering and languishing for ages,
The Christian crossed over, passing through the flame.

1. The Father on His throne; the Son on His right hand.
To meet, the One who is pushed aside on earth in glory.
When Christian saw them inviting him out of his agony
He came out of the furnace saying, "It is finished!"

2. With what would those blind Pharisees see?
That the light has penetrated through the difficulty;
The massive difficulties and disturbing shouts of people.
The hero has completed his race without fainting,
Without being overcome.

3. After wandering for some time from country to country,
His appearance was changed.
Tired from hardships, from whips, from clubs, from cruel fists,
Christian passed away and rested from the kicks.

4. Like Jacob they were stained in blood.
To lay down themselves for their promise, the Gospel,
They've lined up waiting for their turns,
They are saying "Jesus, Jesus, Jesus".

CASSETTE 4

Song IV-1: Your Beauty, My Lord

1. Your beauty, my Lord, was burnt by the sun.
From the excess heat, You were lean and marred.
You had no comfort nor cozy situation, Lord.
For Your creation, You were smitten by pain. (2x)

2. As the death cup was near and my healer worried,
His Father's voice was too far to reach;
There he suffered
His belly so hollow, His ribs clearly seen.
By His death struggle, my Lord, my life He redeemed.

3. You climbed the hill by clinging and crawling.
On my behalf, my Lord, You were made to wander.
For You a day of suffering, for me it was a day of healing.
By offering Yourself, patiently, You made it at last.

Song IV-2: You Who Wander

CHORUS:
You who wander, my dear brother,
Listen and let me advise you again.
Come back to the Shepherd and Keeper of your soul.

1. You ran for nothing, your energy wasted, completely exhausted.
By the burden of sin, your soul was worn out, your bones dried up.
You knew not your destination—lost,

You knew not what to do, but wander.
Come to the Lord Jesus; seek advice from the ransom of the world.

2. Months, ages and years of ignorance
Dreaming in vain to get satisfaction apart from Jesus,
There is no one in this world who constructs and strengthens;
What, then, is best for you?
Receive the wonderful Jesus; He will satisfy you.

3. You who couldn't find knowledge, but just wandered;
Oh, victim of the devil who is ruler of darkness,
There is One who descended from heaven
Seeking a share of the spoils.
If you want to hear the herald, He is Emmanuel.

Song IV-3: Retreat from the Rough Road

CHORUS:
Retreat from the rough road.
Don't step on My blood; that won't do you any good.
Let's be friends instead, for My mercy is full.

1. When you were still a baby, I cared for you.
I put your hands in Mine and taught you to walk.
You learned to walk and knew how to run fast.
You were swift then, but now you have given up.

2. You are burnt by the heat and smitten by thirst,
Your oil all dried up and you have become fruitless.
Your spirituality is now departed from you.
Because you are ruled by your flesh all your grace is finished.

3. I am your God since the time in Egypt.
I am the One Who bought you by My blood.
Stop making me sad.
You know that I love mercy; this is My behavior you know.
Cease to be stubborn and be My friend;
You are My child.

4. My mercy has risen; My heart is stirred.
My hand still remains outstretched.
Come, and let Me put My yoke of love on you.
Give Me your shoulder and let Me plough by you.

Song IV-4: The One Who Was About to Be Lost

1. The one who was about to be lost, defiled by sin,
Barely escaping from the world,
Realizing who he was and becoming wise,
He bitterly confessed his wrong doings from the past.
He has come back in repentance heeding the Lord's words.
He bade farewell to Satan, the world, and the flesh. (Repeat last 2 lines)

2. My hypocrisy hid his thirst.
The pressure of his troubles internally suppressed,
He tarried wonderingly, looking for peace.
He then met the Prince of Peace on the way.
Now he's freed, relieved from his problems,
And he's living comfortable with a life renewed. (Repeat last 2 lines)

3. He loves him full-heartedly and is proud of him.
The Lord has anointed him with oil in the presence of his enemies.
He has raised him up from dust and covered him with honor.
Leading him into victory, He brought him thus far.
Like a fattened calf, he jumps up with joy. "Hallelujah" he shouts with
gladness and joy. (Repeat last 2 lines)

4. The stone thrown aside by wise builders
Saying "It is useless for us", they despised and denied it.
But Jesus of Nazareth is the Cornerstone.
He has become for him the foundation of life.
He said, "Since I am saved and became a new creation,
Let my relatives and friends say whatever they like." (Repeat last 2 lines)

Song IV-5: God of Eternity and King of the Ages

CHORUS:
God of eternity and King of the ages
He is All in All, Jesus of Nazareth.
God of eternity and King of the ages
He is All in All, Jesus of Nazareth.

1. Morning by morning Jesus is new.
Even if you rebel, He never gets bored with you.
The word of His cross is healing for life.
For those who trust and come to Him, He is a foundation.

2. He prepares for battle and girds with power.
Those who were positioned at the top, He casts them down.
By His resurrected authority, He directs the war.
He chases His enemies and says,
"Gather the spoil".

3. By an arrow shot, He drilled the fortress
Having faith in His God, He continued the fight.
"On a bloody street, victory is the Lord's."
Thus was this song sung at the dividing line.

Song IV-6: The Hero Who Was Not Attracted by Pharaoh's Riches

1. The hero who was not attracted by Pharaoh's riches -
His strength was not weakened and still was not drained.
He went out to win in anger of battle
Carrying his God's weapon on his back. (2x)

2. The prison fetters and heavy lashes—
They couldn't cool down his warmth of love.
The young strong man threatened to smash and knock.
He has loaded his right hand with his automatic words. (2x)

3. With his heart's eye widely open and staring,
He set his enemies' camp on fire.

The fire of heaven has visited him mightily.
He stamped snakes and scorpions under his feet. (2x)

4. He is strengthened and his muscles are strong.
The love is burning in him; he is encouraged.
He glorified the Lord by the wounds of his back,
He crossed the river of death by faith.
He glorified the Lord by the wounds of his back,
He crossed he river of death by faith. (2x)

Song IV-7: Oh, Glory

CHORUS:
Oh, glory, glory, glory, hallelujah
To the Lion of the Tribe of Judah who is so unique.
Let me praise Him from the bottom of my heart.
For the favor of my Savior to me is great.

1. Before I knew Him, He knew me.
Before I sought Him, He saved me.
With His wonderful love, He loved me.
From the race of destruction, He diverted my soul.
It was Jesus who pulled me out of the fire.

2. In the time of childhood and youth
When the enemy dragged me into slavery,
Had it not been for His grace and the support of His hand,
Where would I be now, had His wings not covered me?

3. When I got wounded by arrows, I was sad and painful.
He became my breastplate in the time of war.
Being thoughtful about His kindness, let me thank my Lord.
There will never be One Who would help me like Him.

SONG IV-8: YOU SHOULD BE PRAISED, LORD OF HOSTS

CHORUS:
You should be praised, Lord of Hosts.
Whoever was found to untie the seal?
You should be praised; honor should be Yours.
You should be glorified and You should be King.

1. The beginning and the end
Christ Jesus, Who is and Who is to come.
Lamb of God Who was slain,
You Who washed away my dirt.

2. You Who broke our shackles
And You Who broke our yokes, too,
You Who announced our freedom in Your blood,
You are at the right hand of Your Father.

3. You will reward us and give us rest.
By Your unspeakable promise, You will fill us with joy.
To relieve us in Zion,
You will come to comfort us.

SONG IV-9: YOU MULTIPLIED YOUR PEOPLE

CHORUS:
You multiplied Your people
You widened the border of the land.
You stretched out Your hands of salvation for us. (2x)

1. Holding up a banner, Your fierce army is on the march.
The army crossed the sea, stamped and crushed scorpions in the desert.
Your people, so few, were increased with You.
Becoming more than the multitudes, they took up their inheritance.

2. In order to multiply, the Lord sowed a mustard seed on the land.
The rascal came and stamped on it so it would not grow.
But he did not succeed;
Instead it escaped the danger, sprouted and continued to grow.

Praise the Lord, its area enlarged and
It has become a shade for the weak and the tired.

3. O, hallelujah, halle, hallelujah.
Victoriously, He lives forever.
Who is like our God in rescuing?
Whoever competes with Him"
Hearing their cry, He anoints the poor and destitute with oil.
In His courtyard, He plants them and nourishes them as palm trees.

4. Repeat all of stanza 3.

Song IV-10: His Mercy Is Everlasting

CHORUS:
His mercy is everlasting; He is kind forever.
To the One Who showed us His saving hands and
Who visits us in His power,
Offer the good aroma of praise to Him.
Worship Him with shouts of joy.

1. By the rivers of Babylon as we sadly sat down,
We thought of Zion and bitterly cried.
But the God of comfort, looking at us from above,
Wiped our tears and fixed our broken hearts.

2. He won't ignore the cry of the poor.
He never would let His chosen be troubled intentionally.
To disperse their enemies, He flashes His thunder.
Their Savior quickly appears majestically from the sky.

3. Those who became famous in their flesh will utterly fall.
Those who faithfully wait upon the Lord,
Sparkling by the fruits of their tears,
Will ascend by His wings, will run, and will be precious as His jewels.

4. The Lord our God is our refuge.
He is our strength; we will never be afraid.
He will keep us from Satan's snare.
He won't give us to the vultures but will take us home,
Carrying us on His wings.

Song IV-11: What Is Heavy and Beyond Your Ability?

CHORUS:
What is heavy and beyond Your ability?
And what is hard to solve?
What problem is so difficult for You?
You are omnipotent.
You are El Shaddai.

1. With two fish and five pieces of bread
In the desert You fed five thousand.
It is not hard for You to do the same even today.
No matter how weak we are, You can bless by Your word.

2. You Who showered the Hebrews with manna,
You Who made the blind to see and the lame to stand on their feet.
It isn't hard for You to do the same even today,
To send the weakened renewed strength.

3. What disease was difficult for You to cure?
What mighty man ever challenged and held You?
Might of the mighty, King of kings,
Crush Your enemy and pour out Your Spirit.

4. The eyes of all are set on You.
You came to rescue the destitute.
Commander of the winds and of the storms,
In times of trouble, You assist the righteous.

SONG IV-12: AFTER TASTING YOUR POWER

1. After tasting Your power and seeing Your arm,
After seeing Your glory being widely spread,
I forgot all this because I looked at the world,
And I was advised to go away parting from You.
But You, my Lord, see and watch me, Your child.
Divert my feet and be quick to help me. (2x)

2. Your love forces me not to separate from You,
Even if I went astray from Your comfortable gates.
Besides misery - Your grace and mercy.
I could not forget Your nostalgia.
Where would I end fleeing from Your presence?
To whom would I go from your Spirit? (2x)

3. I am badly tossed and missed my target.
I have set my eye to the left and right.
Seeing the sinner succeed and prosper,
Without seeing his end, I became jealous of his deeds.
It was baseless, vanity and vacuum,
But my joy is much better than the world's. (2x)

4. My soul, losing its balance, was about to fall.
But it found a support and my enemy got ashamed.
What kind of deception was it and where was I hurt?
I am firm, and Jesus is on my right side.
The Lord has confirmed that He won't leave me.
Oh, enemy, despair, for you cannot make me fall down. (2x)

SONG IV-13: TO BE IN NEED, TO HAVE PLENTY

CHORUS:
To be in need, to have plenty, to be in hunger and to be satisfied,
I have experienced and learned it all.
I can do all things through Christ Who strengthens me.

1. Sinning by my words, misled by my lips and misleading others;
Thinking I was doing right, I was running into destruction.
All men scared me. I became restless, then the Lord found me.
Stopping my madness,
He looked at me in compassion and gave me forgiveness.

2. Like a strong calf jumping on the mount of life,
In blessed bliss I said to Jesus, "Thank You."
Unconsciously and suddenly I was found in a valley.
Being broken and weeping in the dark, I wished for His light.

3. When the heavenly light seems to fade from his face,
Descending from the Mount of Olives shrinks one
And makes the heart to meditate.
The Lord hasn't left me; He is with me in the valley of life.
He's not only the God of mountains;
He also has not given me over to death.

Song IV-14: I Live by Faith

CHORUS:
I live by faith; I know my Lord.
I have clung to my strong Rock.
Not fearing the storm, I'll fight and conquer.
I'll receive my reward of honor from His hand.

1. Be it above the earth or under heaven,
He always watches your coming in and going out.
Whom have you found like Jesus?
Who can be the ransom and assurance for your life?

2. I won't worry about tomorrow though it's covered with fog.
Even though the vine withers because of heat,
The word in my hand is a light for my feet.
Jesus, commander of nature, is alive.

3. When His will is fulfilled, when I see my Lord honored,
When the earth says "Hallelujah" and heaven applauds,
He is my shelter, my clothes and my bread.
My soul is satisfied by His dignity and glory.

Song IV-15: Keeping That Grace in My Life for Me

CHORUS:
Keeping that grace in my life for me,
In time of trouble, waiting on my Lord,
I would desire to reach that stage
By the strength He gives me, by the walk of faith.

1. Furnace of tribulation, fire of purging,
Fire was the measure, coals of testing.
These two were methods used by past warriors,
The owners of victory, wherever they had trodden through.

2. The standard was the fire for the former generations.
They fought for faith on the battlefield.
For non-perishing glory, for a living hope,
They fought and passed away, greatly despised.

3. Their God is honored in a persecuted worship,
In great hardship, in the health of the Gospel.
They were honored and made the Master of their life to be honored.
They went out to meet the One Who had done them the favor.

4. We, too, are called to be like them—
To see the terrible fire exactly as it is.
Therefore, struggle, you patriot of the Gospel.
Compete with Satan, your rival, and victory is ours.

Song IV-16: The One Who Died for Us

CHORUS:
But to the One Who died for us and Who bought us by His blood –
His salvation and His kingship of all creatures
We shall preach, yes, we shall preach.

1. The Jews ask for signs.
The Greeks ask for wisdom.
Missing the Lord, they wander.

2. Though those who do not understand mock Him,
And though they consider it foolishness,
We don't feel ashamed by the Word of the cross.

3. The call of saving grace comes
For sinners to leave the midst of sin,
Even though they do not receive the Gospel.

4. For us, our sign is Jesus.
Our wisdom is Christ.
The King of Peace is our commander.

5. We never proclaim an empty hope
We do not sow in our flesh.
Our Lord is present; we will not be afraid.

6. Our answer to all who ask us is
Our friend of Calvary.
"Jesus is Lord" we proudly preach.

CASSETTE 5

SONG V-1*: WHY DID YOU SELL YOUR BIRTHRIGHT?

CHORUS:
Why did you sell your birthright?
Why did you trade Jesus?
Glory and wealth vanish away.
Choose what does not vanish away.
The Lord is better for you, the One
Who is eternal life. (2x)

1. You ran after what does not satisfy.
You loved what is not worthwhile.
You sold your birthright
For what is not profitable and helpful!

2. Many have fallen away, trapped;
By the love of money were they snatched away.
Wealth deceives.
Even Judas sold his Lord for this.

3. More than a sword slaughters
The jungle of sin has devoured many.
And what has devoured you?
What is it that holds and chokes your soul?

SONG V-2*: YOU WHO FALL ASLEEP

CHORUS:
You who fall asleep. Jesus calls you.
By the heavenly love, He quickens you.
From the hiding place, the grave of the dead,
He orders you to get up and rise.

1. The heavenly light cleared the darkness away.
Hell got vanquished and death defeated.
To those who are pierced by sin, tired and fallen,
The call is echoing to quicken the dead.

2. Where there is no revelation and no hearing,
Where bitterness, regret and crying prevail,
What dropped you down here and how did you come?
Why did you rush away from the place of the living?

3. This is the hour when you should wake up from sleep.
Examine the time and know the age.
Therefore, wake up, rise and walk.
Come back yourself and also bring back those who are lost.

4. Don't lose your courage, for there is a reward.
By the power of the Holy Spirit, rise up again.
Your weak hands and feeble strength
Will again be strengthened and your life will shine.

SONG V-3: OH, YOU STREET MAN

1. Oh, you street man
Standing on every corner,
You see people and they see you. (2x)
The One Who sees you and rewards you openly,
The One Who makes you walk on high places
Haven't you forgotten Him Who raised you up?

2. Those who sit secretly
And listen to their Lord,

Those who bring the Word of life (2x)
Those who are alert and ready to build men up,
And are fit to do good works -
Blessed are those who know how to intercede.

3. The one who is sent of God is the one who is blessed.
The one who preached only His word. (2x)
Who raised you up and who sent you?
You will be asked to reply at the end and
you will be paid according to what you did.

4. Your labor is so great
Which magnified and puffed you up.
The Lord was hidden, not to be seen. (2x)
Thoroughly examine your life.
See how you stopped praying, thus how naked you are.
You hid Jesus but made yourself to be very visible.

5. Listen to Jesus advising you.
He says to you, "Be still and pray."
Lay your flesh under His feet. (2x)
Then the Lord shall be seen on the upper stage
And His light shall be visible to the world.
Life also increases when the seed of wheat dies.

SONG V-4*: WHEN WILL I HEAR YOUR VOICE?

CHORUS:
When will I hear Your voice?
When will my soul be visited and comforted by You?

1. When You came in the dawn and woke me up,
When You opened my ears and spoke to me,
When You led me in a path of understanding,
When by the living spring of waters You quenched my thirst,
My life was green.
My strength was not weakened like this.
You are my Savior: please remember me.

2. When at night I wake up from sleep,
Your name quickly comes out of my mouth,
I'll tell you my sickness.
Let me hear Your voice and I will be healed.
Oh, Lord, listen to my moaning.
My soul is so weak like this.
How could it continue in distress?

3. The appointed time fulfilled,
The time of sadness completed,
Weakness and numbness overcome.
When shall Your power, descending from on high, fill me?
When will I ever be made happy?
When will I be comforted by Your visit?
When will I be strengthened and stand on my feet?

Song V-5: It's Wonderful to Be at Your Feet

CHORUS:
It is wonderful to be at Your feet.
It is good to study Your word.
Oh, Lord, it is a privilege that shall not be lost.

1. We are disturbed by many things.
We are so worried about our existence.
In flesh and soul, how wasteful we are.
Sitting still and hearing from Your mouth,
Just now I have understood how to hear and obey.

2. As You delight when You are listened to
If we offer you the fat of rams from our hands
That never satisfies You as much as our listening.
I talk too much insisting that I only should be heard,
But to never stop talking prevents one from listening.

3. Without being a disciple and never having been taught,
One who appoints himself will be demoted
When he falls down alone without a helper.
The wise one is reprimanded and gains understanding.
He says, "Let me learn first before racing for service."

Song V-6: Oh, Lord, Cause Us to Grow in Truth

CHORUS:
Oh, Lord, cause us to grow in truth and love.
May our futile pride by left behind.
Oh, Lord, cause us to grow in truth and love.

1. Counting the ages of our Christian life,
Becoming proud of our experience,
And by ceasing to learn in humility,
Our growth stopped because of our pride.

2. We are wise in our own views;
We strain out the gnat.
Without being able to cleanse ourselves
Instead we see the filth of someone else.

3. Asking people to see our growth
We are so vainly proud.
Thus we, too, make You sad.
Unknowingly, how many have we hurt?

4. Make us mild as babies
And put pure hearts in us.
Grant that we open our eyes
And let us walk in Your light.

5. By our words and deeds may we be humble
And be built up in Your love.
Let us grow in truth towards Jesus.
Why should we decline because of our pride?

Song V-7: But I Know One Thing

CHORUS:
But I know one thing.
Because You loved me,
I do love You too. (2x)

1. I won't ask why You love me, for it is certain that You have loved me.
The sign of Your love is that You have been pierced for me.
What You became for me, I have not likewise become.
How great it is I know not, for I haven't the ability to measure.

2. Purchasing me, You freed me from the curse;
Dying You took my burden.
Because You filled me by the Holy Spirit,
You have blessed my soul.
Because You gave me grace in abundance and haven't left me,
How great it is I know not, for I haven't the ability to measure.

3. I long to please You and to honor You in my life.
But I never did profit You; instead I always made You sad.
Worse still, I've bothered You by just disappearing anywhere.
For not bearing much fruit, oh, Jesus, I am weeping.

Song V-8: Jesus of Nazareth

CHORUS:
Jesus of Nazareth, You are with us.
You, Who calmed the storm by Your power.
Praising Your name over and over never makes us tired.

1. We do remember the time we were called.
Wherever he is, everybody runs after his own business.
When seen running to and fro, and when he is called by You,
Whoever said "No" and refused to surrender to You?

2. We were deaf and yet heard the good news.
We understood Your being better than silver and gold.

When You raised the dead and made the blind to see,
Our eyes have seen You and the marvels You did.

3. While we were traveling with You in the storm,
You rebuked the wind lest we drown.
Your comforting voice we never forgot.
Your loved is like the dew for the withered soul.

Song V-9: Oh, My Soul, He Is the Lord; Worship Him

CHORUS:
Oh, my soul, He is the Lord God; worship Him.
To my merciful Lord, let praises abound.
Let me obey Him with all my life.
Let me tell of His kindness, and sing of His mercy.
Let me compose a song of praise and sing it for Him.

1. He is the One who lifted me out of the slimy pit,
Out of the mud and mire,
Who placed my feet on a rock and made me firm,
Who supported me by His grace and kept me alive,
Who hid me from the darts of the evil one by His hands.

2. After seeing weakness, sickness, wounds and brokenness,
When relatives stand afar, Jesus comes close.
Treating us with love, He renews life.
What repayment will there ever be for the favor He shows?

3. My Lord approached and cast away the burden on my shoulders.
The bill of my debt He cancelled by His death.
His mercy that He has shown to me is great.
Let me fall at His feet and glorify my Lord.

SONG V-10*: OTHER THAN THEIR GOD

CHORUS:
Other than their God, not to worship anyone,
Not to bow down before the golden image.
Those who submitted their bodies –
Let the God of Shadrach, Meschach and Abednego be praised forever
Who saved His faithful friends.

1. There is no God like Him Who can save.
He only could save them from the fiery furnace.
Salvation is from Him.

2. The Lord spoke and I heard only His voice.
I realize that power was God's only
I saw Him putting out the fire. (2x)

3. If you give yourselves unselfishly,
Fire does not burn, because God acts.
Glorify His name and be strong. (2x)

SONG V-11*: WHEN GOD ASSISTS

CHORUS:
When God assists, descending from the heavens,
When He wipes out all offences by His justice,
Haven't you seen the trap broken,
The captive freed and telling about His redemption?

1. Though there are many temptations on the pathway of life,
The righteous, calling upon the Lord, shall never perish.
God hears him cry, "Hold my hand."
He pulls him out of the swamp and leads him in victory.

2. When the enemy defies God
And attempts to devour the poor and helpless
By terrifying words which he speaks in pride,
It is only God Who can reach down and save.
Trusting in man is vanity of vanities.

3. Stripped of all he has, deprived of everything,
Only the Lord stands by his side.
For one who is pushed aside in a foreign land,
The only foundation for his hope is his Lord.

4. The help of the saints will come from heaven.
After the ages are past, the Lord will return.
He will wipe away the tears from His children's eyes.
Glory and praise will be given to His name.

SONG V-12*: ALL THOSE WHO WISH TO LIVE

CHORUS:
All those who wish to live in godliness through Christ Jesus
Will be persecuted for the sake of His name and will be tested as gold.
When, at last, they pass the test,
They will inherit eternal life.

1. God's will for His children—
This is the way for the chosen.
Those who rightly understand what they owe
Choose the cross of the Lord.

2. Those who conform to this world
Are the ones who gather rubbish.
They have belittled their birthright.
They are trapped by the comforts of the flesh.

3. Suffering in loving the Lord,
Being throw out anywhere like rubbish –
It's the sign of our salvation and glory
And the cross is our weapon of victory.

4. In your living, be like the Lord.
What have you to do with this perishing world?
Please get out; be separated from it
And be perfect in your heart.

SONG V-13: RISE UP, RISE UP

CHORUS:
Rise up, rise up, rise up, rise up!
Oh, arm of God, rise up as in the past.
Put on Your strength, rise up as in the past.

1. When life became bitter for your people in Egypt
The One Who called Moses out of his shepherd life,
Oh You, God, King of the ages,
Were not You the One Who wounded the dragon?

2. Let the one in error repent, the weak be strengthened.
May the sin-captive be let loose from prison.
We are longing helplessly, waiting for Your arm.
Give us one visit, for we are thirsty.

3. Your past servants made You to be honored.
When power came upon them, they fought lions.
Cripples have run, demons been cast out.
Time doesn't change You.
We have seen You, too.

SONG V-14*: THERE'S NO ONE WHO CAN CHALLENGE YOU

CHORUS:
There is no one who can challenge You.
May Your will be fulfilled in us.
And may Your greatness be proclaimed.
Oh, my Lord, only You be honored.

1. You redeemed your people from earth.
You have begun great works.
Your thoughts cannot be hindered
May Your righteousness and truth flourish.

2. Wherever we reach
You do our works for us.

Before our hands get limp and weak,
Today, as usual, You take the lead.

3. For the sake of Your despised name,
For the sake of Your people in captivity,
May Your arm be held up firmly.
May your honor be widely known today.

4. As we prostrate before You and cry
May Your arm be lifted up, Oh, Lord.
Heaven and earth do honor You
And all will worship before Your face.

Song V-15*: Before My Soul Returns to Her God

CHORUS:
Before my soul returns to her God, my body to the ground,
Let me hurry up and do my job quickly.
Before my soul returns to her God, my body to the ground,
Let me hurry up and do my job quickly.

1. Those who are found active when their Lord comes
Will be rewarded for using their talents.
One who doesn't despise his service but is faithful in little things
Will receive his reward after his work is tested.

2. Those who care less and are negligent about their responsibility
And forgetful about the coming of their Lord –
Their fate is weeping. And lest wailing awaits me,
May Your Spirit always quicken me and let me stand for Your glory.

3. Like steam visible for a while but which disappears after a time,
I know my life is also like that.
Let me run for my Lord without saying,
"I am weary".
Let me be purposefully active.

4. "Now I have fought the good fight;
I have kept the faith and finished the race."
May I say this, as Paul and as Jesus,
"It is finished."
That I may present my praises to the King of hosts.

Song V-16: The Lord's Prayer

The One living in heaven, Oh, our Father,
Holy be Your name; Your kingdom come.
As Your will is done in heaven,
So may it be on earth.
Give us today our daily bread.
Forgive us our sins
As we forgive those who sin against us.
Deliver us from evil.
Do not lead us into testing.
For Yours is the kingdom
The power and the glory. Amen.

CASSETTE 6

Song VI-1*: Oh, God of My Heart

CHORUS:
When You saw me, greatly troubled and pleading,
You said, "Fear not, I am with you."
Your comfort filled me and girded me with joy.
Oh, God of my heart, you're my eternal victory and inheritance.

1. The only hope I have is this God.
Seeing His faithfulness, I surrender all, even my heart.
Fools put their hope in men,
But it is only God Who prepares salvation.

2. The pit which was dug did not swallow me up.
When my strength ran out, You did not desert me.
After You weighed my little faith
You completed the combat for me and made me
Stand on the mountain of victory.

3. As I sing hymns of praise, I rejoice in You.
Before my vain enemies, You have honored me.
Though the world cancels me out,
I am known in the Book of Life.
To the end, my life will stand firm, strengthened in You.

SONG VI-2*: IF HIS HAND WAS NOT STRETCHED OUT

CHORUS:
If His hand was not stretched out,
If He had not helped us
If He had not hastily rescued us like this,
We would have been lost, swallowed by the swamp, sunk in the water.
But Jesus pulled us out and now we're alive.

1. We've heard many times of the death sentence.
In order to live, we've died day by day.
Carrying Jesus' death, we've moved around,
But in spite of all this, we've lived by Your mercy.

2. It's by faith, not by what we see.
Except for the Lord, we've nothing to be proud of.
Even our righteousness is not good enough.
His grace makes us stand; we have not been separated from Him.

3. We are alive and will continue living in Him.
Today, too, we will manifest the work of the Lord saying,
"Glory to His name, honor to His name."
We'll sacrifice all we have to Him.

SONG VI-3*: LET NOT THE WISE BE PROUD IN HIS WISDOM

CHORUS:
Let not the wise be proud in his wisdom.
Let not the strong be proud in his strength.
But let the one who knows that the
Omnipotent God works righteousness and justice on earth
Be proud in the Lord,
Glory in the Lord.

1. My rebellion took me into the wilderness;
It made me wander in a waterless desert.
To my dismay, knowledge taught me pride
While thirst burned me.
Stubbornness wrestled with me,

Truth criticized me; wisdom rebuked me.
And the Spirit won; I found the Lord.

2. Heavenly wisdom opens the eye.
It teaches skills to the lazy.
It's better than gold filigree and rubies.
If you earnestly seek and look for it,
If you would raise your voice and call for wisdom
Then you would know the fear of God.

3. Where is the examiner of this world?
The One Who resolves the problems of the ages?
Jesus is the great omniscient One Who was crucified for us,
He Who caused life to flow out of the desert,
He Who smote and crushed the power of Satan.
When we surrendered to Him, that was the end of the question.

Song VI-4: A New Song

CHORUS:
Let us sing a new song,
For the glory of our Savior.
Let us offer up the sweet aroma of our praises,
With the cries of joy.

1. Those who trusted their Shepherd,
Those who lie down in His pasture,
Following His path, the ones who are called for salvation,
They were spared from the ferocious beasts and slaughter.
They will rejoice because they were not destroyed by the destroyer.

2. He tore off our sackcloth and clothed us with His grace.
Let our reverence sing for Him for His love has consoled us.
Those who wanted to harm us dug a hole and waited for us.
Demons were ashamed—those who ambushed to attack us.

3. Let's sing with a pure heart, rejoicing in our God.
Let's clap our hands, shout the joy cry.
Why should we be reserved?
We'll destroy the fortress by the hymn of our praises.
In spiritual armor, we'll go on winning.

Song VI-5: According to the Mercy I've Received

CHORUS:
According to the mercy I've received,
According to the greatness of Your kindness,
Help me to serve You, Oh, Lord.
And give me the fire of Your Spirit.

1. You cut my chains and broke my yoke.
You have set me free so that my soul glorifies You saying
"No more bondage," You've called me Your child.
By the blood covenant, You have made me your own.

2. So that those who have stumbled be saved from folly,
In order to help the weak by Your word,
Quicken me and wake me up in early morning from my sleep.
Make me a faithful servant, one who gives heart-rest.

3. Banish my laziness with Your reprimanding rod; help me to be diligent
Under the throne of Your grace.
That I may witness saying "Jesus saves!"
Fill up my life by the love of Your cross.

4. To those who lack wisdom and do not understand,
And to the educated who profess they know,
Let me tell the Gospel so that they may believe and be saved,
For my debt is great to all of them.

5. Let not the Gospel be reserved nor limited by any boundaries.
Let Your word go to the end of the earth without being restricted.
Let Your righteousness be distributed far and near,
Let all creation proclaim "Hurrah" in finding Jesus.

Song VI-6*: Oh, Lord, Bless Us with a Blessing

CHORUS:
Oh, Lord, bless us with a blessing.
Enlarge our spiritual territory.
May Your hand be upon us;
You are our hope.

1. You heard Jabez when he prayed.
Likewise You blessed his soul and enlarged his country.

2. We, who are born through the agony and suffering of Your Son,
We, too, are Your offspring.
Gather and keep us.

3. Cast us not from Your presence, we pray.
Remember us by Your favor; visit us with Your healing.

4. May the heavens open, Your Spirit pour down upon us.
May our life be soaked, our soul satisfied.

5. Let us not be lonely. Multiply us by blessing us.
Enrich us by Your grace; make us grow by Your word.

6. Until the earth fills up by knowing God,
Our pleading continues without our strength being weakened.

Song VI-7*: Winners Through Faith

CHORUS:
Those who passed away—winners through faith.
And looking at those ahead of us,
We need to stand for our Lord
For He is the choice of our life, and
He is our assurance.

1. They looked at the best of all.
They wandered from one pit to another.
Abstaining from covetousness which fights the soul,
They crossed the river triumphantly.

2. Abandoning the seemingly right wide road,
We're no refugees on the narrow one.
On this road there is life
Granted to the ones who definitely follow it.

3. While He was rich, He became poor for us.
While He held high rank, He was humiliated for us.
He showed us the true love.
We, too, will walk in His way.

Song VI-8: My God, My God

CHORUS:
My God, my God, I am hurrying to You
I'm running to see Your power and glory.
Show me Your face, then I will be filled with joy.
May your mercy be abundant so that I live in life.

1. While still night, I wake up from my sleep;
I desire to see the light of Your face.
My soul thirsts for You like one thirsty for water.
It longs for You day and night.

2. In Your name, lifting up my hands unto You,
I give praises in my regular prayers.
I submit to You my whole being.
I am ever Yours; I will live in Your house.

3. Rather than to live a thousand futile years in the flesh,
Better to die knowing the truth.
As for myself, I have chosen to carry Your cross.
This, my Lord, is the decision of my soul.

SONG VI-9: WHEN THE POT BREAKS

1. When the pot breaks, the hidden light comes to shine;
When the wheat seed rots, the plant bears much fruit.
My Lord, my God, I need a broken heart.

2. When I hear Your voice, either reproaching or counseling,
Lest I fall and break in the dimness,
My Lord, my God, I need an open ear.

3. To look at You as You walk in front of me,
To walk in light to our place of appointment,
My Lord, my God, I need a healthy eye.

4. To tell about peace, to run with good news,
To say, "Behold, the source of righteousness" to those who thirst for it,
My Lord, my God, I need walking feet.

SONG VI-10: THAT THEY SERVE HIM

CHORUS:
That they serve Him with their whole heart,
That they live in Him and for Him,
The Lord purifies His children;
He cleanses them from their sins.

1. His house smelled of the animals' dung
And lost all that original sweet aroma.
Jesus will not tolerate it;
He will not pass over unless He cleanses it.

2. Dusting away all the unclean things in the temple,
Whipping all the retailers and traders,
He chases them out, for zeal burns in Him.

3. When tares and wheat which grow together
Are cut at the same time,
The wise farmer will use his fork;

He'll separate the produce from the straw
And give the chaff to the wind.

SONG VI-11*: TO DO YOUR WILL

CHORUS:
Now then, my Lord, make me understand
To do Your will the rest of my life.
Teach me.

1. I did all I desired without fearing God.
I piled up problems for years to come.
In the life I lived, sowing in sin,
Your grace gave me beauty by changing my life.

2. Knowing Your will enabled me to obey.
Staying far from sin made me wise.
Being taught over and over of Your good rules
As a stranger in the land, I sing today.

3. Your will which You have completed in me is marvelous.
My eyes are upon You today, and for tomorrow.
Show me the way I should walk
For the rest of my life.
Let me know Your will.

SONG VI-12*: ALLOWING THE WILL OF HIS GOD

CHORUS:
Allowing the will of his God to become his will,
Trusting in his Lord with his whole soul
Being satisfied in all of life,
The righteous shall live, abiding in His Word.

1. The lust of the flesh, desire of the eye
And the love of the world deceived his heart.
He thought being in the Lord to be foolishness;

He took off his Christianity and threw it away.
Look at that person running towards death.

2. Running ahead of God's will, and
Diving into the sea of lust, he got drowned.
Searching for fame, he went roaming.
He bustled as he threw off contentment.
Thirsty, but never quenching his thirst, he died.

3. Oh, stranger of the desert,
You who covet that which is worthless
You who forgot who you are,
How could you miss it all?
Covetousness begets sin, and sin, death.

4. Carnal racing must henceforth be cut off.
Useless consumption needs now to be stopped.
Know His will and obey.
Be supplied by His word and advice
Lest you disobey again and be punished.

Song VI-13*: Be Glad, My Brother

CHORUS:
Be glad, my brother, that your accuser has been cast away.
The price of your sin is paid by the Lord.
Accept His mercy; forget your sorrow.
After you repent, let joy fill your heart.

1. The One who wipes out the accusation of your enemy
Is your advocate standing before the Father.
Repent from the burden of your sin and just relax.
Tell it to Jesus; He'll wash your sin burden by His blood.

2. Your body is all covered up by your filthy cloth.
Your guilt is magnified; you are immersed in shame.
Say, "No matter what, I decide not to be hopeless.
I am determined that I will not flee from His grace."

3. By casting out your enemy, releasing your bondage,
Wiping out your accusations and changing the judgment,
That Father of love, He has proclaimed mercy;
So that your garment may be changed,
He has issued a decree.

Song VI-14: Do Not Turn Your Inheritance Over to Mockery

CHORUS:
Do not turn your inheritance over to mockery.
Do not let your holy temple be destroyed by the enemy.

1. The one who pardons wrongs passes over iniquity.
The one who hovers over His people to save them from destruction—
Who is a God like You, whose mercy is abundant
When Your saints are persecuted, when trouble multiplies?

2. The inheritance of God, it is written, is His people.
In order that they worship Him, serve Him,
He took them as migrants from Egypt.
Who would attempt to replace their freedom by slavery?
Who would dare to claim them?
The people belong to God!

3. Until this day, You are honored and feared by Gentiles.
You have turned the curse of the enemy to blessing.
You have drowned the pursuers' horses in the sea.
You have kept Your inheritance,
Defending it by Your mighty hand.

Song VI-15*: Oh Lord, My Lord, Come

CHORUS:
Oh, Lord, my Lord, come.
Has not the time arrived?

1. Your people are waiting for You.
Oh, Lord, my Lord, come.

They are longing for Your revelation.
Oh, Lord, my Lord, come.
Please come without delay.
Oh, Lord, my Lord, come.
Hasn't the time come yet?
Oh, Lord, my Lord, come.

2. For she loved Your name.
Oh, Lord, my Lord, come.
My soul is filled up with insults.
Oh, Lord, my Lord come.
For she thinks of her blessings.
Oh, Lord, my Lord, come.
Today my soul trusts in You.
Oh, Lord, my Lord, come.

3. Before weakness worsens,
Oh, Lord, my Lord, come.
Before the patriot gets defeated,
Oh, Lord, my Lord, come.
The combatant's hope,
Oh, Lord, my Lord, come.
Be strong against Your enemy.
Oh, Lord, my Lord, come.

4. The idol is being smashed.
Oh, Lord, my Lord, come.
Let me watch Your name be glorified.
Oh, Lord, my Lord, come.
As You were known in ancient days,
Oh, Lord, my Lord, come.
Let the earth know You.
Oh, Lord, my Lord, come.

CASSETTE 7

SONG VII-1: HE SEES YOU

CHORUS:
He sees you (4x)
He sees you, Jesus sees you;
He sees you, yes, He sees you.
He's concerned about you,
And He is coming to rescue you.

1. You who are in the wilderness,
You who weep as Hagar,
If you would see the One Who sees you,
You would have a hopeful ending.

2. If life gets messed up,
And what you've got is all scattered,
And when you think the Lord has left you,
When your enemy ridicules you . . .

3. When your heart is sad and sorrowful,
Your life's firm staff,
Comforter and encourager
Is none but the Lord.

4. The Lord Who unloads all burdens,
Protector of the needy,
And a faithful shepherd.
It is Emmanuel Who is for us.

SONG VII-2*: WHEN WOULD GOD EVER WANT THE SINNER TO PERISH?

CHORUS:
When would God ever want the sinner to perish?
Even the one who is fallen, He would not want to perish.
He deals with him in thoughtful counsel.

1. The Lord, full of mercy, truth, love and kindness -
Let us draw near in repentance and receive forgiveness.
None should perish; the Savior has died for us.
Christ Jesus has become a ransom for us.

2. Why does a person feel hopeless in his fallen life?
Why is it easy for him to go to the deeps?
The one who says, "Though the Lord lets me die, I will wait for Him" -
The one who stands by faith will not remain wretched.

3. God punishes the child whom He loves for his good.
He advises, rebukes and straightens him out.
He looks at him with a fatherly look.
When He sees him stumble, He quickly supports him.

SONG VII-3: YOU BECAME MY REDEEMER

CHORUS:
You became my redeemer, Jesus my Lord,
My life's anchor, support of my steps.
I have seen Your salvation and righteousness.
Therefore I will praise Your name with joy. (2x)

1. Whether by gold, by silver, wisdom or knowledge,
Whoever was saved from sin, from the fall,
O Lord, You are the One Who clothes me in righteousness.
In mercy You mediated and reconciled me with the Father. (2x)

2. Through Christ Jesus' work on the cross I've been saved from eternal death and suffering.

I've been endowed with a free gift of righteousness.
I offer a sacrifice of thanksgiving to the Lord Who ransomed me. (2x)

3. You surmised my childishness and my weakness.
You, strong Lord, revealed Yourself to me;
You bruised the enemy who overpowered me.
Jesus, it is You who gave me victory. (2x)

4. By accomplishing Your good work in my life,
That You might be magnificently seen in my daily walk—
This is my plea, my constant prayer.
You are my honor, my satisfaction, and
You are my pride. (2x)

Song VII-4: He Never Breaks His Promises

CHORUS:
He never breaks His promises, for He's a faithful God.
We have seen the fulfillment of all He has said.
We exalt Him, above all, in praise.

1. The city of sin, the work of the devil -
We have witnessed that He has destroyed that fortress and that mountain.
Our Lord Jesus is revealed, the Light of our life.
By His death, saving us, He completed His word of hope.

2. In peace, in life, in His good counsel,
In doing away with our misery and sorrows,
The Lord God saw all our needs.
He heard our wailing, and broke our yoke.

3. The threat of hell, the howling winds of trouble,
The cruelty of powers, the breath of their anger,
All the noises of the storm, the songs of unrighteousness,
He silenced them all by the rebuke of His authoritative words.

4. He is a wall of appeal, a refuge for the poor.
A comfortable hiding shelter is none other than Jesus.
Many will be safe by entering this shelter.

Song VII-5: Oh Lord, Our Lord

CHORUS:
Oh, Lord, our Lord, let us praise You
And say to You "Be honored" as a response to Your favor. (2x)

1. Satan wished to winnow us as wheat.
He threatened he would dim our faith and hope.
Though he arises outrageously
We have seen him silenced, defeated by You.
For You have contended for our faith and life.
We praise You, Lord.

2. Even if our enemy put an obstacle in our way to cut our journey short,
No matter how high the walls of the fortress,
You destroyed them, praise You, Jesus.
You make the crooked ways straight
And You open up closed doors.

3. You put away Your people's reproach.
You wipe off the tears from their faces.
You graciously anoint their heads with oil.
You reign in their praises.
For such a small folk, Your kindness is so abundant.
Be glorified, our God.
You are the eternal Most High.

4. After preparing a feast You called us with honor.
Wow! You caused us to sit at the King's table
By Jesus Christ, in the place of honor.
Our souls were feasted on the Bread of Life.
From our hearts, we willingly do thank You
And we will forever be loyal to You. (2x)

Song VII-6: On Whatever Road I Walked

CHORUS:
On whatever road I walked, He cared for me
Up to the present, He has kept me from evil.
The Lord will help me stand until the end.
And I'll reach my home country without my faith weakened. (2x)

1. Before the storm caused me to fall or the water drowned me,
He grabbed my hand in His and took me across the river.
Before the flame of temptation's fire hurt me,
By the grace of my Lord, I passed through alive.

2. With the living ones that I might glorify You;
In passing through temptation that I might thank You,
Jesus stood at my side and strengthened me.
He repeatedly saved me from the lion's mouth.

3. I commend my life unto my God.
I live without fear under His shepherding.
I am confident under His wings.
In His care and watchfulness, I will enter my home country.

4. I will remember the marvelous works the Lord performed.
I'll thank Him for the years passed.
I'll depend on Him for whatever my future holds.
I'll live in His bosom, in His everlasting arms.

Song VII-7: May Your Temple be A House of Prayer

CHORUS:
May Your temple be, Lord, a house of prayer. (2x)
May Your temple be, Jesus, a house of prayer. (2x)

1. By the blood of your Son You said,
"May there be life and peace."
You proclaimed pardon for our sin.
Be praised, O God, for reconciling us.
You made us Your temple, Your dwelling place.

2. You, the King Whose throne is in heaven,
Hallowed be Your name among us on earth.
Accept the sweet aroma of our sacrifice
As a thanksgiving from our lives.

3. Angels saying "Holy, holy, holy"
Diligently adore You day and night.
And may our song of praise reach You
Our supplications, prayers, praise, adoration.

4. May Your lamp be lit and the Light be seen.
Fill your house with Your glory.
Let people come to Your brightness.
Let them worship You and be saved by Your holy name.

5. Lest it be a world market center, a profit-making place,
Sanctify and keep Your dwelling place.
Make it a place of healing, of eternal life.
May Your house be the dwelling place of the Holy Spirit.

Song VII-8: Your Dwelling Places

CHORUS:
How lovely are Your dwelling places!
Which by Your Holy Word, by Your Spirit, You blessed.
Oh, my Lord, in the temple, on Your exalted throne
May adoration be presented to You. (2x)

1. Precious stones, living children
People ransomed by the blood of the Lamb
They are built to be a temple,
And become the dwelling place for the King.

2. In the world, millions who lack satisfaction
Came from afar hearing of Your fame.
Rather than sitting in the tent of sinners
They chose to be called Your dwelling place.

3. In Your house there are precious things;

There are great stores of Heaven's treasures.
By light and by your ointments,
Your children have become very shiny.

4. Your priests with trumpets,
Singers with musical instruments,
Their voices went forth in unison.
They highly exalted Him in their songs of praise.

5. By His everlasting mercy
The Most High visited us in His generosity.
The Lord gave His people His favor.
God filled His temple with His glory.

SONG VII-9: WHO WOULD SEEK THE LOST?

CHORUS:
Who would seek the lost?
Who would treat the hurt?
Who would repair the broken?
Who would renew the ruins?

1. Watching God's house in ruin,
While you seek your own charming life,
Wishing to get rich without the Lord –
Until today you have been running
But your hand is empty of any fruit.

2. The sheep have become the wild beast's prey.
They've gone astray because of lack of a Shepherd.
While you ministered to yourself and worked for luxury.
Try to see, my friend, the flock's misery.

3. Where is your talent, oh, my brother?
Have you buried it like the lazy man?
The One who gave it to you will require it from you.
Where did you put the thing that was entrusted to you?
The lost soul will seek from your hand.

4. The one who is called to gather souls,
The one who is compassionate and kind,
The one who proclaims the Good News,
He'll receive rewards at the end.
He'll shine forever like the brilliance of the sky.

Song VII-10: It's Love That I Lack

CHORUS:
It's love, love, love that I lack.
I'm a type who counts wrongs.
Lord, make me one who forgives.
Cut off my root of bitterness.
Give me a life sweetened by Your love.

1. Had I prophecy, wisdom and revelation,
Had I faith which destroys a mountain,
Even if I speak in tongues of men or angels
If I don't have love it's of no use to me.

2. Love is patient; it does kindness.
It rejoices in truth but doesn't delight in evil.
It is not jealous nor boastful; it humbles itself.
While it is hurting, yet it forgives all.

3. After meeting his enemy at a convenient place
Who would accompany him on the right way in love?
Who among humankind would let go in peace?
David did this during his time.

4. While we were Your enemies, by dying, You made us friends.
Since You gave us life by Your love on the cross
In order to save lives by loving all men,
Overwhelm us, Lord, by true love.

SONG VII-11: JESUS CHRIST

CHORUS:
Jesus Christ
Yesterday, today
And forever, You God, are the same.

1. When the heavens get old and pass away with the earth
And the mighty ones in them all vanish away,
You, dear Lord, are the same forever.
You do not change. You stay bright as ever.

2. The One we worship never tires nor weakens,
But lives forever, powerful and praise-worthy.
Jesus is Alpha and Omega, Lord.
His hand is stronger than those who are stronger than we.

3. While we were yet guilty sinners,
We saw God's love through Christ.
He took our curse by dying on the cross.
Tearing our sackcloth, He clothed us with His righteousness.

4. Your love upon us, which you had in mind in Ancient times
We've seen it today; Your purpose is love.
We've relied, lived under the shelter of Your wings.
We'll get through triumphantly being held by Your hands.

Hallelujah, hallelujah, hallelujah,
We've been kept by you. (Repeat chorus)

SONG VII-12: GREATER THINGS THAN THIS

CHORUS:
We will yet see greater things than this
When the Lord's power is revealed
When the earth is filled with the clouds of His glory
And the Lord's praise.

1. When the Lord, by His Spirit and His examining word,
Told us our works, listing them in detail,
We marveled at His knowledge and were ashamed of our lifestyle.
We repented, asking Him to forgive us.

2. By His blood He cleanses our sins.
The forgiveness of our Lord Jesus is plentifully abundant.
By His power He casts out evil spirits
By the authority of the Gospel, His Kingdom expands.

3. To the one who groans, "Oh, my Lord"
His salvation will come, His righteousness be revealed.
Herald God's mercy to all people.
Behold the rain of abundant blessing.

4. When the hungry are fed, when the Most High gives His word,
Then the earth shakes with the joy cries of the righteous
In the songs of praises, in hymns of joy,
In the great harvest, the fruit of service.

Bibliography

Aren, Gustav. *Evangelical Pioneers in Ethiopia: Origins of the Evangelical Church Mekane Yesus*. Stockholm: EFS Förlaget, 1978.

Armstrong, Sonya L., Hope Smith Davis, and Eric J. Paulson. "The Subjectivity Problem: Improving Triangulation Approaches in Metaphor Analysis Studies." *International Journal of Qualitative Methods* 10 (2001) 151–63.

Balisky, E. Paul. "African Indigenous Songs and Church Growth." A paper in partial fulfillment of an M.A. at the Institute of Church Growth, Fuller Theological Seminary, 1972.

———. *Wolaitta Evangelists: A Study of Religious Innovation in Southern Ethiopia, 1937–1975*. ASM Monograph Series. Eugene, OR: Pickwick, 2009.

Balisky, Lila W. "Heavenly Liturgy." In *Worship and Mission for the Global Church: An Ethnodoxology Handbook* edited by James R. Krabill et al., 350. Pasadena, CA: William Carey Library, 2013.

———. "I Refuse, I Refrain by Tesfaye Gabbiso." In *Sorrow and Blood: Christian Mission in Contexts of Suffering, Persecution, and Martyrdom*, edited by William D. Taylor et al. 350. Pasadena: William Carey, 2012.

———. Personal Diaries of Lila Balisky 1967–2015.

———. "Theology in Song: Ethiopia's Tesfaye Gabbiso." *Missiology: An International Review* 25 (1997) 447–56.

Balisky, Lila, and Ralph Lee. "Ethiopian Hymnody." In *Canterbury Dictionary of Hymnology*. Canterbury Press, 2015. https://hymnology.hymnsam.co.uk/e/ethiopian-hymnody?q=Ethiopian%20hymnody.

Barz, Gregory F. "Confronting the Field(note) In and Out of the Field: Music, Voices, Texts, and Experiences in Dialogue." In *Shadows in the Field: New Perspectives for Fieldwork in Ethnomusicology*, edited by Gregory Barz and Timothy J. Cooley, 206–23. New York: Oxford University Press, 2008.

Bediako, Kwame. "Christ in Africa: Some Reflections on the Contribution of Christianity to the African Becoming." In *African Futures: 25th Anniversary Conference at University of Edinburgh*, 447–58. Edinburgh: University Press, 1987.

Begbie, Jeremy S. "The Powers of Music in Worship." In *Imagination and Interpretation: Christian Perspectives*, edited by Hans Boersma, 109–27. Vancouver, BC: Regent, 2005.

———. *Theology, Music and Time*. Cambridge: Cambridge University Press, 2000.

Best, Harold M. *Music Through the Eyes of Faith*. San Francisco: Harper, 1995.

Bevans, Stephen B., and Roger P. Schroeder. *Constants in Context: A Theology of Mission for Today*. Maryknoll, NY: Orbis. 2004.

Blacking, John. "The Structure of Musical Discourse: The Problem of the Song Text." *Yearbook for Traditional Music* 14 (1982) 15–23.

Bolay, Anne. "The *Azmari*: Voices of Ethiopian Memory." In *Proceedings of the XIVth International Conference of Ethiopian Studies, November 6–11, 2000* (I) 75–83. Addis Ababa, Ethiopia: Institute of Ethiopian Studies, Addis Ababa University, 2000.

Bosch, David J. *Transforming Mission: Paradigm Shifts in Theology of Mission*. Maryknoll, NY: Orbis, 1991.

Brueggemann, Walter. *Praying the Psalms: Engaging Scripture and the Life of the Spirit*. Eugene, OR: Cascade, 2007.

Butler, Sue. "Considering 'Objective' Possibilities in Autoethnography: A Critique of Heewon Chang's *Autoethnography as Method*." *The Weekly Qualitative Report* 2 (2009) 295–99. http://www.nova.edu/ssss/QR/WQR/chang2.pdf.

Cameron, Lynne, and Robert Maslen. *Metaphor Analysis: Research Practice in Applied Linguistic, Social Sciences and the Humanities*. Studies in Applied Linguistics. London: Equinox, 2010.

Chaillot, Christine. *The Ethiopian Orthodox Tewahedo Church Tradition*. Paris: Inter-Orthodox Dialogue, 2002.

Charter, Vernon. "Contested Symbols: Music, Revolution, and Renewal in Ethiopian Protestant Churches." *EthnoDoxology* 3 (2006) 1–13.

Chitando, Ezra. *Singing Culture: A Study of Gospel Music in Zimbabwe*. Uppsala, Sweden: Nordiska Afrikainstitutet, 2002.

Corbitt, J. Nathan. *The Sound of the Harvest: Music's Mission in Church and Culture*. Grand Rapids, MI: Baker, 1998.

Creswell, John W. *Qualitative Inquiry and Research Design*. Thousand Oaks, CA: Sage, 2007.

Cumbers, John. *Count It All Joy: Testimonies from a Persecuted Church*. Kearney, NE: Morris, 1995.

Dickson, Kwesi. *Theology in Africa*. Maryknoll, NY: Orbis, 1984.

EECMY. "God Is Here: Fifteen Songs from Ethiopia," (*Ǐgziabhér Ale*), 1984. Mimeographed with music transcription by Marianne Nilsson and text translation by Hartmut Schoenherr with Jim and Aurelia Keefer. Prepared by EECMY (Ethiopian Evangelical Church Mekane Yesus) for the AACC (All Africa Council of Churches) worship but never published due to constraints during the Ethiopian revolution. Mimeographed copies in both English and Amharic exist.

Eide, Oyvind M. *Revolution & Religion in Ethiopia: The Growth and Persecution of the Mekane Yesus Church, 1974–1985*. Oxford: James Curry, 2000.

Ellis, Carolyn, et al. "Autoethnography: An Overview." *Forum: Qualitative Social Research* 12 (2011) 1–13. http://www.qualitative-research.net/index.php/fqs/article/view/1589/3095.

Ephrem Alemu and Tewodros Tadesse. *Sǐle zemenu zǐmaré yeǐdǐget dereja kezemariyan andebet* ("Current Development of Songs from the Mouths of Singers Themselves") Magazine interview. *Éftah*, Tǐkimt 2007 EC, 4–5.

Eyob Denio. *Yemezmurǐna yemezemǐran hǐywet* ("Song and the Singer's Life"). 2nd ed. Soddo, Ethiopia: Kale Heywet Church Office, 2002 EC.

Fargher, Brian. "The Charismatic Movement in Ethiopia 1960–1980." *Evangelical Review of Theology* 12 (1988) 344–58.

———. *The Origins of the New Churches Movement in Southern Ethiopia, 1927–1944.* Leiden: E. J. Brill, 1996.

Ferran, Hugo. "Lila W. Balisky Private Ethiopian Music Collection." 2013. http:hugoferran.wordpress.com/publications.

Fikre Tolossa. *The Ethiopian Herald* (no date) 21.

Finnegan, Ruth. *Oral Literature in Africa.* World Oral Literature Series 1. Cambridge: Open Book, 2012.

Fritsch, Abba Emmanuel. "Liturgy and Culture in Ethiopia Today." In *Faith and Culture in Ethiopia: Towards a Pastoral Approach to Culture*, 61–77. Addis Ababa, Ethiopia: Capuchin Franciscan Institute of Philosophy and Theology, 1997.

Geertz, Clifford. *The Interpretation of Cultures.* New York: Basic Books, 1973.

Gezahegn Mussie. *Amlïko yekït lïbs ayïdelem (yehodos ïngïda)* ("Worship Is Not a Fashionable Suit!"). Guest of the magazine in *Hodos*, Megabit-Ginbote, 2000 EC, 4–6.

———. "Christian Worship and Music Syllabus" (Self-published pamphlet in Addis Ababa, Ethiopia), 2008.

———. "LivingWorship International Ministry" brochure, Addis Ababa. n.d.

———. *Zïmaré tïlant zïmaré zaré* ("Songs of Yesterday; Songs of Today"). *Birhan* 51 (1996 EC) 1–5.

Girma Bekele. "A Pastoral Letter to Ethiopian Christians." http://christianserviceworker. org/a-pastoral-letter-from-girma-bekele. Accessed April 21, 2015.

———. *The In-Between People: A Reading of David Bosch through the Lens of Mission History and Contemporary Challenges in Ethiopia.* Eugene, OR: Pickwick, 2011.

Hansen, Rich. "Transforming the Dualistic Worldview of Ethiopian Evangelical Christians." *International Bulletin of Missionary Research* 39 (2015) 138–41.

Hawn, C. Michael. *Gather Into One: Praying and Singing Globally.* Grand Rapids, MI: Eerdmans, 2003.

Helen Berhane and Emma Newrick. *Song of the Nightingale: One Woman's Dramatic Story of Faith and Persecution in Eritrea.* Kent, UK: Release, 2009.

Hiebert, Paul G., R. Daniel Shaw, and Tite Tiénou. *Understanding Folk Religion: A Christian Response to Popular Beliefs and Practices.* Grand Rapids, MI: Baker Books, 1999.

Higashi, Guy Scott Shigemi. "Musical Communitas: Gathering Around the Ukulele in Hawaii and the Foursquare Church." (D.Miss dissertation, Fuller Seminary), 2011.

Hof, Eleonora. "A Missiology of Lament." *Swedish Missiological Themes* 101 (2013) 321–38.

Howell, Allison M. *The Religious Itinerary of a Ghanaian People: The Kasena and the Christian Gospel.* Frankfurt am Main: Peter Lang, 1997.

Kaplan, Steven. *The Monastic Holy Man and the Christianization of Early Solomonic Ethiopia.* Wiesbaden, Germany: Franz Steiner Verlag, 1984.

Kidula, Jean Ngoya. "Making and Managing Music in African Christian Life." In *Music in the Life of the African Church*, edited by Roberta King et al., 101–16. Waco, TX: Baylor University Press, 2008.

Kimberlin, Cynthia Tse. "The Music of Ethiopia." In *Musics of Many Cultures*, edited by Elizabeth May, 232–52. Berkeley: University of California Press, 1980.

King, Roberta R. "Beginnings: Music in the African Church." In *Music in the Life of the African Church*, edited by Roberta King et al., 1–16. Waco, TX: Baylor University Press. 2008.

———. "Bible; *Lex Canendi, Lex Credendi*." In *Music in the Life of the African Church*, edited by Roberta King et al., 117–32. Waco, TX: Baylor University Press, 2008.

———. *Pathways in Christian Music Communication: The Case of the Senufo of Côte de'Ivoire*. ASM Monograph Series. Eugene, OR: Pickwick, 2009.

———. "Toward a Discipline of Christian Ethnomusicology: A Missiological Paradigm." *Missiology: An International Review* 23 (2004) 294–307.

Krabill, James R. *The Hymnody of the Harrist Church Among the Dida of South-Central Ivory Coast (1913–1949)*. Frankfurt am Main, Germany: Peter Lang GmbH., 1995.

Lakoff, George, and Mark Johnson. *Metaphors We Live By*. Chicago: University of Chicago Press, 1980.

Leedy, Paul D., and Jeanne Ellis Ormrod. *Practical Research Planning and Design*. Boston: Pearson Education, 2013.

Levine, Donald N. *Wax and Gold: Tradition and Innovation in Ethiopian Culture*. Chicago: University of Chicago Press, 1965.

Love Ethiopia Press Release at http://www.palau.org/news/media-resources/press-releases-item/love-ethiopia/press/release.

Magesa, Laurenti. "African Christian Spirituality." In *African Theology on the Way*, edited by Diane B. Stinton, 68–78. London: SPCK, 2010.

McGann, Mary E. *Exploring Music as Worship and Theology: Research in Liturgical Practice*. Collegeville, MN: Liturgical, 2002.

McLuhan, Marshall. *Understanding Media: The Extensions of Man*. Boston: MIT Press, 1994.

Molyneux, K. Gordon. *African Christian Theology: The Quest for Selfhood*. Lewiston, NY: Mellen Univerity Press, 1993.

Moreau, A. Scott. *Contextualization in World Missions: Mapping and Assessing Evangelical Models*. Grand Rapids, MI: Kregel Academic, 2012.

Nachmanovitch, Stephen. *Free Play: Improvisation in Life and Art*. New York: Penguin, 1990.

Nettl, Bruno. *The Study of Ethnomusicology: Thirty-One Issues and Concepts*. Urbana: University of Illinois Press, 2005.

Nilsson, Marianne. "Evangelical Hymns in Amarinya." *Swedish Missiological Themes* 91 (2003) 80–172.

Okullu, Henry. *Church and Politics in East Africa*. Nairobi, Kenya: Uzima, 1974.

Parks, Sharon. *Leadership Can Be Taught: A Bold Approach for a Complex World*. Boston: Harvard Business School Press, 2005.

Phiri, Lazarus. "The Great Shift: Africa in Missions." In *Evangelical Missions Quarterly* 50 (2014) 401–4.

Ryan, Gery W., and H. Russell Bernard. "Techniques to Identify Themes in Qualitative Date." 1985. http://www.analytictech.com/mb870/readings/ryan-bernard_techniques_to_identify_themes_in.htm.

Saliers, Don E. *Music and Theology*. Nashville: Abingdon, 2007.

Samuel Wolde-Yohannes. "The Vision of Man and Humanity in Ethiopian Culture, a Politico-Philosophical Perspective." In *Faith and Culture in Ethiopia: Towards a Pastoral Approach to Culture*, 93–100. Addis Ababa: Capuchin Franciscan Institute of Philosophy and Theology, 1997.

Sanneh, Lamin. "The Horizontal and the Vertical in Mission: An African Perspective." *International Bulletin of Missionary Research* 7 (1983) 165–71.

Schreier, Margrit. *Qualitative Content Analysis in Practice.* Thousand Oaks, CA: Sage, 2012.

Seleshi Kebede. "The Cooperation of Trinitarian Churches in the Mission and Transformation of Ethiopia." (D.Min. diss., Bakke Graduate University, 2008).

Shelemay, Kay. "Crossing Boundaries in Music and Musical Scholarship: A Perspective from Ethnomusicology." *The Musical Quarterly* 80 (1996) 13–20.

Sïbhat L'Amlak. (Various editions) MekaneYesus (EECMY, Ethiopian Evangelical Church Mekane Yesus) hymnbook—assortment of editions through the years. EECMY is the second largest evangelical church in Ethiopia, connected to European Lutheran churches.

Spradley, James P. *Participant Observation.* New York: Holt, Rinehart and Winston, 1980.

Stapert, Calvin R. *A New Song for an Old World: Musical Thought in the Early Church.* Grand Rapids, MI: Eerdmans, 2007.

Steinhovden, Jan Magne. "*Mäzmur* and *Zäfän*: Within and Beyond the Evangelical Movement in Ethiopia." Submitted in partial fulfillment of the MA in World Music Studies, Department of Music, University of Sheffield, 2012.

Stinton, Diane. "Africa, East and West." In *An Introduction to Third World Theologies*, edited by John Parrott, 105–36. Cambridge: Cambridge University Press, 2004.

Sumner, Claude. *Ethiopian Philosophy, III.* Addis Ababa: University Press, 1978.

Sun, Irene Ai-Ling. "Songs of Canaan: Hymnody of the House-Church Christians in China." *EthnoDoxology* 4 (2010) 1–10.

Sunquist, Scott W. *Understanding Christian Mission: Participation in Suffering and Glory.* Grand Rapids, MI: Baker Academic, 2013.

"Tesfaye Gabbiso." *Keston News Service (Profile)* #217, 22, 1985.

Tesfaye Gabbiso. *Beziyan Gizé.* Addis Ababa: Ethiopian Full Gospel Believers' Church, 2002 EC. (Currently in process of publication in English with the proposed title of *Those Days*).

———. "Day of Salvation," TV program. Yemedan Ken (*yemedan ḵen*) www. yemedanken.net. part I with Kebede Mergia, 2011.

———. Love Ethiopia Press Release. http://www.palau.org, 2013.

———. *Mïhïretu Ayalqïhïma 1967–2005 EC* (His Mercy is Everlasting). A book of Tesfaye Gabbiso's songs (words only). Hawassa, Ethiopia: *Mulu Wengél Amanyoch Bête Krïstiyan* (Full Gospel Believers' Church), 2013.

———. "Music and Worship." (A practicum project at Ethiopian Graduate School of Theology. Addis Ababa), 2004.

———. *Yetesfayé Gabbiso Mezmuroch: The Songs of Tesfaye Gabbiso.* Amharic/English diglot compiled by Lila Balisky and translated by Haile Jenai. Addis Ababa: SIM Press, 2011.

Tewelde Beyene. "Inculturation and Evangelization in the History of Ethiopian Christianity." In *Faith and Culture in Ethiopia: Towards a Pastoral Approach to Culture*, 5–20. Addis Ababa, Ethiopia: Capuchin Franciscan Institute of Philosophy and Theology, 1997.

Tibebe Eshete. *The Evangelical Movement in Ethiopia: Resistance and Resilience.* Waco, TX: Baylor University Press, 2009.

Ullendorff, Edward. *The Ethiopians: An Introduction to Country and People*. London: Oxford University Press, 1960.

Vanhoozer, Kevin J. "One Rule to Rule Them All? Theological Method in an Era of World Christianity." In *Globalizing Theology: Belief and Practice in an Era of World Christianity*, edited by Craig Ott and Harold A. Netland, 85–126. Grand Rapids: Baker, 2006.

Wallace, W. J. "Hymns in Ethiopia." *Practical Anthropology* 9 (1962) 271.

Walls, Andrew F. *The Cross-Cultural Process in Christian History*. Maryknoll, NY: Orbis, 2002.

———. "Globalization and the Study of Christian History." *Globalizing Theology: Belief and Practice in an Era of World Christianity*, edited by Craig Ott and Harold A. Netland, 70–82. Grand Rapids: Baker Academic, 2006.

———. *The Missionary Movement in Christian History: Studies in the Transmission of Faith*. Maryknoll, NY: Orbis Books, 1996.

Wudasé Amlak #2 ("Praise to God"). Published in Addis Ababa, Ethiopia, by Geja Kale Heywet Church Communications Department, 1984 EC.

Wright, Christopher J. H. *The Mission of God: Unlocking the Bible's Grand Narrative*. Downers Grove, IL: InterVarsity, 2006.

Wright, N. T. *Surprised by Hope: Rethinking Heaven, the Resurrection, and the Mission of the Church*. New York: Harper Collins, 2008.

Yin, Robert K. *Case Study Research: Design and Methods* (3rd edition). Thousand Oaks, CA: Sage, 2003.

Zelalem Mengistu. *Hïyasé mezmurat: yidres lezemariwoch: sïle mezmuroch hïṣeṣoch yeḵerebe his* #2 ("Critique of Songs; To All Singers Whom This May Concern: Critical Review on Flaws in Songs"). Brooks, Alberta: Ezra Literature Services, 2009.

———. *Yidres lezemariwoch* #1 ("To All Singers Whom This May Concern"). Brooks, Alberta: Ezra Literature Services, 2007.

Amharic Articles: Tesfaye Gabbiso
Special Collection

With special recognition to Binyam Negussie Gebre/Heywot for his work in preserving this collection.

CODE: The articles are numbered from 1–10 and indicated thus when referred to in the text.

Tesfaye, #1 - *Beïlïlta sïgïdulet* ("Worship Him with Illiltas") *Birhan*, #43, 1971 EC, 6 and 13.

Tesfaye, #2 - *Ïgziabhér sireda kesemayat werdo- ketesfayé gabbiso gar* ("When God Descends from Heaven—with Tesfaye Gabbiso") Question and Answer in *Birhan* #7, 1985 EC, 10–13.

Tesfaye, #3 - *Ïgziabhér sireda kesemayat werdo- yetesfayé gabbiso mïsïkïrnet* ("When God Descends from Heaven, with Tesfaye Gabbiso") Question and answer #2 following the previous article in *Birhan* #6, 1985 EC, 10–12.

Tesfaye, #4 - *Tesfayé Gabbiso*. (Guest speaker) *Mïsïkïr*, Tahisas, 1995 EC, 12–15.

Tesfaye, #5 - *Zemarina yezemari hïwet* ("The Singer and the Singer's Song") *Yehiwet Birhan* #4 Sene, 1998 EC, 10–11.

Tesfaye, #6 - *Menfesïn ataṭifu* ("Do Not Quench the Spirit") *Miiraf I*, Tir-Yekatit #3, 1999 (EC?), 9–11.

Tesfaye, #7 - *Ḳoïta ketesfayé gabbiso gar* ("Interview with Tesfaye Gabbiso") Part 1 in *Miliat*, 2nd year #8 Ginbote, 1999 EC, 3–6.

Tesfaye, #8 - *Ḳoïta ketesfayé gabbiso gar* ("Interview with Tesfaye Gabbiso") Part 2 in *Miliat*, 2nd year #9 Nehasae, 1999 EC, 2–8. This also includes a brief interview with Tesfaye's wife, Hannah on p. 8.

Tesfaye, #9 - Yewïbdar Amsala. *Tesfayé gabbiso, keyet wedét?* ("Tesfaye Gabbiso, From Where to Where?") *Meytanoya* #1, Tahesas, 2001 EC, 9 and 19.

Tesfaye, #10 - *Beïnéna begwadenyoché laï sïlederesewu ïsïratna ïngïlt* ("The Imprisonment and Incidents that Happened to Me and My Friends") Question and Answer in *Matetes*, Ginbote 2002 (EC?) 24–25.

Additional Sources of Information

EMAILS

Bekele Wolde-Kidan. Printed interview by Brian Fargher with Bekele Wolde-Kidan entitled "Good News from Ethiopia" on October 10, 2014, in Calgary, Alberta.

Brant, JoAnn, to Lila Balisky. September 5, 2014, re: song the KHC missionaries take with them.

Clermont, Krista, to Lila Balisky. October 1, 2014. Full answers to my questions about Ethiopian missionaries and the song they are using in Chad.

Gezahegn Mussie to Lila Balisky. May 10, 2014. In response to email from Lila Balisky to Gezahegn Mussie dated April 29, 2014.

Kruse, Angela, to Lila Balisky. August 5 and 8, 2014. First Gumuz worship song coming through a dream. Creating scripture songs.

MacLachlan, Mark. October 1, 2014. Song has become primary to evangelism strategy of SIM among Gumuz.

Nilsson, Marianne. Email to Lila Balisky. February 6, 2014.

Solomon Akalu to Lila Balisky. September 10, 2014, re: EKHC Global Missionaries Allocation Internationally.

Zelalem Mengistu to Lila Balisky. September 25, 2014, re: his articles and bibliography information.

EMAILS BETWEEN LILA BALISKY AND TESFAYE GABBISO

April 30, 2013; May 2, 2013; June 2 and 7, 2013; July 5, 9, and 17, 2013; September 4, 2013; December 18, 19, and 23, 2013; January 19, 2014; February 1 and 12, 2014; April 5 and 24, 2014; August 7 and 29, 2014; September 1 and 4, 2014; January 2, 2015; March 30, 2015; May 7, 2015; May 27, 2015. Following completion of dissertation, a significant email on April 27, 2017, regarding his family generations' spiritual experience and brief discussion of metaphor.

INTERVIEWS

Dawit Getachew. Interview with Lila Balisky at Mekane Yesus Seminary, Addis Ababa, Ethiopia, January 27, 2015.

Ezra Abate. Interview with Lila Balisky and Helen Afewerk at Yared School of Music in Addis Ababa, Ethiopia, March 4, 2008.

Feleke Hailu. Interview with Lila Balisky and Helen Afewerk at Yared School of Music in Addis Ababa, Ethiopia, March 4, 2008.

Gezahegn Mussie. Interview with Lila Balisky at SIM, Addis Ababa, on January 6, 2015.

Hugo Ferran. Personal conversations in Balisky home in Grande Prairie, AB, Canada, August 1–11, 2012.

Mimi Shesterniak. Interview with Lila Balisky and Hugo Ferran in Grande Prairie, AB, Canada, August 7, 2012.

Minas Biruk. Interview with Lila Balisky at SIM, Addis Ababa, January 26, 2012.

Moges Berassa. Interview with Lila Balisky at The Cottage, Addis Ababa, June 19, 2013.

Tesfaye Gabbiso. Interview with Lila Balisky, Addis Ababa, Ethiopia, June 12, 1990.

Tesfaye Gabbiso. Interview with Lila Balisky, Addis Ababa, Ethiopia, June 8, 2013.

Tesfaye Gabbiso. Interview with Lila Balisky, Hawassa, Ethiopia, January 9, 2015.

Tibebe Eshete. Interview with Lila Balisky, Addis Ababa, July 11, 2013, and telephone interview, July 8, 2015.

Yigezu Desta. Interview with Lila and Paul Balisky and Vernon Charter, SIM Guest House in Addis Ababa, Ethiopia, July 9, 2002.

Yohannes Girma. Interview with Lila Balisky, Addis Ababa, Ethiopia, January 7, 2015.

Zelalem Mengistu. Interview with Lila Balisky, Brooks, AB, Canada, May 31, 2014.

Index of Names

Note: Page numbers followed by n and a number indicate footnotes.

Index of Subjects

Note: Page numbers followed by n and a number indicate footnotes. Page numbers in italics indicate illustrative material.

CPSIA information can be obtained
at www.ICGtesting.com
Printed in the USA
LVHW011924030519
616632LV00002B/2/P

9 781532 634949